Altman and After

Multiple Narratives in Film

Peter F. Parshall

THE SCARECROW PRESS, INC.
Lanham · Toronto · Plymouth, UK
2012

Published by Scarecrow Press, Inc.
A wholly owned subsidiary of The Rowman & Littlefield Publishing Group, Inc.
4501 Forbes Boulevard, Suite 200, Lanham, Maryland 20706
www.rowman.com

10 Thornbury Road, Plymouth PL6 7PP, United Kingdom

British Library Cataloguing in Publication Information Available

Library of Congress Cataloging-in-Publication Data

Parshall, Peter F., 1937–
  Altman and after : multiple narratives in film / Peter F. Parshall.
    p. cm.
  Includes bibliographical references and index.
  ISBN 978-0-8108-8506-6 (cloth : alk. paper) — ISBN 978-0-8108-8507-3 (ebook)
  1. Motion picture plays—History and criticism. I. Title.
  PN1995.P28 2012
  791.43'6—dc23
                              2012009176

The paper used in this publication meets the minimum requirements of American National Standard for Information Sciences—Permanence of Paper for Printed Library Materials,
ANSI/NISO Z39.48-1992. Printed in the United States of America.

Contents

CONTENTS

Acknowledgments

This book began as a series of classes entitled "Crash Cinema" that focused on films telling multiple stories. I am indebted to the students in those courses whose enthusiasm for the subject spurred me to continue my research into the topic.

I owe a particular debt to the Lilly Endowment for granting me a Faculty Open Fellowship for a year of postdoctoral study in film back in 1988. That sabbatical was spent at the University of Wisconsin, and I cannot express sufficient gratitude to the film faculty for their warm welcome. I especially thank David Bordwell and Kristin Thompson, whose friendship for the past twenty years has meant a great deal. Everyone who writes in the area of narrative structure owes an enormous debt to David for his extensive and lucid writing on that subject. He is particularly knowledgeable in the area of multiple-plot films and was generous in providing me with materials and suggestions.

The library staffs at the Wilson Library of the University of Minnesota and the Hennepin County Library system were unfailingly helpful. I also want to thank Nancy Andreasen, Mary Jo Nissen, Marcia Pankake, and Sheila Summerfield, friends and fellow cinephiles, who read the entire manuscript and offered exceptionally helpful corrections and suggestions.

I offer particularly warm thanks to my colleague, David Desser. His thoughtful comments sharpened my central argument, his keen eye eliminated superfluous material, and his careful copyediting caught numerous errors. His support for the past year has been critical in bringing this project to completion.

My thanks to the congenial people at Scarecrow Press/Rowman and Littlefield who contributed their skills to this project. Sally Craley in the production department made useful suggestions. My production editor, Jayme Bartles Reed, kept things smoothly on schedule. I am particularly indebted to Stephen Ryan, the senior editor at Scarecrow, who has been unfailingly patient and supportive.

My fine son, Jonathan, besides providing inspiration by getting his book published first, also helped untangle the conundrums of Adobe's InDesign so I could do the layout to my satisfaction. My darling daughter, Julie, contributed absolutely nothing to the creation of the book but contributes every moment to the joy of my life.

Finally, this book is dedicated to my wife, Carol Marie. For fifty years she has loved and cherished me beyond all reason and supported my endeavors, including this one. She is my treasure.

Arolcay Emanlay

1

Introduction

The Potential of Complex Narratives

When Ilsa Lund walks into Rick's Café Américain twenty-five minutes into *Casablanca* (Curtiz, 1941), the Hollywood dream machinery swings smoothly into action. Preceding her husband, Victor Laszlo, by a few steps and slightly to his left, she is foregrounded to the camera. Obligingly, it tracks back from three-quarters in front, keeping her carefully framed while teasing the viewer by letting lamps and screens block her momentarily. Dressed in a simple white suit, she pops from the screen, luminescent even in the café's subdued lighting. Played by the young Ingrid Bergman, with flawless skin and a shy smile, Ilsa needs minimal help from the camera to be irresistible. The audience's empathy is further increased by the wary look she casts about as the waiter shows them to a table (Figure 1.1).

1.1
Creating audience identification: Ilsa in Rick's Café Américain.

She is undoubtedly worried about the safety of her husband, a leader in the resistance and a high priority target for the Nazis. Her concern is well-founded because Major Heinrich Strasser has arrived in Casablanca with the express purpose of ensnaring Laszlo and now sits only a few feet from the table where Victor and Ilsa will be seated. The audience has been carefully filled in on these dangers and so can share Ilsa's concern, further allying them to her. The exposition has also shown the horde of refugees already trapped in Casablanca, unable to obtain the requisite exit visas, seeming to make the city a dead-end for Victor and Ilsa. Thus story, camera, costume, makeup, and lighting combine to link the audience as closely as possible to the star. Even the music helps: Sam is playing "Speak to Me of Love" as Ilsa enters, quietly announcing the romance at the heart of the narrative.

Strong empathy with the central characters is one key feature in the classic film; a second is the story's relentless forward drive. The goals of the protagonist impel the action (Rick wants to get Ilsa to safety), obstacles block his path (Strasser tries to trap Laszlo), and deadlines increase the pressure (the plane to Lisbon is about to leave). Nonessential scenes (Laszlo's resistance meeting) are elided and the editing cuts each scene at the moment of greatest intensity, so that the action leaps forward. The result is a dramatic world where every decision is critical, imparting a heightened vitality to the characters. The intensity of this experience pulls viewers irresistibly into the story, emotionally linked to these attractive personages living in a world of romance. Further supporting this format's appeal is its ontological resonance. That is, this narrative structure supports the comforting worldview that human life has meaning. The camera's intense focus on the central characters makes human activity of paramount importance in the cinematic universe. The tight causal structure supports the idea that reasoned actions can solve problems and generate happy endings. We are not (as we secretly fear) being tossed about randomly on the ocean of life—we are steering successfully through the storm toward some safe harbor. Given the uncertainties that beset us on every side, it is no wonder we enjoy retreating to a world that allows escape from our troubles and sustains our sense of self-worth. A director who abandons these tried-and-true formulas and proposes a less sunny or less certain view of reality does so at his/her peril.

Altman the Rebel

But that is exactly what Robert Altman does in *Nashville* (1975). His story has no fewer than twenty-four characters, precluding close identification with any of them. Other devices further reduce emotional linkage. Altman generally keeps his camera at a distance, rarely moving into tighter shots, and avoids shot/reverse shot entirely. (Roughly 50 percent of *Casablanca*'s shots are shot/reverse shot, melding us to Rick and Ilsa as they gaze intensely at one another.) *Nashville*'s screen is often filled with a number of characters competing for our attention (Figure 1.2). The sound track is equally busy, with voices overlapping and key conversations

1.2
Altman's crowded frame with multiple characters.

sometimes indistinct. Instead of a driving plot line, there are simply five days of life in Nashville, with the camera jumping from place to place, making sure to show all twenty-four characters on each of the days. (The narrative is far less random than it first appears, but does not drive forward like most Hollywood films.) The dangers of abandoning the accepted format seem borne out in the case of *Nashville*, which did poorly at the box office, completely overshadowed by *Jaws* (Spielberg, 1975).[1] And yet *Nashville* is now regarded as a classic: Helene Keyssar calls it the most important film of its decade.[2] Through careful accretion of detail the film paints a finely nuanced portrait of American culture at the time of the nation's two hundredth birthday. Altman was willing to trade the immediate appeal of the classic plot for the greater richness of meaning provided by complex narrative structure.

Altman's experiments were encouraged because his career began when the rules of studio filmmaking were being challenged by the innovators of the '60s and '70s: Scorsese, Lucas, Nichols, Coppola, Penn, Kubrick, and others. Unfortunately, their revolution was short-lived, lasting barely ten years. Although some of the early upstart films were successful—*Bonnie and Clyde* (Penn, 1967), *The Graduate* (Nichols, 1967)—classical style soon reasserted itself. Altman's fellow rebels either accommodated themselves to the studio system or disappeared. Experiments with style and story were quickly subsumed into standard Hollywood storytelling; successful films hewed to a central story line, notably true of *The Godfather* (Coppola, 1972) and *Jaws,* both directed by (formerly) upstart directors. George Lucas who had interwoven story lines so creatively in *American Graffiti* (1973) retreated to a formulaic narrative line (supplemented by spectacular special effects) in *Star Wars* (1977). Altman, however, enjoyed creating by ensemble and intermixing narratives, a format he began with *M*A*S*H* in 1970. While many of his films had a central plot line—*Brewster McCloud* (1970), *McCabe and Mrs. Miller* (1971), and *The Long Goodbye* (1973)—many others used interwoven stories. After *Nashville* came *A Wedding* (1978), *Short Cuts* (1993), *Prêt-à-Porter* (1994), *Kansas City*

(1996), *Gosford Park* (2001), *The Company* (2003), and finally *A Prairie Home Companion* (2006). Altman was ahead of his time with *Nashville*. Although some experiments with story structure continued—e.g., Woody Allen's multiple story lines in *Hannah and Her Sisters* (1986) and *Crimes and Misdemeanors* (1989)—the real explosion of the form would not come until fifteen years after *Nashville*.

The '90s Narrative Revolution

In the 1990s the independent film movement blossomed and many directors began to take unprecedented liberties with narrative convention. *Pulp Fiction* (Tarantino, 1994) violently jumbles the time order of its three stories; *Groundhog Day* (Ramis, 1993) repeats a single day's action until the main character finally "gets it right"; *Memento* (Nolan, 2000) tells its story in reverse order. Gus Van Sant presents slice-of-life stories with no exposition in *Elephant* (2003) and *Last Days* (2005), leaving the viewer to interpret events as best she can. *Adaptation* (Jonze, 2002) and *Swimming Pool* (Ozon, 2003) suggest the rules of narrative can take control of reality. Fincher's *Fight Club* (1999) has a narrator with dual personalities; *A Beautiful Mind* (Howard, 2001) presents John Nash's schizophrenic delusions as real. *Eternal Sunshine of the Spotless Mind* (Gondry, 2004) abandons objective reality altogether and attempts to show the internal workings of a character's consciousness. While these new forms—"complex narratives" in Janet Staiger's terminology[3]—do not dominate theater screens, they have received wide acceptance.

The independent film movement of the '90s waned somewhat in the following decade with many of its innovations integrated into "standard" storytelling— exactly as happened in earlier periods. A major strength of classical narrative structure is its ability to adapt to new trends. It incorporated the ideas of foreign directors in the '30s, borrowed elements of German Expressionism for the '40s *film noir,* and absorbed the experiments of the so-called New Wave directors.[4] But the impact of these narrative experiments is undeniable and the profusion of new forms—Charles Ramirez Berg has identified no fewer than twelve "deviations" from standard narrative structure[5]—provides a multitude of possible avenues for exploration. As one would expect, critics have begun to explore them along with the filmmakers. The essays in Warren Buckland's *Puzzle Films* look at films that deliberately mislead the viewer, such as *The Sixth Sense* (Shyamalan, 1999) and *A Beautiful Mind*, arguing they reflect the contemporary sense of fragmented reality. Alan Cameron's *Modular Narratives in Contemporary Cinema* studies films with scrambled story order such as *Pulp Fiction*, suggesting they exhibit a new sense of time.[6] David Bordwell, in particular, has studied complex narratives in depth, showing how they mix in traditional devices to keep the viewer oriented despite the new story twists and turns.[7]

Given the richness of new forms, this book will not try to sample all of them and will, in fact, focus specifically on just two modes: films that tell multiple stories and films that repeat the same story with variations. Examining them, it asks an obvious question: have these new forms produced any significant artistic advantages? Given the risks of abandoning classic narrative structure, there need to be offsetting rewards. Obviously, one gains novelty. Bordwell suggests that filmmakers are in a constant race to generate audience appeal through incorporating new devices while still constructing stories that make sense to viewers.[8] Particularly following television shows such as *Hill Street Blues* in the 1980s that interwove story lines, filmmakers could count on greater audience acceptance of such forms. The instant success of *Pulp Fiction* showed that multiple stories, sudden jumps in time, shifts in tone, cartoonish filming, and random violence could be jumbled together and find eager acceptance. Its success, in turn, attracted other directors seeking to entice viewers with strategies more innovative than bigger explosions and fancier CGI effects. In some cases, sadly, the new forms were used simply as gimmicks, attempting to liven up tired story lines. However, in other instances serious filmmakers embraced complex narratives because they opened up new artistic possibilities. Like their fellow artists in written fiction, filmmakers are eager to find fresh ways of telling stories and of presenting the world.

Eight Significant Films

So it is with the eight films selected for study here. These are not works that toss in exciting narrative twists to titillate viewers but that lack serious purpose or a compelling artistic vision. They are, in general, smaller independent films rather than mainstream offerings. While complex narrative forms have been pulled into some big budget films, the results have seldom been artistically noteworthy. In contrast, the independent directors represented here—Altman, Iñárritu, Tarantino, Akin, Haneke, Tykwer, Hong, and Kieślowski—are known for their creativity. The one film which might be considered "main stream" because of its extraordinary success, *Pulp Fiction*, is included not only because of its innovation but because it is generally regarded as a mere popular success lacking serious meaning. Thus Dana Polan concludes his eighty-page study of the film by saying it shows "style winning out over substance"[9]—a too-hasty dismissal. Each of these films, then, has expanded the cinematic vocabulary in some significant fashion. Many other directors and films might have been selected, but this group had the advantage of covering a broad geographic span and more than thirty years of cinematic history, giving a sense of how widely this revolution has spread and how durable it appears to be.

A final important consideration is that the eight films fall into two broad categories which are completely opposed and, at the same time, strangely congruent. Five of the eight films may be labeled generally as ***multi-plot films***. Instead of following a narrow cast of characters in a single story arc these films interweave two, three, or even—as with *Nashville*—dozens of stories. However, they use varying patterns, employ unique artistic methods, and present radically different visions of the world. The other three films fall into an entirely distinct mode, the ***multiple-draft film***. They tell the same story two or even three times, as if the filmmaker wanted to experiment with alternate outcomes. While quite different, these modes share an important trait: *both emphasize thematic patterns*, most typically similarities in the case of multi-plot films and contrasts with the multiple-draft films. Thus the multi-plot film will often reveal connections among the interwoven stories, to emphasize human commonalities. Lives following similar paths encourage us "to notice how characters are sharply similar or different from one another."[10] By contrast, the multiple-draft film directs one's attention most strongly to the differences in competing versions of what is essentially the same story. In both cases, the viewer can most deeply understand the film by identifying the themes being compared or contrasted. These eight films, in sum, present intriguing explorations of the potential inherent in these new complex narrative forms.

The Multi-Plot Film versus the Ensemble Film

With this general overview in mind, let us examine briefly the history and theory behind these two forms of complex narrative starting with the multi-plot film. First, it must be distinguished from a related form, the ***ensemble film***. While Hollywood stories generally feature just one or two main characters, films with multiple protagonists have existed almost since movies began. Studios discovered early on they could increase a film's appeal by cramming in as many major stars as possible. Hence Reisner's *The Hollywood Revue of 1929* featured Jack Benny and Conrad Nagel as Masters of Ceremony, John Gilbert and Norma Shearer doing a scene from *Romeo and Juliet*, plus a host of other stars including Laurel and Hardy. As the title indicates, it is simply a revue showcasing the talents of its performers. In other films of the '30s, particularly those with a strong supporting cast, associated stories might be developed to complement the main one. Thus, Cukor's *The Women* (1939) portrays a group of friends that "counsel" one of their number going through a divorce. There is a nod to the idea of multiple stories, since each woman is given a back story that shows related problems with male-female relationships. However, the film has a strong central plot in which Mrs. Haines learns how undependable the majority of her friends are and decides to return to her husband.

Most studio films with an expanded cast from the '30s and later fall into this ensemble film category.[11] They enjoyed a particular burst of popularity in the '60s and '70s with such productions as *Judgment at Nuremberg* (Kramer, 1961), *Advise and Consent* (Preminger, 1962), and *How the West Was Won* (Ford and Hathaway, 1962) where the attraction of multiple stars reduces the risks of a high cost, large-scale production.[12] A particularly popular variety features a group adventure, ranging from Wilder's *Stalag 17* (1953) to Aldrich's *The Dirty Dozen* (1967). In these cases, as in disaster movies like *The Poseidon Adventure* (Neame, 1972), although the viewer's interest is spread over a group of characters, there is really one basic story line, be it escaping a Nazi prison camp or a sinking ocean liner. The opportunity for increased horseplay in a film like *Robin and the 7 Hoods* (Douglas, 1964) is counterbalanced by minimal character development and predictable plotting.

While ensemble films popped up from time to time, the film telling multiple stories seldom appeared in the first decades of cinema despite the great success of one early attempt. MGM's *Grand Hotel* (Goulding, 1932) interwove four stories whose clichéd nature was offset by the combined star power of Greta Garbo, John and Lionel Barrymore, Joan Crawford, and Wallace Beery. This is a true multi-plot film whose separate stories take place within the confines of a posh Berlin hotel. For all its hackneyed scripting, *Grand Hotel* did extremely well at the box office, won an Oscar, and spawned a host of later imitators and remakes, including *Hotel Berlin* (Godfrey, 1945), *Hotel* (Quine, 1967), and various TV offshoots. Despite this early success, further attempts at multi-plot films in classic Hollywood were decidedly sporadic, e.g., *Tales of Manhattan* (Duvivier, 1942). This conservatism is not surprising. Hollywood had struggled during the '20s to move from the short film to feature-length productions and regularize story structure. Then came the upheavals caused by the coming of sound, the Great Depression, studio mergers, and the Hays Code. Little wonder the studios adhered tenaciously to proven formulas.

European directors, like those in Hollywood, tended to stick to strong central narratives, although some explorations occurred. Jean Renoir, as much ahead of his time in 1939 as Altman in 1975, portrayed the decadence of French bourgeois society prior to WWII in *Rules of the Game* through the intermingled people at a country house outside Paris: hosts, house guests, and servants. Renoir's portrait of the society is as despairing as Altman's and was as strongly rejected by audiences and critics. Not until the rise of the French New Wave twenty years later was narrative experimentation taken up vigorously again. Most of it involved playing with genres, but Jacques Rivette used multiple plots in *Paris nous appartient* (1961) and *L'amour fou* (1969). Jacques Tati employed the ensemble situation for comic effect, seen notably in *Play Time* (1967) which has no real plot line, dozens of characters, and a screen filled with sight gags. Robert Bresson produced at least one interesting experiment in *Au hasard, Balthazar*

(1966), a series of vignettes tied together by the progress of a donkey through the hands of various owners. Multi-protagonist films in other European countries included Federico Fellini's *I vitelloni* (1953), Otar Iosseliani's *April* (1961), and Anthony Asquith's *The Yellow Rolls-Royce* (1964). These experiments, like those in the Hollywood Renaissance in the 1960s, pushed at the boundaries of standard narration, but with limited impact.

After decades of neglect, the multi-plot film came into its own as one of the complex narrative forms explored in the 1990s. While it has multiple protagonists like the ensemble film, it differs in having truly separate plot lines. Evan Smith, who uses the term ***thread narrative*** for the multi-plot film, separates it from ensemble films such as *The Poseidon Adventure, The Big Chill* (Kasdan, 1983), and *Steel Magnolias* (Ross, 1989), which "feature only one main story, a single dramatic journey." In contrast, a thread narrative develops "multiple story threads." Each of these "is a separate main story and all threads have roughly the same dramatic weight."[13] Bordwell's term for the film with multiple plots is ***network narrative***. He agrees with Smith that such films are unlike ensemble films where "all of the players are defined by their roles in the overriding project," e.g., raiding a Las Vegas casino in *Ocean's Eleven* (Milestone, 1960). Network narratives have multiple protagonists, "but their projects are largely decoupled from one another, or only contingently linked."[14] In the ensuing discussion, the terms "thread narrative" and "network narrative" will be used interchangeably, although the latter term seems more appropriate, emphasizing that the separate story lines often end up showing connections, particularly thematic ones.

This ability to create complex relationships between two or more story lines attracted many directors in the '90s at a time when studios became more willing to distribute independent films. Their willingness was undoubtedly encouraged by the success of *Pulp Fiction,* which, though influential, did not single-handedly begin this trend, since a host of such films was springing up worldwide. Among them one finds Jarmusch's *Mystery Train* (1989), Sayles's *City of Hope* and Linklater's *Slacker* (1991), Wong's *Chungking Express* and Altman's *Prêt-à-Porter* (1994), Minghella's *The English Patient* and Sabu's *Dangan Runner* (1996), Tarantino's *Jackie Brown* (1997), Liman's *Go,* Anderson's *Magnolia,* and García's *Things You Can Tell Just by Looking at Her* (1999), and Iñárritu's *Amores Perros* and Haneke's *Code Unknown* (2000). Eventually the multi-plot format went mainstream and achieved Hollywood respectability: Steven Soderbergh's *Traffic* (2000) won four Oscars including Best Director, and *Crash* by Paul Haggis was chosen Best Picture for 2004. Other well-received exemplars included Altman's *Gosford Park* and Sprecher's *13 Conversations about One Thing* in 2001, Iñárritu's *21 Grams* and Curtis' *Love Actually* in 2003, Roos' *Happy Endings* and Gaghan's *Syriana* in 2005, and Iñárritu's *Babel* in 2006.[15] As Murray Smith proposes, "now that the 'meme' [of parallel plots] has successfully been transplanted into the meme pool of American film-making, it is fair to assume that it will reappear."[16]

Advantages of the Multi-Plot Film

Viewers may be intrigued by the twists and turns of a multi-plot story but this does not guarantee a strong film. Having more characters may weaken viewer identification and less time per story means less opportunity for character development. Evan Smith argues that the need to "condense, or even omit, psychological transitions might be the greatest weakness of the thread construct."[17] Further, some filmmakers may try to substitute story convolutions for real narrative depth. (Michael Newman makes a convincing argument that this is true in the case of *21 Grams*.[18]) However, when used intelligently, the network narrative offers compensating strengths. For one thing, "our immersion in film and television has trained us to fill in gaps" and "to give underdeveloped characters the benefit of the doubt. . . . We no longer demand a single, driving, fully realized story; now, we are just as happy to enjoy the mass momentum of multiple mini-dramas."[19] That is shown with the success of a film like *Love Actually* which tells of the British Prime Minister falling in love with his tea girl, his sister worrying about her husband's fidelity, a widower helping his young son court a classmate, an office girl whose romantic aspirations are repeatedly dashed by needing to care for her mentally ill brother, two porn film stand-ins who start to find one another attractive, a man who falls in love with his Portuguese housekeeper despite not speaking her language, a young Brit who goes looking for richer sexual pastures in America and—oh, yes—a broken-down rock -'n'-roll singer. Sketchily presented as many of these stories are, their combined momentum is compelling. Besides multi-plot films, narrative experimentation of all kinds is no longer restricted to art houses but increasingly finds an audience in mainstream cinema. An example is *The Sixth Sense* which received six Oscar nominations and grossed $672 million worldwide, second best for the year.

While network narratives lose some of the straight-line drive of the classic story, they can provide a compensating benefit in their ability to interweave stories in interesting ways. A story told from varying viewpoints can potentially provide a "play of perspectives."[20] In watching the stories, we are intrigued by "the way the various lines of action interweave with one another," and gain an "'architectural' pleasure" in the artfulness of the construction.[21] Each of the five multi-plot films to be discussed here shows how effectively—and in what varied fashion—this mode can be employed. No two of them interweave their stories in similar fashion or to illustrate similar ideas. In fact, the five films exemplify no less than three different modes of construction within the multi-plot format.

Mosaic Narrative

The first complex narrative form to be studied is the *mosaic film*, with just one exemplar, *Nashville*. Admittedly, the term is problematic. Margrit Tröhler would not consider *Nashville* a mosaic film, reserving the term for network narratives in which the characters, rather than belonging to an established group, are scattered geographically.[22] Most other critics are less restrictive, using "mosaic" as generally synonymous with network narrative. Thus Stephen Farber describes *Syriana* as "a complex cinematic mosaic with multiple story lines."[23] Berg doesn't use the term "mosaic' in his taxonomy and assigns *Nashville* to his category of "Polyphonic or Ensemble Plot," with multiple protagonists in a single location, much like *Grand Hotel*.[24] In his view, it is simply another film telling multiple stories. David Bordwell thinks most films with interwoven stories produce a mosaic effect: "When we back off from the tiny bits, we discern a larger composition."[25] Bordwell prefers the term "network narrative" because it emphasizes the way the stories usually are webbed together, and uses that term for *Nashville*.

It seems useful to distinguish between two forms of complex narrative, using "network" for films that interweave two or three stories and "mosaic" for a film that, like Altman's, is an assemblage of multiple characters and minor events, a sort of pointillist narrative. *Nashville* jumps from person to person over the five days of the plot, giving quick snippets of their lives. More important than any individual's story is the collective picture of the country music world that emerges—the performers, associates, fans, and hangers-on. Mixed in also are elements of a political narrative, for John Triplette, an advance man for Hal Phillip Walker, arrives in town to recruit those stars to appear at a rally for his candidate. Over the course of the film, the singers who present themselves on stage as good old boys, warm and welcoming, turn out to be petty, self-centered, and back-stabbing. They are creating a public image to sell themselves to their audience and their similarity to politicians is all too obvious. By managing to weave so many characters and stories into a coherent work of art, this film becomes one of the greatest achievements of the mosaic form. (Fellini's *Amarcord* from 1973 may be the other most successful example.) This complex montage is held together by the interwoven themes, prostitution prominent among them.

Network Narrative

The next four films, more common varieties of the multi-plot film, can all be labeled *network narratives* as described by Bordwell. In these films, the separate story strands may each have a strong forward causal drive as in a classic plot, but the viewer's interest is shifted to the story connections. He says, "As story action becomes less goal directed, we're asked to form an abstract sense of structure," adding that these may sometimes be "remote and fragile connections," almost "poetic linkages."[26] Where a standard narrative arouses the viewer's interest in what will happen next, the network narrative arouses interest in how the stories are connected, how they intersect, or how they are similar. It is true that the classical Hollywood film often juxtaposes contrasting stories, but as Bordwell notes such contrasts are generally subsumed to the causal plot structure. For example, in *Jerry Maguire* (Crowe, 1996), the problems in Jerry's marriage are highlighted by the stronger connection of Rod Tidwell to his wife. However, these contrasts are integrated into the central thrust of each man's drive for success.[27] Much less common, Bordwell notes, are films that reverse this priority, "stressing parallels at the expense of causal connections."[28] One of the few "standard" films to do so, *The Godfather Part II* (Coppola, 1974), simultaneously tells the story of the rise to power of Vito Corleone and, two decades later, of his son, Michael. The two men are equally ruthless, but the parallel permits a crucial contrast, for "Vito builds his empire by expanding his circle of friends and helping the weak" while Michael "strips himself of personal ties" and ends up alone at the end.[29] Thus, while each story drives forward, the two plot lines are not linked causally and the focus is strongly on parallels and contrasts. This device of thematically related story lines, less common in standard films, is what the network narrative exploits most strongly.

The first of the network narratives to be examined, *Pulp Fiction*, shows that emphasizing parallels and links does not mean that causality is abandoned. The three story lines are all linked to Los Angeles crime boss Marsellus Wallace, whose presence is felt, on stage or off, throughout. At the same time, the various story lines all drive forward relentlessly and intersect fairly strongly, although the film's startling jumps in time conceal some of the connections until the end. There is also tight temporal unity, with the various actions occurring over the space of just a few days. Despite these suggestions of classical construction, the film's pop culture references, exaggerated violence, and cartoonish filming have led critics to dismiss it as "empty of social and moral content."[30] Such judgments overlook how Tarantino has juggled time order to emphasize important themes. Thus the film begins with a pair of amateur robbers leaping to their feet to hold up the coffee shop where they are eating breakfast. The story breaks off just as they draw their pistols, to be picked up again at the very end of the film. Now we see that among their intended victims are two professional hit men and the eager amateurs soon find large caliber weapons pointed at their heads (Figure 1.3). Before drawing their pistols in the first place, those amateurs had asked—primarily in jest—if they should consider a different line of work. Now the question arises again in far more serious fashion. In the end, what links the stories is not Marsellus or the city of Los Angeles so much as the fact that four characters make critical decisions about the future direction of their lives. Thus thematic issues suggest meanings initially obscured by the high caliber fireworks.

1.3 Let's reconsider our path in life: Jules and Pumpkin.

Hub and Spoke Narratives

The next two films studied may be termed **hub and spoke** narratives. This is Berg's term for a subcategory of the **network narrative** in which the various stories connect at a single point but follow independent paths before and after. Inherently, this means the stories will show less interconnection than other forms of network narrative in which lives may be tightly interwoven. Furthermore, many hub and spoke stories "emphasize chance, coincidence, and the freakish nature of fate." That is, Berg argues, small events and off-hand decisions often bring characters together in what turns out to be a life-altering event.[31] Such a philosophy underlies a film like *11:14* (Marcks, 2003), where coincidence plays a large part in the disasters that occur.

The two examples of hub and spoke narratives studied here, *Amores Perros* and *Code Unknown*, intend to do far more than demonstrate the quirkiness of fate. Alejandro González Iñárritu's *Amores Perros,* might seem at first to illustrate the power of chance, as three sets of characters are brought together in a car crash, the film's hub event (Figure 1.4). The car crash has become a salient trope in the network narrative, "as conventional as a Main Street shootout in a Western."[32] It is an all-too-convenient device for bringing characters together and sending their lives in new directions. But Iñárritu uses the device with particular intelligence. For one thing, he repeats the crash four times, revealing more of the causes and ramifications with each repetition. Further, the lives of the three sets of characters involved—a young man from a poor family, a publisher and his super-model girlfriend, and a garbage scavenger living with a pack of mongrel dogs—turn out to be thematically linked despite the social gulfs that separate them. In each story, the male allows *machismo* to destroy the family ties he holds most dear. As we come to see, the car crash is merely the symbolic capstone to histories of destructive behavior.

1.4
A hub
event:
The car
crash in
*Amores
Perros.*

In the other hub and spoke film, Michael Haneke's *Code Unknown*, the collision is far less violent, a brief scuffle on a street in Paris with apparently limited consequences. Thereafter the characters follow their separate lives, shown in fragmentary episodes. The events from each are scattered among brief moments from the others, so none of the lives seems to show a clear trajectory. Furthermore, most of the events seem minor: friends chatting at dinner or a farmer and his son raking the barn. The film demands analysis, first, because Haneke takes the multiplot film in a whole new direction. Rather than revealing human commonalities, he emphasizes disconnection, with each scene separated from its neighbors by a three second blackout. The scenes themselves show the breakdown of ties between the characters and those around them. That meaning only becomes evident, however, as the thematic parallels in the film's four stories gradually emerge.

Fatih Akin's *The Edge of Heaven* (2007) is appropriate to round out the category of network narrative because it is the most recent film and also a masterful example of thematic linkage. Throughout, the film creates links between culturally disparate characters whose story arcs intersect only at a few brief points. The action takes place in locales as much as 1,800 miles apart, over the space of more than a year. Yet the film creates thematic unity by juxtaposing two stories centered on parent-child conflicts—father/son and mother/daughter—even though one family is Turkish and one German. Akin is particularly skillful in creating resonant visual images to emphasize story parallels. Thus, shortly into the film, the camera holds in long shot as a coffin slowly glides down a conveyor belt from an airliner sitting on the runway in Istanbul. The coffin carries the returning body of a Turkish woman, killed accidentally in Germany. Fifty-seven minutes later, the camera occupies precisely the same position at the same airport and observes a coffin slowly riding up the conveyor into the plane. This time a young German woman is being returned home after her accidental murder in Turkey. The deliberate visual parallel emphasizes the parallel tragedies that have occurred and encourages the viewer to ponder the reasons that underlie them. This film is a classic and moving example of the **network narrative**, showing human lives interwoven in ways the protagonists only gradually come to realize. All five of these multi-plot films, then, juxtapose characters, scenes, even visual elements, to build a complex picture of the interplay of human lives. In so doing, they almost invariably expand their portrait beyond these individuals to the society at large.

The Multiple-Draft Film

The second major mode examined here, the **multiple-draft narrative**, essentially tells a single story with variations. Its alternative label, the **database narrative**, conveys the idea that these films generate a pool of narrative events and then shuffle their order, their timing, or their outcomes. In effect, the filmmaker gets to "try out" different ways of putting his story together.[33] Because they juggle the order of events or show those events from different points of view, these films may undercut our sense of a coherent world. Although literary examples can be found of characters pursuing alternative paths, there is little early history of the mode in the film world. Some early films told more than one story, most famously Griffith's 1916 *Intolerance*, but there seem to be no significant examples of exactly repeated stories.[34] One delightful exception is Buster Keaton's *Three Ages* (1923), which has a little man attempting to win the affections of a girl and defeat his rival as a Stone Age caveman, a Roman soldier, and a denizen of the Roaring Twenties. The same five actors play the same roles—boy, girl, villain, and girl's parents—and the story differences function to create an abundance of sight gags. Thereafter, the form seems little used until the 1990s, its rise possibly inspired by the appearance of video games[35] which allow a protagonist who has "died" to restart the story.

The closest thing to a film antecedent may be Kurosawa's ground-breaking *Rashomon* (1950) which tells the same story from the viewpoint of four different characters. Their divergent accounts of a samurai's murder can be attributed to human selfishness, as each character tries to put events in a light most favorable to himself or herself. Subsequent films have shown the variety of ends that can be served by telling a story from different perspectives. In *He Said, She Said* (Kwapis and Silver, 1991), the purpose is comic, highlighting the differences in male and female viewpoints. Liman's *Go* uses the device to maintain dramatic tension: one character's part of the story is carried to near catastrophe at which point the story switches to another character. *Lawless Heart* (Hunsinger and Hunter, 2001) unfolds the events of a weekend from the perspective of several characters, starting over each time. Each re-telling reveals the motivations behind actions that (as seen by others) seemed selfish or stupid. The shifting perspectives ultimately give the viewer a more sympathetic understanding of each character.

The *database narratives* studied here move beyond these hints of subjective viewpoints and uncover a reality which may be uncertain or have new dimensions. The first of them, Hong Sangsoo's *Virgin Stripped Bare by Her Bachelors* (*Oh! Soo-jung,* 2000), like *Rashomon* tells a single story from different perspectives, in this case a courtship as seen by the young man and the young woman. Trivial differences such as a fork falling off a table in one version and a spoon in the other change significantly the picture we get of the two characters. But where Kurosawa presents such differences as a reflection of human self-centeredness, Hong is far more radical, presenting differences so profound that one must question whether any knowable "reality" exists at all. He uses the form, in other words, to suggest the opacity of our world and the people in it.

The second film, Tom Tykwer's *Run Lola Run* (*Lola rennt,* 1998), is a variation of the database narrative commonly referred to as a *forking paths narrative*.[36] The term derives from the famous Borges story, "The Garden of Forking Paths," which proposes that a person's life diverges with each decision he makes, resulting in "an infinite array of possible worlds."[37] This format is familiar to many viewers from Howitt's *Sliding Doors* (1998) where a woman's life follows two different paths depending on whether she catches a particular subway train. Forking paths films often emphasize how a chance difference can significantly change one's life. A famous early exemplar, Kieślowski's *Blind Chance* (1981), begins with a young Polish medical student running to catch a train. Depending on whether he catches the train, misses it and is arrested, or misses it and simply returns home, he goes on to become either a member of the Communist Party, a member of the underground, or a doctor and family man. Tykwer in his film might seem to emphasize chance as much as Kieślowski. His heroine, Lola, needs to obtain 100,000 Deutschmarks in twenty minutes to save her boyfriend, Manni, and fails miserably the first two times before succeeding on her third try. This is not a single story told from different viewpoints but, like Kieślowski's film, a narrative comprising three separate stories. Also, rather than suggesting that the variations are due to human psychology there is a sense that events are shaped by larger forces. To begin with, Lola's miraculous ability to resurrect herself and then Manni after the first two attempts suggests a world of magical reality. And if one seeks to understand what leads Lola to ultimate success, the answer seems to lie not so much in different choices as from coming to see the world in a new way.

The final film, Krzysztof Kieślowski's *The Double Life of Véronique* (*La double vie de Véronique,* 1991), presents two young women, one living in Poland and one in France, who appear to be *doppelgängers*—the same person living two separate lives. This is the most complex permutation of the database narrative. For one thing, the story does not simply stop and start over as in *Lola.* Instead, we follow the life of Weronika in Poland and, when she dies suddenly, the story switches to Véronique in France. So is this the story of one woman or two? The underlying similarities in their lives—both are musicians and have heart conditions—and the fact that the same actress plays both roles suggest that this is a single life taking two different directions, another forking paths narrative. The same idea is suggested by the title, which is "The Double Life of Véronique," not "The Two Veronicas." On the other hand, there are not the exactly similar events or returning characters found in most forking paths narratives. Only ephemeral details link the two stories—mysterious dreams, a musical theme, the color red, a transparent ball. Further, there is a moment in the story when the two women encounter one another, with Weronika catching sight of her double and recognizing her. (At that moment, they are dressed identically.) This might suggest they inhabit the same reality or realities that somehow overlap. Here is a particularly startling use of juxtaposed stories, as Kieślowski uses the mode to probe liminal worlds that normally lie outside our ken.

Multi-Plot, Multi-Path, and Classical Narrative

Looking at these various forms of complex narrative, one sees, in the first place, the range of possibilities opened up by the new play with story forms. Further, the network narrative and the database narrative share a key similarity: both rely heavily on thematic patterns. In the network narrative, stories placed side by side cry out to be compared. Frequently, the filmmaker is uncovering similarities in what first appear to be divergent lives—for example, Germans and Turks inhabiting the same geographic space but immersed in different cultures. By contrast, database narratives, which repeat a single story filled with identical elements, impel one to look for differences. We consider how Véronique's life differs from Weronika's and ponder if things turn out better or worse for her. The all-important similarities and differences most often manifest themselves in patterns which may range from the relationships of parents and children to animal motifs to colors. If filmmakers have been attracted to these new modes, one reason is that they encourage the viewer to be attentive to subtle similarities and differences.

In sum, the single plot with a central protagonist has been the narrative mainstay since Aristotle first described it (and before) because of its obvious strengths. Audiences identify strongly with the protagonist, share her tribulations vicariously, and gain insight as she does. The narrative's strong drive toward its climactic reversal heightens the story's emotional charge. Of course, classic films still allow contrasts and comparisons through conflicts and subplots, but these elements are subsumed to the central narrative thrust. The multi-plot and multi-path films expand these possibilities and do not necessarily lose the strengths of classic story format. The narratives of *Pulp Fiction, Amores Perros, The Edge of*

Heaven, The Double Life of Véronique, and *Run Lola Run* drive forward resolutely and the number of central characters remains limited enough to permit audience identification. And where the single protagonist story derives its "lesson" from the problems he faces and the actions he takes, the story with multiple plots or with multiple versions can do the same—sometimes for a variety of characters. Now that audiences are comfortable with complex narrative modes, serious directors worldwide have understandably been attracted to forms that can be shaped in so many fascinating ways. That variety is clearly seen in the films studied here, ranging from the cartoon kineticism of *Run Lola Run* to the somber meditativeness of *Code Unknown.* Most important, complex narratives can paint a finely nuanced portrait of life as these eight fascinating films illustrate. Little wonder they attract creative filmmakers and knowledgeable filmgoers alike.

Notes

1   *Nashville* has earned around $11 million in the thirty plus years since its release; *Jaws* has taken in over $400 million. Jan Stuart, *The Nashville Chronicles* (New York: Limelight, 2003), 299-300.
2   Helene Keyssar, *Robert Altman's America* (New York: Oxford University Press, 1991), 134.
3   Janet Staiger, "Complex Narratives: An Introduction." *Film Criticism* 31, nos. 1/2 (Fall/Winter 2006): 2.
4   David Bordwell, Janet Staiger, and Kristin Thompson, *The Classical Hollywood Cinema: Film Style & Mode of Production to 1960* (New York: Columbia University Press, 1985), 70-84, 370-77; David Bordwell, *The Way Hollywood Tells It: Story and Style in Modern Movies* (Berkeley: University of California Press, 2006), 72-73.
5   Charles Ramirez Berg, "A Taxonomy of Alternative Plots in Recent Films: Classifying the 'Tarantino Effect,'" *Film Criticism* 31, nos. 1/2 (Fall/Winter 2006): 5-61.
6   See also Jonathan Eig, "A Beautiful Mind(fuck): Hollywood Structures of Identity," *Jump Cut* 46 (Summer 2003). htttp://www.ejumpcut.org/archivejc46.2003/eig/mind-films/text.html (28 July 2010).
7   Bordwell's examination of these new forms in *The Way Hollywood Tells It* is further expanded in chapter 7 of *Poetics of Cinema* (London: Routledge, 2008).
8   Bordwell, *Poetics of Cinema,* 191.
9   Dana Polan, *Pulp Fiction* (London: BFI, 2000), 86.
10   Bordwell, *The Way Hollywood Tells It,* 211.
11   For an extended discussion of the ensemble film see Maria del Mar Azcona, *The Multi-Protagonist Film* (New York: Wiley-Blackwell, 2010).
12   Bordwell, *The Way Hollywood Tells It,* 95.
13   Evan Smith, "Thread Structure: Rewriting the Hollywood Formula," *Journal of Film and Video* 51, nos. 3/4 (Fall/Winter 1999-2000): 88, 90.
14   Bordwell, *Poetics of Cinema,* 192.
15   Bordwell lists two hundred such films as of mid-2007 and the number grows annually although perhaps at a slackened pace (*Poetics of Cinema,* 245-50).
16   Murray Smith, "Parallel Lines," in *American Independent Cinema,* ed. Jim Hillier (London: BFI, 2001), 160.

17   Evan Smith, "Thread Structure," 90.

18   Michael Newman," Character and Complexity in American Independent Cinema: *21 Grams* and *Passion Fish*," *Film Criticism* 31, nos. 1/2 (Fall/Winter 2006): 89-106.

19   Evan Smith, "Thread Structure," 94.

20   Bordwell, *Poetics of Cinema*, 208.

21   Murray Smith, "Parallel Lines," 155-56.

22   Margrit Tröhler, "Les films à protagonists multiples et la logique des possibles," *Iris* 29 (Spring 2000): 85-86.

23   Stephen Farber, "A Half-Dozen Ways to Watch the Same Movie," *New York Times* (13 November 2005): A18.

24   Berg, "A Taxonomy of Alternative Plots," 14-18.

25   Bordwell, *Poetics of Cinema*, 193.

26   Bordwell, *Poetics of Cinema*, 198, 199.

27   Bordwell, *The Way Hollywood Tells It*, 93.

28   Bordwell, *The Way Hollywood Tells It*, 93.

29   Bordwell, *The Way Hollywood Tells It*, 93-94.

30   Peter Brooker and Will Brooker, "Pulpmodernism: Tarantino's Affirmative Action," in *Pulping Fiction: Consuming Culture across the Literature/Media Divide*, ed. Deborah Cartmell, et al. (Chicago: Pluo, 1996), 137. The Brookers are summarizing the attitude of a host of critics whom they cite.

31   Berg, "A Taxonomy of Alternative Plots," 40.

32   Bordwell, *Poetics of Cinema*, 204.

33   David Bordwell uses the term "*multiple-draft* narrative" in "Film Futures," *SubStance* #97, 31, no. 1 (2002): 102. The rapid pace of innovation has left critics struggling to develop a consistent terminology and a variety of terms has been proposed for films that present alternative story versions. Marsha Kinder assigns the term "database narrative" to narratives which "reveal the arbitrariness of the particular choices made, and the possibility of making other combinations which would create alternative stories." "Hot Spots, Avatars, and Narrative Fields Forever—Buñuel's Legacy for New Digital Media and Interactive Database Narratives," *Film Quarterly* 55, no. 4 (2002): 6. She includes *Run Lola Run* among such films. Allan Cameron uses the term "modular narrative" as akin to database narrative, designating "narratives that foreground the relationship between the temporality of the story and the order of its telling." *Modular Narratives in Contemporary Cinema* (New York: Palgrave Macmillan, 2008), 1. That is, the jumbling of time in a film like *Pulp Fiction* calls attention to the fact that the story elements could have been presented in a variety of orders.

34   Kristin Thompson mentions another early example of multiple stories: Fritz Lang's *Destiny* (*Der müde Tod*, 1921) in which a girl makes repeated attempts to rescue her lover from Death (Personal correspondence).

35   Bordwell, "Film Futures," 102.

36   Edward Branigan suggests that "forking paths" be used for more simple juggling of time, "leaving the name 'multiple-draft' narrative as a way to cover a more general phenomenon." "Nearly True: Forking Plots, Forking Interpretations: A Response to David Bordwell's 'Film Futures,'" *SubStance* #97 31, no. 1 (2002): 108.

37   Bordwell, "Film Futures," 88.

Mosaic

Narrative

2

Nashville

Pitching Songs and Selling Politicians

Robert Altman, unquestionably a major force behind the new narrative trends, exhibits breathtaking levels of innovation in *Nashville* (1975), leaping ahead twenty years in cinematic storytelling. Unfortunately, few viewers of the time were ready to make the leap with him. Despite rave reviews by Pauline Kael, Roger Ebert, Andrew Sarris, Molly Haskell, and others, the film did not catch on and was firmly snubbed at the Oscars. If average viewers were unimpressed, those in the city where it was filmed were openly hostile. One Nashville luminary said the best part was the ending, "when they shot that miserable excuse for a country-music singer," and another opined that if Altman were to return to the city he'd likely be hung.[1] Their disdain is understandable—how could a film presume to represent the city eponymous with country music without casting a single authentic Nashville star? A larger problem was its ideology. Capturing the social climate at the time of America's two hundredth birthday, *Nashville* is filled with reminders of Watergate, Vietnam, the civil rights upheavals, and political assassinations: Altman called it "my metaphor for America."[2] Despite moments of warmth and humor, the aimless lives of the characters were a discomfiting metaphor for a nation that seemed to have lost its collective way—a sense that Americans were anxious to put behind them.

Equally problematic was the aspect seen today as marking the film's particular genius: its narrative invention. Despite having no real predecessors to draw on, the film uses the multi-plot format with exceptional skill. Dispensing entirely with the idea of a central protagonist, Altman creates a ***mosaic film***, a pointillist narrative built up of multiple stories and minor events. No fewer than twenty-four characters are involved, each appearing on every one of the film's five days. While most of them are secondary and quickly sketched, there are still eight or more central characters to be fleshed out. To do so, Altman uses a key strength of the thread narrative, building up nuanced portraits through a gradual accretion of detail. For example, in one scene, the would-be singer Sueleen appears laughable as she performs ineptly, while in another, forced to do a striptease, she is highly sympathetic. Furthermore, characters are juxtaposed as the threads interweave, showing parallels and contrasts. Thus the calculated performance of a country music star in one recording studio seems cold compared to the enthusiastic gospel choir shown next door. In this fashion, *Nashville* demonstrates how the film with multiple plots can dispense with overdetermined, stereotypic characterization and depend instead on small details and subtle contrasts.

Further, for the most part the film jettisons the forward-driving action, plot obstacles, and emotional confrontations that typify the Hollywood film. The story is built from vignettes that appear random and insignificant. Most of the scenes unfold at a relaxed pace, with no fast cutting or jumpy camera work designed to create artificial excitement. Although the scenes unfold chronologically and all occur within the bounds of Nashville, the action jumps from place to place with no apparent connection. It seems no more than a "slice of life" of a few days in the country music capital. While the plot moves toward the final political rally, that is not put forward as a crucial moment. Rex Reed was one of many critics who decried the film's lack of structure, saying, "The whole picture just falls apart."[3] Reed missed how the accumulated effect of low-key moments can build into a meaningful portrait. Thus one extended traffic jam scene has the characters simply sitting in their cars waiting for an accident to be cleared away. But this nicely shows their narcissism, sitting isolated in their vehicles, chatting aimlessly, and making no attempt to help the accident victims. Instead of driving toward a climactic scene that "explains" everything—showing who is right and who is wrong—the film's meaning emerges steadily in the behavior patterns exhibited over the course of five days.[4]

Notably, the multitude of characters, short scenes, and constant jumping from one story to the next prevent close identification with any one character. The camera divides the viewer's attention by filling the screen with people and actions, seldom moving into close shot. Crucial events are not always foregrounded and the sound track is notably busy, as in the scenes at the night clubs where the sound comes from one table, then another, providing bits of various conversations amid the music and audience noise.[5] Here again, Altman is using one of the potential strengths of the complex narrative: creating a more subtle, complex emotional tone. While many of the characters are engaging and bits of humor pop up constantly, other scenes reveal petty, egoistic behavior as performers vie for the position of primacy.

Altman maintains an ironic stance—enjoying these colorful characters but keenly aware of their shortcomings—and his techniques encourage viewers to do the same. He wants them to pay close attention, to sort out crucial details without their being foregrounded, and to evaluate the characters and their actions intellectually rather than just responding to them emotionally. Observing events in this fashion, one appreciates how the characters develop complexity and the various stories merge into a meaningful portrait as they interweave. In other words, twenty years before other directors begin to experiment with narrative form, Altman presents a fully-developed, tightly integrated example of just how artistically effective the mosaic film and thematic structuring can be.

Story Summary

Nashville's apparently random narrative actually has clear starting and stopping points. It begins with John Triplette's arrival in Nashville. A front man for Hal Phillip Walker, the Replacement Party's presidential candidate, he has come to recruit as many Nashville stars as possible to perform at an upcoming Walker rally. The story closes when the rally ends abruptly because Kenny, an unbalanced young man, shoots Barbara Jean, the lead star. However, the rally plot line remains in the background, serving mostly to underscore the major theme of the film: that politics and popular music are equally hypocritical in the way they pander to their publics. Over the course of five days we meet a mélange of Nashville regulars and visitors. Haven Hamilton, a vain country music star, appears in scenes in his recording studio, at home, in a local music club, in church, and performing at Grand Ole Opry. Besides going after Haven, Triplette recruits a trio of folk singers, Tom, Bill, and Mary. (Tom spends his time bedding every woman in sight, including Mary, Bill's wife.) We meet Linnea, a sympathetic housewife with two deaf children, and her husband, Del, a lawyer who works with Triplette trying to recruit the Nashville stars. The singer they most want to recruit is Barbara Jean, just returning to Nashville after a nervous collapse. She promptly collapses again and is hospitalized. Her irascible husband and manager, Barnett, initially refuses Triplette's overtures, but is forced to let her appear at the Walker rally after she goes into a rambling monologue during a performance at another country music show. A host of minor characters also appears. Sueleen, a cafeteria waitress, wants desperately to be a music star and hasn't got a lick of talent. Opal claims to be a BBC reporter but is most likely another hanger-on. Mr. Green is an older man who brings his niece, L. A. Joan, to the hospital to visit his sick wife, only to have her run off with Buddy, Haven Hamilton's handsome son. Albuquerque, newly come to town, runs away from her husband, desperate to see the Grand Ole Opry. These characters appear in various scenes over the five days of the story and all show up for the finale at the Walker Rally.

Characterization by Accretion

One of the potential strengths of thread narrative is that characterization can be more subtle, using small details like pointillist dots rather than the broad strokes of stereotype. While some of its twenty-four characters are presented sketchily, *Nashville* fleshes out the central ones surprisingly well through bits of behavior in scattered scenes. This requires the viewer to be sensitive to small details and then step back and see how, as in an Impressionist painting, they coalesce into a meaningful whole. Further, the portraits that emerge are often multivalent. While there are many cynical digs at the vanity and self-centeredness of the performers, more sympathetic aspects are also shown, something Alan Karp terms Altman's "bisociative" structure,[6] which avoids the simplified character types of Hollywood films.

One character portrayed almost entirely negatively is Haven Hamilton, a big-name country music star with an ego to match. His initial appearance in his recording studio allows the viewer to contrast the backstage reality with the onstage persona. Haven is recording a song for the Bicentennial: "We Must Be Doing Something Right (to Last Two Hundred Years)." The song's thesis is that America's survival for two centuries can be attributed to its moral superiority. As many critics have noted, the film will spend its remaining two hours and thirty minutes refuting that thesis. Like all the country music stars, Haven presents himself as a warm and welcoming person, but the scene neatly undercuts that image. Strongly up-lit when first seen in his recording booth, Haven appears sinister, peering around into the darkness, looking positively paranoid (Figure 2.1). Cut off from the backup group

2.1 Characterization by accretion: Haven in the recording booth.

who sing in a separate booth, he talks through a microphone to his son, Buddy, emphasizing his isolation. He wears his white spangled cowboy shirt even in the booth, suggesting a constant concern for his image. Spotting Opal, the supposed BBC reporter who enters with her tape recorder in hopes of an interview, Haven immediately stops the session and orders Buddy to remove her. "If she wants a copy of this record, she can buy it," he snaps, and then launches into a diatribe about the piano player's long hair, snapping "You don't belong in Nashville." So much for the image of the warm and welcoming South. Thus while Haven's song lyrics proclaim him a man of the people, his visual isolation and imperious treatment of everyone in the studio reveal him for the vain, petty tyrant he is.

Haven's character is further adumbrated when Triplette shows up a day later at Haven's home, hoping to persuade him to appear at the Walker rally. Although Lady Pearl insists that Haven never takes sides politically, after she has left, Triplette tells Haven that Walker thinks "you'd make a fine governor" and would support him with his organization. Haven doesn't respond, but asks Triplette if he'll be coming to his performance at the Grand Ole Opry that evening—Triplette hastens to assure him he'll be there—and Haven says he'll give his answer then. In other words, Triplette must be willing to play Haven's game if he wants to succeed. And of course Triplette does succeed, because Haven shows up at the Walker rally at the end. The canny maneuvering in this scene underscores the film's equation of the worlds of politics and entertainment. That equality is further emphasized by the filming, with Haven and Triplette shown six times in a balanced two-shot, the longest being the twenty-six second moment where Triplette offers support for a governor's race (Figure 2.2). Putting the two men nose to nose

2.2
Two canny players: Haven and Triplette.

in these shots—Triplette is savvy enough to sit down so as not to tower over the diminutive Haven—shows them as equal players, shrewdly sizing one another up. Haven's toughness in this scene (not to mention his desire to be governor) suggests that his rise to the top of the Nashville world has been due more to political than musical talent. This apparently random scene, where nothing conclusive happens, still adds precise details to Haven's portrait.

With this background on Haven, viewers can appreciate the ironies in the image he projects as he appears at the Grand Ole Opry. He first sings, "For the Sake of the Children, We Must Say Goodbye," about a man who breaks off an affair to return to his family. The hypocrisy is palpable, since Haven is separated from his wife and Lady Pearl is obviously his mistress. Nor is he any better as a father. Although he always has Buddy take a bow at public appearances, Haven consigns his son to serve as his chauffeur and generally treats him "with less affection or respect than he accords a domestic servant."[7] Haven's second song, "Keep a-Goin'," extols his strength in adversity and "is delivered with the paranoiac eye-gleam and bared teeth of a 1950s conformist-executive who will do anything to win his next promotion."[8] As the song lyrics say, "It takes work to reach the top," and Haven is determined not only to maintain his position in the music industry but possibly to wriggle onto the governor's chair. While the image is of a genial, family-oriented, God-fearing man, the reality is a vain, ruthlessly ambitious entrepreneur.

Triplette

Triplette's character is harder to pin down for the simple reason that he constantly changes, telling everyone what they want to hear. Sensing Haven's ambition, he promises political support. Recruiting folk singers Bill and Mary, he says he's got a lot of local yokels on the bill and would like a broader appeal. Undoubtedly aware they have released only one record, he mentions that the Walker program will be syndicated. Needing Sueleen to do a striptease, he offers her the chance to appear onstage alongside Barbara Jean. Knowing Haven will only appear if Barbara Jean does, he promises Barnett there will be no political paraphernalia onstage—an obvious and outright lie. Since he makes each of these offers with a smile and a straight face, he appears entirely genuine. However, the viewer is privy to every one of these scenes and sees how Triplette smoothly changes his story to fit the situation. The point is all too obvious that politicians get elected by sensing what people want to hear and promising it to them.

Triplette's real face becomes more apparent in the scene at Grand Ole Opry. As Haven preens for his audience at the front of the stage, Triplette is sitting with Del in the "family benches" at the rear. The preceding scene at Haven's house had emphasized their parity in cynical calculation, and Triplette shows himself Haven's equal in hypocrisy here. As pint-sized Haven lowers the microphone for his song, Triplette asks Del with quiet sarcasm, "How tall is that guy?" and the two of them laugh together. Triplette mocks Haven's rhinestone-studded outfit (echoing Haven's disdain for the piano player's long hair), "He's got the entire galaxy on the back of his shirt." Taking note of Connie White's costume (a singer filling in for the ailing Barbara Jean), Triplette comments to Del, "Last time I saw a dress like that, I was headin' to the junior prom." Like Haven, Triplette is all image. He talks to the singers with seeming sincerity, lauding their talents and respectful of their position, but scorns them behind their backs. This, in turn, reflects on Hal Phillip Walker, for whom he serves as a stand-in. Triplette's cynical manipulation of his clients undercuts any credence for Walker's claim to represent the common man, to stand for honesty in government, and to bring a new spirit of openness to politics. With slow but careful brush strokes the film paints its picture of Triplette the front man and, by implication, of American politics.

Del

A particularly deft portrait is given of Del Reese, Linnea's husband, who first appears at the airport to meet Triplette, hoping to serve as his go-between with other Nashville personages. In a typical film their meeting would occur in a quiet space, using close shots, and a tightly scripted dialogue to characterize the two principals. Altman, however, stages the meeting in long shot in the middle of the airport corridor, with people hurrying by, so the viewer must struggle to extract the relevant details. Focusing on the two men is particularly difficult because hippie L. A. Joan is standing prominently at screen right, dressed in short shorts, bandeau top, long multicolored stockings and thick clogs—a distracting spectacle indeed. The sound track is as cluttered as the visual field, with other characters talking as they walk by and the airport P. A. system nattering on in the background.

In the corridor, Del calls out "John Triplette" at a man standing nearby, who ignores him, and then the real Triplette walks up and introduces himself. As the two shake hands, Bill and Mary, the young folk singers, push past them and then the two men walk off. During this meeting, the camera has moved in slightly and other people have cleared the screen so the encounter can be seen and heard, but the scene is very brief and we have no sense of who either man is or why they are meeting. However, the attentive viewer can pick up clues about Del. He put on his sunglasses while still indoors, vainly attempting to look like a mover and shaker for his meeting with Triplette (Figure 2.3). However, having made his

2.3
Del trying to look like a mover and a shaker.

initial appearance in the airport cafeteria amid a group of outsiders, especially the hopelessly subtalented Sueleen, he is immediately marked as another "would-be." This is reinforced by his guessing wrong at which man is Triplette and then awkwardly apologizing for his sunglasses, donned so self-consciously a moment before. Being Haven's lawyer does not make him an insider, for when he tries to introduce Triplette to Barbara Jean's husband and manager, the ever-irascible Barnett brushes him away with, "I got no time now! Jesus!"

Del is also marked as a lecher. His interested glance at Sueleen in the cafeteria foreshadows his later attempt to hit on her. He fails to spot Triplette because he is too busy sizing up L.A. Joan and he says, "Hello," hopefully to the pretty Mary when she brushes by. As he walks along with Triplette, Del is constantly glancing over his shoulder, apparently searching for new prospects, financial or female. These small details can be assembled into a coherent picture of an inept, sleazy hustler, but this is not something the film hands out on a platter. Portraits of the other characters, similarly, are built up by small details in brief scenes, many of whom turn out to resemble Del in key regards, being long on ambition and short on ethics. Thread structures always require close attention by viewers, but *Nashville* uses very fine details and mixes them in with a welter of visual information.

Linnea

Not all the characters in Nashville are portrayed so negatively. Linnea is generally sympathetic, although it takes a while for the dots in her picture to coalesce. Her first appearance is puzzling—a lone white woman singing in the midst of the Fisk gospel choir—but makes sense juxtaposed with Haven Hamilton in the studio next door. Where he is isolated in his recording booth, she stands in the midst of her fellow singers, dressed in a matching blue choir robe, her spontaneity in clear contrast to Haven's calculated endeavors. (Altman signals where his sympathies lie, putting his credit as director and producer over Linnea's enthusiastic singing [Figure 2.4].) In another telling juxtaposition, Linnea is seen at home with her family after two scenes in Nashville music clubs. The clubs were dimly lit, with people crowded together, the camera generally distanced, and the sound track busy. In contrast, Linnea's dining room is bright, tasteful, and orderly, and as Del walks into it to join his wife and two children, the camera tracks into

2.4
Linnea:
The real
mover and
shaker.

successively tighter shots. Their son, Jimmy, is telling about his swimming class; he is deaf and so speaks somewhat indistinctly and signs some of his story. Close-ups emphasize how intensely Linnea is involved in his story, in contrast to Del, who is obviously bored and uncomprehending. He cannot sign to the children as Linnea can, breaks awkwardly into Jimmy's story to speak to her, then asks his son a question which the boy does not understand. Although there is nothing as obvious as a fight, Del seems unable to offer emotional support to his wife and children. Showing them in separate shots further emphasizes the disconnection. In this light, Linnea's enthusiastic gospel singing may be an attempt to compensate for the lack of spiritual sustenance from her spouse.

Given Linnea's positive portrait, viewers are justifiably dismayed when, after fending off several invitations from Tom, the lothario singer, she shows up at the Exit Inn where he is performing. Announcing a new song dedicated "to someone special who might be here tonight," Tom launches into a touching rendition of "I'm Easy." The camera cuts among various women in the front—previous conquests—and then very slowly zooms in to Linnea sitting in the rear in her white suit (the shot lasts twenty-six seconds). She listens intently, her face betraying no expression. She does not move a muscle, but as the song finishes, she exhales soulfully. The viewer is disappointed when this sympathetic character then turns up in Tom's bed, apparently having descended to the same level as the callow Opal and feckless Mary.

However, there are key differences. Where Opal had been pictured sound asleep and Mary draped adoringly across Tom's chest, Linnea is in her slip, wide awake, and positioned higher than Tom in the frame. Mary had crooned, "I love you, I love you" to the sleeping Tom, but now he asks Linnea to teach him "I love you" in sign language and he ends up saying those words rather than an adoring female. Linnea screws up her face at the smell of his toke, but asks to try it, takes a speculative drag, and hands it back (Figure 2.5). This action signals her basic

2.5 Linnea trying Tom and trying a toke.

attitude in this encounter: she has no more serious interest in dope than in Tom but is curious enough to try them each once. And where the other women had clung to Tom, now it is he who asks Linnea to stay longer when she heads into the bathroom and begins dressing. Instead of being another adoring sycophant, Linnea appears very much Tom's equal and, if anything, is more in control than he is.

This impression continues as the scene finishes. With a scowl, Tom picks up a phone and calls another woman, his typical ploy to exert his dominance. Dressing in the background, Linnea can obviously hear but only glances casually in his direction. While Tom continues his phone seduction, she finishes putting herself together, gives Tom a warm kiss in passing, waves good-bye from the door and is gone. Tom quickly terminates his phone conversation and sits in bed, looking sulky. Linnea's marital cheating is sad, but one guesses being romanced by a hot stud provided a welcome respite from her child-caring duties. She appears to have used Tom as much as he used her, letting him flatter her with his song and provide more excitement between the sheets than she finds at home. Now the fling is over, she puts on her watch and her clothes, gives him a kiss that says, "Thanks for the fun time," and heads back to the real world and her life of serious responsibility. In the end, Linnea comes across as a complex, engaging, and genuine person, although not without foibles. Her portrait is another triumph of Altman's subtle pointillist technique.

Thematic Juxtaposition

A second key strength of thread structures is their ability to bring out thematic relationships, seen throughout in the linking of the entertainment industry and politics. Thus the film opens with a frenetic pitch for a hit record containing the songs of *Nashville*. (The record was actually made.) It touts "twenty-four of your very favorite stars," as if the various singers are popular country western stars rather than minor TV and movie actors not known for their singing. As the hokey commercial finishes, the sound track segues immediately into the (equally canned) sound of the "Walker Wagon" which rolls out to cruise the streets of Nashville, spouting its commercial for Hal Phillip Walker. (The visual field also segues, with the word "Nashville" in the titles, shown in white letters on a black screen, becoming the same word in black letters on the Walker sign over the garage door.) These visual and auditory links connect the two scenes, with the voice of one carnival barker replaced immediately by another's. In case anyone has missed the point, a second pair of visual and sonic dissolves connects politics and entertainment as the camera follows the Walker Wagon for a few moments, and then the sounds of guitar, banjo and rhythm section creep onto the soundtrack under Walker's voice. The scene dissolves into the studio where Haven is recording his fiercely patriotic song. These juxtapositions announce the film's central thesis: politicians and performers must both sell themselves to their publics. Both spheres are ultimately rooted in the same values: self-promotion, creation of an appropriate image, vicious infighting, and total cynicism.

The juxtaposition means that the character of the performers, in turn, reflects on the nature of politicians. After mouthing platitudes like the Walker Wagon, Haven shows in the recording studio that his real interest is not patriotism but selling records. The very fact he can be enticed by Triplette's offer of support for a gubernatorial campaign further emphasizes how closely entertainment and politics overlap. The film's final scenes, with the Nashville musicians assembled on the stage beneath Walker's political banner, is the image clinching the merger of these two branches of the performing arts. This is particularly ironic given that all the singers there assembled have loudly proclaimed their total disinterest in politics. Lady Pearl said Haven doesn't "take sides politically," folk singer Bill stated "I don't care about politics," and Barnett announced, "No politics, no government, no nothin'." Nevertheless, they all show up. Their attitude mirrors that of the American public in most eras: assume an attitude of disdain, treat politics as mostly entertainment, and only become involved when there appears to be some possibility for personal gain. The result, the film suggests, is that the public gets the politicians it deserves.

Barbara Jean at the Hospital

More meaningful juxtapositions occur in the scenes that follow Barbara Jean's collapse at the airport. She is seen in her hospital room, deluged with visitors and gifts. Immediately after this, L. A. Joan is taken to the hospital by Mr. Green to see her aunt Martha, but starts flirting with Buddy and heads away with him. Next, having escaped from her husband during the traffic jam, Albuquerque walks down the road alongside Kenny announcing her wish to go to the Grand Ole Opry. Finally, Sueleen is shown alone in her room practicing her act in front of a mirror. The thematic center of these various scenes lies with Barbara Jean in the hospital, where show business and illness are equated. The nurse acts as a stage manager, telling Barbara Jean cheerfully, "We're settin' up for you" as Buddy hurries around hanging objects on the wall. Del comes in wanting to introduce Triplette, the candy-stripe girl brings flowers, Barnett yells at Buddy's hammering, and Tommy Brown and his wife pay a visit: the scene resembles nothing so much as the backstage pandemonium before a show. There is even a guard at the door. In effect, the hospital room is transformed into a performance space, emphasizing that, even when ill, Barbara Jean must be "on stage" (Figure 2.6).

2.6 Barbara Jean in the hospital: Show business as illness.

Juxtaposed to this scene, L. A. Joan is another performer, changing costume in an instant and more interested in a sexual conquest than in her sick aunt. She appears in new togs in every scene, her shifting outfits suggesting she is all external appearance, like most of the Nashville performers. Her need for new partners mirrors the need of the musicians for audience applause, for public approval, for attention. Albuquerque suffers from it too, declaring to Kenny her determination to be a country western singer. (Since Kenny is unbalanced, this continues the link of stardom and illness.) The hunger to be noticed is expressed with particular pathos by Sueleen's trademark song, "Let Me Be the One." Her desperate wish to be somebody special is particularly painful because of her all-too-evident ordinariness. She stuffs white socks into her bra, stands in a room full of tacky furnishings, dressed in a home-sewn purple dress, and practices her tawdry routine with entirely unspontaneous hand gestures (Figure 2.7). We are not intended to laugh at Sueleen, anymore than at Barbara Jean, exhausted by the demands of her career, or plucky Albuquerque with her torn stockings. All three women are prisoners of the dream of stardom, trapped and sickened like Barbara Jean.[9]

2.7 More show business sickness: Sueleen.

Grand Ole Opry

Through further juxtapositions, the performance at the Grand Ole Opry reveals fissures in the supposed camaraderie of the country music clan. Connie White and Barbara Jean are presented as bitter rivals who would never appear on the same stage. Further, as Tommy Brown walks off stage past the waiting Haven, he remarks sarcastically that the audience is "dead." Haven mutters under his breath, "You're lucky to be alive." The genial Haven, then, is very much a product of the Old South and partial to an earlier time when a Negro like Tommy Brown who aspired to be the equal of Whites would quickly have been taught the error of his ways. (At the NASCAR races the next day, Haven will turn and pass a slice of watermelon to Tommy and his wife in another subtle racist gesture.) The Grand Ole Opry segment is given particular resonance as Barbara Jean and Barnett listen on the radio in the hospital. Barnett insists on hearing all of Connie's performance, seeming deliberately to torment his wife, but claiming this is necessary so he will be able to thank Connie for filling in. When Barbara Jean objects, he snaps, "Don't tell me how to run your life!" and tells her not to go "nutsy" on him. Shattered, she stumbles back into bed and whimpers alone in the room after he leaves.

The juxtaposition again associates the idea of illness with show business. In stark contrast to the brightly lit stage, with the audience applauding and family members gathered in the benches nearby, Barbara Jean and Barnett sit alone in the darkened hospital room. Crammed with flowers, it suggests a funeral parlor: being shut away from the stage and applause is a kind of death. Locked in her isolation cell, Barbara Jean must endure the hectoring of her husband, whose continued irascibility might well suggest that, on some level, he is jealous of the attention she receives. Saddest of all is the inescapable trap in which she is caught. Her fans demand she remain the sweet young girl, dressed always in white with childish ribbons in her hair, and her husband similarly keeps her in a child-like role. However, few children are equipped to deal with the politics, the pressure, and the constant public scrutiny required in this dog-eat-dog profession. The somber setting here reveals the dark interior of the entertainment world, contrasting with its glittering exterior (especially glittering in the case of Haven's jacket). One is left to ponder whether the performers have been driven to the stage in a search for emotional contact missing in their lives, or whether their emotional emptiness is the result of too long immersion in this world. Belying the apparent casualness of events, these carefully juxtaposed scenes throw the tawdriness of Nashville lives into sharp relief.

Symbolic Snapshots

A third important use of the thread structure is thematic—interweaving strands to present a symbolic picture of Nashville and, through it, of America. A first good example is the traffic jam that occurs after the airport scene, forcing all the characters to wait in their cars while the highway is cleared. Each behaves characteristically. Sueleen flirts with boys in the surrounding cars; Tom collects girls' addresses; Haven, self-promoting as always, signs autographs and bickers with Lady Pearl; Mr. Green natters on about Martha, his sick wife, while L. A. Joan ignores him; supposed BBC correspondent Opal invents scenes of catastrophe (while being careful not to go near the actual accident site), and practical Linnea calmly orders popsicles to cool herself and Opal.

As Helene Keyssar notes, this scene is emblematic of the film's structure, capturing the Nashville world in microcosm and revealing the essence of each character.[10] In this case, everyone goes on doing what he or she normally does and ignores everyone else. That, in turn, comments on the American mythos. A favorite American belief holds that, in times of crisis, everyone pulls together—a myth given credence in countless musicals where even rivals cooperate to put on the final grand show. Since Altman delights in inverting generic structures,[11] in his version of the musical, the characters sit calmly in their cars without giving the slightest thought of helping the accident victims. This scene can be taken as a metaphoric image of the American political situation in 1975: everything is in chaos, forward progress has ground to a halt, and people just ignore the problem. They sit in their individual vehicles, their isolation emphasized by many shots through car windows, and wait for someone else to fix things. And throughout this chaotic scene, the beer truck, the ice cream vendor, and the turtle stool salesman do a brisk business while the Walker volunteers continue passing out materials and pasting on bumper stickers. Commerce and politics go merrily on in the midst of catastrophe.

Seduction and Striptease

All these elements—complex characterization, thematic juxtaposition, and symbolic portraiture—are combined in the sequence that alternates Tom singing "I'm Easy" at The Exit Inn with Sueleen doing her striptease at the smoker across town. The camera cuts constantly between the two scenes, linking them. At the smoker for Hal Phillip Walker, after Del has invited the men to write out their checks, the music starts and Sueleen is lowered on a platform from the ceiling, nicely suggesting the degradation that awaits her. Wearing one of her obviously homemade gowns and a feathered mask, she launches into an off-key rendition of "I Never Get Enough (of the Love I'm Hungry For)." The derisive applause that begins while her number is still going on forms a sound bridge to the applause back at The Exit Inn where Tom is launching into "I'm Easy." His beautiful ballad becomes, in this setting, a masterpiece of deception. The singer portrays himself as completely in the thrall of his beloved, unable to help himself. "Say you want me, I'll come runnin'/Without takin' time to think/Because I'm easy" (Figure 2.8). This is the same Tom who arrived at the Nashville airport with three pretty

2.8
"I'm easy":
Musical
seduction.

stewardii in tow and who marched to the phone to call the next woman on his list while Opal was still searching for her clothes. But while aware the image Tom is projecting is totally fraudulent, the viewer is drawn into the scene. The song is beautiful, Tom sings it movingly (in stark contrast to Sueleen's sad performance) and the camera tracks in steadily to increase the intensity of the moment. Everything in the scene emphasizes how talented he is.

Back at the smoker, Sueleen is forced to flee the stage in the middle of her second song as the men yell and throw things scornfully. Triplette quickly intervenes, telling her she can sing at the Parthenon with Barbara Jean if she'll strip. She stands stunned for a moment, then asserts, "I'm gonna be as big a star as Barbara Jean is one day." Triplette agrees, "You can't miss." She returns to the stage, the band breaks into a burlesque beat, and piece by piece she removes her clothing. The camerawork shows measured objectivity. Sueleen's humiliation is ugly and could have been accentuated with close-ups of tears running down her cheeks or of the leering faces of the men. No such shots appear. Instead, the camera generally stays at a middle distance, preserving her modesty by letting the musicians and heads of the men block her out. She pulls the socks out of her bra and tosses them to the audience, turning her back to the camera in the process (Figure 2.9). She steps out of her skirt, walks around as she takes off her bra, and then peels off her panties, concealed behind the piano. The men whistle and applaud as she disappears in the rear, shown in long shot. As filmed, the routine is unerotic, sad, and tawdry.

Sueleen is not made an erotic spectacle nor a melodramatic object of pity. Rather, the camera creates a Brechtian distance, encouraging the viewer to remain emotionally detached and consider the wider meaning of these juxtaposed scenes.

2.9 Sueleen's striptease: The prostitution of politics.

For one thing, Tom and Sueleen are linked by the theme of prostitution. Her degradation is awful, but so is his, all the more so because he does it to himself. He uses his considerable musical talents for the sole purpose of bedding as many females as possible. (To emphasize his narcissism, his seduction scenes are always accompanied by a tape of him singing one of his own songs.) In using his music to satisfy ego needs, Tom mirrors all the Nashville artists for whom career advancement takes precedence over artistic achievement. Further, if Sueleen is being exploited and demeaned, so are the men and so is the political process. No discussion of the merits of the candidate is going on in this room. Instead, Triplette is creating support for Walker by pandering to the carnal instincts which Tom embodies. Triplette is stage-managing the entire show, and it comments on him, on his candidate, and on the state of American politics. He has succeeded with all his targets—Haven, Bill and Mary, Barnett, and Sueleen—by intuiting what they are dreaming of and promising to supply it. By implication, politicians tap into the dreams of their constituents to get elected. The juxtaposed scenes also equate Tom and Hal Phillip Walker. Like Tom, politicians sell a pretty face and a song, crooning what people want to hear. The Walker Wagon spouts its platitudes of looking out for the little guy, but Walker's representative shows himself totally disdainful of ordinary people, promoting his candidate by whatever means necessary. This hearkens back to Haven recording his patriotic song to create a marketable image. Entertainers and politicians, the film makes clear, are both performers whose public image seldom corresponds to their true characters.

Finally, these scenes complete the film's complex portrait of Sueleen. After her act, Del drives her home and tries to come on to her, but hurries off when Wade, Sueleen's coworker at the cafeteria, shows up. Wade asks about the show and she confesses, "I had to do me a striptease tonight in front of all those men." Outraged, Wade finally dares speak the truth, telling her she cannot sing. "They gon' tear your heart out if you keep on." Totally unfazed, Sueleen smiles at him smugly.

She can too sing, she insists, and he's welcome to come and hear her at the Parthenon with Barbara Jean. She waggles her fingers saucily in his face and waltzes inside. Having seen repeated examples of her dreadful lack of talent, the viewer can only look on with sorrow. Unlike the image familiar from many films—the unknown star whose talent finally emerges—Sueleen represents the "aspiring entertainer as untalented, stubborn, self-deluded dope."[12] Here is another nuanced character to whom we respond in constantly changing ways. We smile at her eagerness to sing in the diner and her obvious lack of talent. Those smiles continue as she practices her silly routine alone in her room during the Grand Ole Opry broadcast. Then we feel sorry as she is demeaned in the striptease and are truly embarrassed when she scurries away like a whipped dog at the end. As a final humiliation, she must endure Del's sleazy come-on. But then she turns a deaf ear when Wade tries to talk sense to her, forcing us to realize that she sets herself up for these humiliations because her dreams are so unrealistic. Sueleen's portrait, in turn, implies a comment on the American political process. We may feel disgust for cynical manipulators like Triplette, but we are also forced to realize how many dolts are eager to sell out to anyone who will stroke their egos.

The Walker Rally

The film closes with the Walker rally in a scene that encapsulates Altman's view of American society and politics coming up to the bicentennial year. It is staged at the Parthenon, Nashville's concrete replica of the famous Grecian marble edifice. As Del explains to Triplette, the building was constructed for a centennial celebration and then rebuilt because people began calling Nashville "The Athens of the South." This fake setting for Walker's rally is an obvious commentary on Nashville and on American politics. Far from being a democratic Athens, Nashville has shown itself and its music business to be a rigid aristocracy run by a few cynical oligarchs. Walker himself is never seen. His motorcade drives up, Walker stays in the car to work on his speech, and when Barbara Jean's shooting occurs, the motorcade is gone in a flash. Walker's invisibility is another suggestion that politicians are created images rather than real people. The complete cynicism of the political process is shown when Barnett arrives and finds Triplette has reneged on his promise to remove the political paraphernalia. When Barnett protests, Triplette dares him to withdraw Barbara Jean, knowing full well Barnett cannot take the risk. With everyone now totally in his control, Triplette can drop his mask of congeniality. Then, no sooner does Barbara Jean launch into "My Idaho Home" when Kenny fires from the audience and the rally ends.

There are no good rationales for Kenny's shooting of Barbara Jean, although many theories have been advanced. It is true that the setting and filming link her to Walker. Walker posters were seen in the rear seat of Kenny's car, abandoned during the traffic jam, and he later passed the Walker headquarters carrying his instrument case with the pistol inside and Walker's picture pasted on the outside. Given America's history of political assassinations at the time, it is possible that Kenny's original intention was to shoot Walker. Another theory would suggest that, given his troubled relationship with his mother (revealed in a short phone call to her), Barbara Jean's song about her childhood, which she dedicates "For Mama and Daddy," strikes some chord in him. But Jane Feuer argues that assigning any motive misses the point. "The assassination is of necessity capricious. Anyone could be the killer and anyone could be the victim in a world where violence runs very close to a surface of complacency."[13] Such violence obviously permeates American society, as the Vietnam demonstrations, the civil rights struggles, the Nixon legacy, and the political assassinations—all alluded to in the film—attest. After the shooting, Haven calls out angrily, "This isn't Dallas, it's Nashville." In this, he mirrors the general American attitude that racial discrimination and brutality exist elsewhere in the country but not in one's hometown. The intercut shots of Kenny moving through the crowd suggest he is about to do something, but what he takes from his instrument case is concealed, and at the moment of the shooting the camera cuts to a high angle, extreme long shot from the rear of the crowd, with Barbara Jean a distant figure slumping to the stage. The camera placement deliberately conceals actions and puts the viewer at a distance, directing our focus to the larger picture, not one individual's motives.

Conclusion

The film ends with a series of fascinating images. Taking the microphone, Albuquerque launches into "It Don't Worry Me." She picks up steam with her singing, the Fisk choir and the band join in, and soon the audience is singing with her, with children clapping along (Figure 2.10). Then the camera cuts to a high angle, extreme long shot of the stage and the audience; it pulls back still farther, tilts up to a shot of the sky and clouds, and slowly fades to black.

2.10
The
sing-along:
A multi-
valent
ending

The end titles roll. This ending is classic Altman in its multivalency. It rejects the neat closure of the typical Hollywood film, since the viewer doesn't understand Kenny's motives, never sees Hal Phillip Walker, doesn't know if Barbara Jean survives, and can't be sure how to respond to the final song. This ending inverts the typical ending of a musical, where a fresh new star emerges, since it is unclear that Albuquerque's success is now assured. Further, where musical finales generally emphasize community, all these performers are participating for selfish reasons and this closing number, rather than being a unifier of diverse groups, "is used to emphasize the disintegration of America."[14] Nor can we fail to appreciate the irony of the Walker rally turning into a public sing-along, further emphasizing the overlap of politics and entertainment. Leonard Quart and Albert Auster argue that the irony of this song is "accentuated by the fact that a black choir leads the singing," especially given the refrain, "You may say that I ain't free/But it don't worry me."[15] Michael Klein suggests that the audiences is retreating into fantasy, and calls the song "bleak satire: passive acceptance of economic exploitation and cultural oppression."[16]

But the film's meanings are never so simple. One finds here the "bisociative" structure Karp speaks of, where scenes and characters evoke conflicting reactions, as when we are angered at Sueleen's exploitation and simultaneously frustrated by her own complicity. In this case, we can feel some pleasure that Albuquerque has finally gotten a few moments of fame—and can actually sing. Virginia Wexman in particular sees many signs of hope, including Haven's sincere attempt to protect Barbara Jean without regard for his own safety and the older stars leaving the stage, as if to make room for new blood. The singing by the hardscrabble Albuquerque, the Fisk choir, and the children in the audience shows that "the young and the disenfranchised have been given a voice." In her view, the song shows the expression of "spontaneous human feeling" that gives a sense of hope.[17] Altman himself laid out the simultaneous cynical and optimistic aspect of the song. "That song is double edged. In one way you can say, Jesus, those people are sittin' there singing right after this terrible thing happened; that shows their insensitivity. And on the other hand, no matter how bad things get, there's always a positive hope for the future."[18] In truth, the song is catchy and encourages the audience to sing along. The camera first includes the rally crowd and then adopts a position uniting the audiences at the rally and in the movie theater. The lyrics clearly announce the problems of the country—"all the world is takin' sides. . . . Life may be a one-way street. . . . Tax relief may never come." But it concludes, "Economy's depressed, not me." It's up to the viewer to decide if this determination to ignore problems represents fatuous complacency or determined optimism that America will somehow find a way to carry on.

Afterword on Narrative Structure

The great advantage of the classic plot, with its limited number of characters and driving narrative arc, is that complex issues can be simplified. Thus the problems looming as the United States entered World War II are made manageable in *Casablanca* by reducing "a large, abstract issue (American intervention) to a particular melodrama (the Rick-Ilsa-Laszlo triangle)."[19] This movement from the international to the personal is nicely signaled by the opening credits that move rapidly from a spinning globe to the streets of Casablanca and shortly thereafter to Rick brooding in his café. Once he and Ilsa have reaffirmed their love, the defeat of the Third Reich will obviously be as simple as his dispatching of Strasser—at least, by Hollywood logic. Altman reverses this pattern because his aim is not to solve the romantic problems of a few glamorous individuals but to take a serious look at the issues facing American culture. For this purpose, the *mosaic* film, with its range of characters and stories, is the ideal narrative form. Altman simplifies only to the extent that he shrinks all of the United States down to a single city.

The resulting *tour de force* creation can only present its ideas through thematic patterns since there is no central plot "problem" and since the audience's emotional connection with the characters is more tenuous. Hence the wonderful concatenation of scenes linking politics to entertainment and then entertainment to egoism, illness, and prostitution. This final link is the saddest, suggesting that both entertainment and politics have been irreparably corrupted by money. One of the film's most touching moments occurs on the stage of the Opry Belle as, pausing in the midst of her performance, Barbara Jean begins a rambling monologue about her life. It ends with the story of her earning fifty cents as a little girl by learning to sing two songs from a record in less than an hour. Becoming more and more distracted, she mumbles, "I think ever since then I been workin', and supportin' myself," at which point Barnett takes her off the stage. The monologue poignantly links Barbara Jean's breakdown to the first time she received money for performing. Her plight seems emblematic of the commercialization of country music, causing it to lose touch with its roots in personal experience. By implication, politics has also lost touch with the people it is supposed to represent and America has lost touch with its core values.

Keyssar states flatly, "If there is a most important film of the 1970s, it is *Nashville*."[20] It marks a pivotal moment in American society, looking resolutely to the past, especially the Sixties, both in its manner of creation,[21] its structure, and its concerns. It touches on all the issues that roiled the preceding decade, from Vietnam to the civil rights movement to Watergate. But while the film looks back at these problems, the Keith Carradine song that closes the film, "It Don't Worry Me," is sadly prescient.[22] It perfectly encapsulates the attitude of the American public on the country's two hundredth anniversary, wearied by years of strife. The film's method of storytelling would have been problematic in any case, but the film's cynical vision of America rubbed salt in the wound. Audiences of the time had had their fill of social turmoil, political skullduggery, and military misadventures. The nation had already suffered serious blows to its sense of self-worth and idealism. What the public longed for, it found in *Jaws*, released just three months earlier and which grossed over $400 million in contrast to the $11 million *Nashville* has earned in the twenty years since its release.[23] Here were obvious good guys and bad guys, a hero who could triumph over his fears to do the right thing, and a fearful beast that could be definitively dispatched (until the sequel). All the amorphous threats to the American way of life could be embodied in the shark's solid corporeality and erased in a very satisfying explosion.[24] But *Nashville*'s marvelous use of actors, its inversion of the musical genre, its innovative use of sound, its bits of improvisation, its subtly juxtaposed scenes, and its constant challenging of the viewer make it a landmark film. None of the directors who began exploring multi-plot stories in the 1990s would equal Altman's narrative complexity, but they could not help but be inspired by this masterful demonstration of thematic structuring.

Notes

1   Jan Stuart, *The Nashville Chronicles* (New York: Limelight, 2003), 292-93.
2   Charles Michener, with Martin Kasindorf, "Altman's Opryland Epic," *Newsweek* (30 June 1975): 46.
3   Cited in Stuart, *The Nashville Chronicles*, 285-86.
4   Helene Keyssar describes the film's structure succinctly. Altman links scenes through dialogue and visual elements, as is common, but the film "is also powerfully propelled by a mode of montage in which the key connecting elements present themselves initially in metaphoric rather than syntactical relationship to each other." *Robert Altman's America* (New York: Oxford University Press, 1991), 136.
5   *Nashville* pushed Altman's experiments in sound to a new level, with each character individually miked and captured on a separate tape track, allowing very subtle fading in and out of particular voices. Stuart, *The Nashville Chronicles*, 141-47.
6   Alan Karp, *The Films of Robert Altman* (Metuchen, N.J.: Scarecrow, 1981), 3-4.
7   Stephen E. Bowles, "*Cabaret* and *Nashville*: The Musical as Social Comment," *Journal of Popular Culture* 12, no. 3 (1978/1979): 554.
8   Norman Kagan, *American Skeptic: Robert Altman's Genre-Commentary Films* (Ann Arbor, Mich.: Pierian, 1982), 130.
9   The rapid jumping from scene to scene, epitomized here, has led James Bernardoni to charge Altman with succumbing to the "television fallacy," eschewing "coherent meaning" in favor of the TV comedy show pattern where an odd group of characters create gags by rebounding off one another. *The New Hollywood* (Jefferson, N.C.: McFarland, 1991), 26-27. This critique overlooks both the satirical intent and the thematic unity found in these apparently disjunctive scenes.
10   Keyssar, *Robert Altman's America*, 157.

11   Norman Kagan notes Altman's predilection for genre inversion throughout his study, *American Skeptic: Robert Altman's Genre-Commentary Films.*

12   Kagan, *American Skeptic,* 137.

13   Jane Feuer, "*Nashville*: Altman's Open Surface," *Jump Cut* 10/11 (June 1976): 32.

14   Rick Altman, *The American Film Musical* (Bloomington: Indiana University Press, 1989), 324.

15   Leonard Quart and Albert Auster, *American Film and Society since 1945,* second edition (Westport, Conn.: Praeger, 1991), 114.

16   Michael Klein, "*Nashville* and the American Dream," *Jump Cut* 9 (October/December 1975): 7.

17   Virginia Wright Wexman, "The Rhetoric of Cinematic Improvisation," *Cinema Journal* 20, no. 1 (1980): 39-40.

18   Cited in Stuart, *The Nashville Chronicles,* 271.

19   Robert B. Ray, *A Certain Tendency of the Hollywood Cinema, 1930-1980* (Princeton, N. J.: Princeton University Press, 1985), 92.

20   Keyssar, *Robert Altman's America,* 134.

21   Jan Stuart's fascinating study of the film's creation in *The Nashville Chronicles* identifies it as perhaps the apogee of the Altmanesque methods of creation. The cast lived for two months in a giant commune on the outskirts of Nashville, working feverishly during the day and then partying as they watched the rushes every night. There was a carefully honed script by Joan Tewkesbury and Altman, but during many of the scenes (e.g., the car crash), actors were encouraged to improvise bits of business as Altman rushed from one group to another filming, and no one—least of all he—knew which scenes would end up in the final film. It was the complete embodiment of the hippie lifestyle, with all the actors pretty much equal and Altman the chief bong-master.

22   Carradine played the piece for Altman (along with his other composition, "I'm Easy") and the two songs were key inspirations for the film, appearing in every draft of the script. Stuart, *The Nashville Chronicles,* 35-37.

23   Stuart, *The Nashville Chronicles,* 299-300.

24   J. Hoberman does an insightful analysis of the competing ideologies of the two films, with that of *Jaws* clearly more to the public's liking. "*Nashville* contra *Jaws*, or 'The Imagination of Disaster Revisited.'" In *The Last Great American Picture Show: New Hollywood Cinema in the 1970s.* Thomas Elsaesser, Alexander Horwath, and Noel King, eds. (Amsterdam: Amsterdam University Press, 2004), 195-222.

Network

Narrative

3

Pulp Fiction

Pop Culture's Poster Child

No discussion of recent narrative experiments can avoid mentioning *Pulp Fiction*. It was a phenomenon at the time—earning more than $200 million, garnering eight Academy Award nominations, and winning the Palme d'Or at Cannes. Despite this success, many critics remained unimpressed. They granted the film's inventiveness and clever script turns, but saw the work as "empty of social and moral content."[1] Robin Wood spoke for many in saying "Pulp Fiction is a work of phenomenal cleverness and no intelligence whatsoever."[2] In retrospect, however, the film's importance is undeniable. Tarantino did not single-handedly create the 1990s explosion of narrative experimentation—earlier exemplars can be found, including many Altman films, Jarmusch's *Mystery Train* (1989) and Sayles' *City of Hope* (1991). Nonetheless, numerous directors credited Tarantino with encouraging them to innovate and the success of *Pulp Fiction* undoubtedly helped attract financing and distribution for other ground-breaking projects. Tarantino seems prescient in heralding an era of greater inventiveness, with his visual panache taken up by films like *Amores Perros* and his cartoonish scenes forecasting the vogue that would soon take off with the Wachowski brothers and *The Matrix* series.

Some aspects of *Pulp Fiction* have worn less well than others. The stylized violence, overdone in so many subsequent films, including Tarantino's own, seems clichéd. Tarantino's insatiable need to be over-the-top, attractive as it is to some of his geeky fans, becomes forced. Butch the boxer may need to redeem himself, but using a samurai sword to rescue his crime boss from sodomizing by a corrupt L.A. cop seems gratuitously outrageous, not to mention racist and homophobic. On the other hand, Tarantino's juggling of time order is innovative and creative. Classic Hollywood films are careful to keep the time order clear. Flashforwards are almost never used. Flashbacks are permitted only when clearly motivated and signaled by a host of obvious devices. When Rick thinks back to his happy days in Paris with Ilsa, the camera tracks in to his face, Sam's playing of "As Time Goes By" segues into an orchestral version, and a dissolve transforms the scene from the café's nighttime interior to a sunlit street in Paris down which Rick and Ilsa drive in a convertible. The transition and the reasons for it are absolutely clear. Tarantino throws these rules to the wind and cuts from one story to another with no forewarning, jumping forward and backward at will among four different story lines.

These unmotivated transitions can be seen simply as Tarantino announcing his directorial control, juggling time as freely as he does genre and tone, flaunting the rules for the sake of doing so. But in fact these time shifts sharpen the character contrasts and highlight important story moments. Thus the film begins with a couple, Honey Bunny and Pumpkin, sitting in a coffee shop and asking, "Should we change our lives?" They joke back and forth and end up deciding they *will* change: they will start robbing restaurants since liquor stores have become too dangerous. But while they don't take the question seriously at this point, the issue comes up again at the end when Pumpkin finds a large caliber pistol under his chin, held there by an unsmiling hit man. Now the question is a matter of life and death. In fact, each of the main characters faces serious decisions, and for all the verbal and cinematic fireworks going on, those decisions lie at the core of the film. Contrary to Wood's dismissive judgment, it is possible that, thanks to its astutely overlapped stories, *Pulp Fiction* has some overlooked specks of intelligence. For all the film achieved its fame by "stand-alone bits of virtuosity," a jokey script, and "the show-off quality of the cinematic style," creating a "roller-coaster experience,"[3] at its core, somewhat surprisingly, one finds serious thematic concerns.

Story Summary

The story begins when Pumpkin and Honey Bunny, a pair of semi-pro robbers, leap up from their table at a coffee shop to announce a stick-up. The story jumps to earlier that same morning as Jules and Vincent, two hit men working for Marsellus Wallace, drive to a job. They enter an apartment where three young men are eating breakfast, recapture Marsellus's briefcase, and gun down two of the men for failing to fulfill their assignment. That evening, Vincent goes to the house of his dealer, Lance, buys some potent heroin, shoots up, and puts the remainder in his pocket. Vincent has been asked by Marsellus, who is very black and very ominous, to entertain his wife Mia for the evening, she being very pretty and very white. They go to a retro-fashion juke joint, win a dance contest together, and return home. While Vincent is in the bathroom, Mia discovers his bag of heroin, thinks it is coke and snorts it. Vincent rushes her comatose body to Lance's house, gets a syringe of adrenaline that he must plunge directly into her heart, and she revives. Badly shaken, he drives her home.

The story jumps to the night of Butch's fight—he's an over-the-hill boxer paid by Marsellus to take a dive. A flashback shows Butch as a boy receiving his father's watch, preserved by a buddy who was with him when he died in Vietnam. Butch wins his fight and has made a killing with the bookies (who knew the fix was in) but must stay alive long enough to collect his bets, something Marsellus will do his best to prevent. Discovering that his girlfriend, Fabienne, forgot to pack the precious watch, he sneaks back to their apartment the next day and gets it, but ends up shooting Vincent, who is staked out there. Marsellus spots Butch driving away, gets flipped over the car hood, survives, and a foot chase ensues. It ends with both men knocked cold in a pawnshop by the owner, Maynard, and tied up in the basement. When Marsellus is dragged into the adjoining room by Maynard and his policeman friend, Zed, for a round of sodomy, Butch frees himself, grabs a samurai sword from the pawn shop shelves, kills Maynard and frees Marsellus. In return, Marsellus permits Butch to leave L.A. alive.

The final segment returns to Jules and Vincent immediately after they have shot the two young guys in the apartment. When a fourth boy suddenly appears and empties his pistol at them, they quickly dispatch him. Astounded by the missed shots, Jules calls the event a miracle and announces he will quit the business. As he and Vincent are debating this issue in their car, Vincent's pistol accidentally goes off, scattering the brains of Marvin (the third guy, their confederate) all over the backseat. They rush to the house of Jules's friend, Jimmie, and manage to get the mess cleaned up with the help of Winston Wolf, sent by Marsellus. During their breakfast afterward, the robbery by the amateur couple begins, ending when Jules captures Pumpkin but, having decided to amend his life, lets the couple go free. He and Vincent then calmly exit the coffee shop into the bright Los Angeles sunshine.

This chaotic plot is even crazier as a viewing experience, very much the emotional "roller coaster" ride Dana Polan suggests. Tarantino throws in a host of elements to build excitement—witty dialogue, fast-paced action, ample violence, cartoonish camera work, and sudden swerves in the plot line.[4] Although it may seem patently absurd to seek serious meaning in a film which advertises itself as being pulp fiction, the choices made have grave consequences: eight people die in the various stories and others come perilously close. Furthermore, the thread structure sets up contrasts between the decisions of the various characters. Tarantino's shifting of time order, in particular, foregrounds important narrative themes.

Prologue: The Hawthorne Grill

The balance of farcical and serious moments begins immediately in the pro-logue where a young couple, seated in an orange vinyl booth in the Hawthorne Grill, is in the midst of a vigorous argument, the subject of which remains unclear at first. Pumpkin says, "Too risky. I'm through doing that shit." They banter back and forth as couples will do, with Honey Bunny accusing him of sounding like a duck, and going "quack, quack, quack" at him. Finally the conversation clarifies as Pumpkin argues liquor stores have become too dangerous to hold up because of-ten the owners are foreigners who "don't even speak fucking English." This could result in their killing someone and both agree they don't want that. Pumpkin pro-poses that restaurants are perfect targets—they aren't prepared for robberies, the help won't resist, and the customers provide lucrative pickings. Honey Bunny is sold. "I'm ready." They kiss; then Pumpkin leaps up on the seat, flourishing his gun, and Honey Bunny screams: "Any of you fucking pricks move and I'll execute every motherfucking last one of you!" The screen freezes on the pair, Dale and the Del-Tones come in with "Miserlou," and the opening titles roll.

This scene establishes the conflicting forces that will characterize the film, moving from jokes to serious action in the blink of an eye. The lighter tone is enhanced by many moments of cartoon stylization as exhibited in the scene's final freeze frame—the camera sharply upangle, Honey Bunny and Pumpkin standing in parallel poses with outstretched pistols. They contrast strongly with the bright window behind them and are framed geometrically by the window structure. The curvature induced by the wide-angle lens increases the visual distortion (Figure 3.1). Further, the wild swings in emotional tone have begun. The viewer first can't

3.1
Tarantino toying with narrative: Halting the action *in medias res.*

understand what the argument is about and when the topic turns out to be armed robbery, wonders if characters named "Pumpkin" and "Honey Bunny" are to be taken seriously. She, who had earlier thanked the waitress sweetly for refilling her coffee cup and cooed "I love you" to Pumpkin, suddenly begins shouting oaths worthy of a pirate. Third, the film begins in the style of screwball comedy, as

Tarantino specified, with rapid patter between a man and a woman.[5] And just as those films used verbal fireworks as a stand-in for sexuality, the same is true here, as Honey Bunny says, "Let's do it. Right now, right here," Pumpkin's slaps his phallic pistol on the table, and they kiss passionately. It is obvious that the banter has served as "verbal foreplay" for the orgasm which will be the robbery.[6] The fast-paced dialogue, the teasing shifts of tone, the scatological language, the sexuality, and the freeze frame that stops the scene just as it reaches its climax all announce a clever, self-conscious filmmaker who delights in toying with his audience.

While this playfulness seems to justify critics who see the film as mindless hi-jinks, the scene has also introduced important issues. For one thing, it foregrounds the sexuality underlying the screwball comedy, the gangster film, and many other standard film genres. Sexuality and masculinity will be important themes in all the film's stories, with early scenes supporting the conventional view of mascu-linity being tied to large caliber weapons. However, in the latter half of the film, rescuing watches and cleaning brains out of the backseat of a car will create new perspectives on masculinity and the use of such weapons. More crucially, this prologue raises the issue of how to live one's life, which the couple treats superfi-cially but which will arise again in the ending.

Jules and Vincent

In a startling shift, the story jumps to two new characters who seem to have no relationship to the opening events. In fact, their scene occurs much earlier the same day in the same city, Los Angeles. Jules and Vincent (Samuel L. Jackson and John Travolta), two gangsters in the employ of Marsellus Wallace, are on their way to an early morning job. Vincent has apparently been in Europe for a time and describes the pleasures of legalized marijuana in Amsterdam and is amused by a quarter pounder with cheese being called a "royale with cheese." Then a sud-den disorienting cut occurs, with the camera inside the car trunk as Jules opens it, commenting "We should have shotguns for this kind of deal." As they load their pistols, the two discuss how many people are "up there." As in the opening scene, the obvious first impression here is of a comical, pop culture style, supported by the cartoonlike camerawork, which constantly changes angle and distance. After two-shots of the men in the car, it jumps inside the trunk (Figure 3.2), tracks them walking into the building, cuts to a very high angle from the corner of the lobby and then drops to a low-angle two-shot of the pair in the elevator. This showy cam-erawork is matched by the clever dialogue. There are many outrageously funny lines—Richard Alleva notes acerbically that "If gangsters really had this sort of wit, they'd be writing screenplays"[7]—and the rapid changes in tone throw the viewer off balance. On top of this, both scenes exhibit an undercurrent of sexuality

3.2
More
flashy
camerawork:
Inside the
car trunk.

and the sudden explosion of violence—elements guaranteed to generate audience appeal (and corresponding critical disdain).

However, the interwoven structure emphasizes numerous parallels with the preceding scene of Pumpkin and Honey Bunny: a trivial conversation between two partners begun *in medias res*; an ordinary setting (the coffee shop, a Chevy Malibu); references to food; blatant prejudicial biases, in this case toward foreigners who put mayonnaise on french fries; sudden cartoonish cuts (a close-up of the waitress's face bringing coffee, the cut to inside the trunk); and a steady movement toward violence that belies the trivial conversation, in both cases announced by the appearance of weapons. A further parallel is the scene's sexuality, as Jules and Vincent get into a highly scatological discussion of foot massages reminiscent of the sexual banter of Pumpkin and Honey Bunny. But where the earlier pair made robbery an exciting game, we now find serious men living in a world with far more stringent rules. These parallels encourage the viewer to compare the two sets of characters, especially since they will encounter one another in the final scene.

Particularly interesting is the discussion of Mia, the boss's wife. It seems that Marsellus had Antwan, one of their confederates, thrown out a fourth story window for giving Mia a foot massage. Jules remarks, "Since then, he kind of developed a speech impediment." (This nicely foreshadows the subsequent scene where Vincent will find himself attracted to Mia on their date but not anxious to acquire a permanent stutter.) Vincent forces Jules to agree that a foot massage can be sexual (by asking Jules to give him one), but Jules argues that Marsellus went too far. Just as Pumpkin and Honey Bunny raised a potentially serious question— what direction shall we take our lives?—so underlying this discussion is another sober philosophical issue: is Marsellus just? Marsellus is, after all, the ultimate arbiter in the world of Jules and Vincent, and Jules is suggesting that getting thrown out a window for touching Mia's feet seems a consequence disproportionate to the offense. The discussion might not seem at all serious, since it devolves into a highly scatological consideration of how foot massages rank in relation to other sexual acts. Like the earlier discussion of European fast food, it appears to be just trivial banter to amuse the audience, but it serves to differentiate the two men.

Vincent operates by a simple code: the boss gets to make the rules. Jules, in contrast, seems to expect some system of justice to be observed. Already key thematic questions have been raised: what is justice and how shall we live our lives?

Ezekiel

As Jules and Vincent carry out their assignment, the portrayal of Jules's is critical, preparing for the changes in him at the end. Here he is totally in charge and utterly ruthless. At the apartment, they find their victims having breakfast. (Pumpkin had noted the advantage of robbing restaurants—you catch people with their pants down—and Jules and Vincent show their professionalism by doing exactly that.) Jules takes charge and is filmed slightly upangle against a dark wall that makes him all the more sinister. With deceptive mildness, he apologizes to the first boy, Brett, for interrupting his meal, calmly asks if he might try his Big Kahuna burger and takes an appreciative bite. Continuing his psychological intimidation, he asks for some of Brett's drink and proceeds to finish it off. The close-up of Jules's face, his eyes staring fixedly at Brett (off camera), combined with the gurgle of the cup being drained foreshadows chillingly the young man's fate (Figure 3.3). The two men reclaim Mar-

3.3
Eyeing his
hapless
victim, Jules
drains the
cup.

sellus's briefcase and prepare to finish things up, with Jules becoming increasingly demonic. When Brett stammers his apologies for messing up, Jules casually pulls the pistol from his waistband and kills the boy on the couch with a single shot at point-blank range. Looking back at Brett, he inquires, "Oh, I'm sorry. Did I break your concentration?" He leans in ominously, peppers Brett with questions, shoots him in the shoulder, and then begins the quotation of his favorite Bible passage, Ezekiel 25:17. "The path of the righteous man is beset on all sides by the inequities of the selfish and the tyranny of evil men." Jules's voice gets steadily more intense. "Blessed is he who in the name of charity and good will shepherd the weak through the Valley of Darkness for he is truly his brother's keeper and the finder of lost children. And I will strike down upon thee with great vengeance and furious anger those who attempt to poison and destroy My brothers." Jules is in close-up now, yelling: "And you will know My name is the Lord when I lay My vengeance upon thee!" On those words, he and Vincent raise their guns and blow Brett away.

This scene clearly establishes Jules as the lead dog. He drives the car, walks ahead, knows most about the situation, and takes charge once they enter the boys' room. His foregrounded position will continue in subsequent scenes with Vincent. He totally embodies the ruthless killer. He does not simply dispatch his victims: he toys with them like a cat with a mouse. First he teases Brett about his eating habits—"Hamburgers! The cornerstone of any nutritious breakfast"—and a few moments later he is shrieking at him that he has tried to fuck Marsellus "like a bitch"! The casual way Jules shoots the boy on the couch without so much as looking at him is more awful than the sadistic pleasure exhibited by many movie villains. This partly seems to be an assumed persona, for Jules said to Vincent as they walked to the door that it was time to "get into character." (Pumpkin and Honey Bunny employed the same process, switching into "tough guy" mode to intimidate the coffee shop customers.) But unlike those amateurs, anxious not to kill anybody, the only concern of the two men here is whether they brought sufficient firepower. This is no longer the amateur league, with Jules the embodiment of the cold-blooded killer. He may question the ethics of Antwan being thrown out a window, but he does not hesitate to carry out his assignments with ruthless efficiency.

Vincent Revealed

With Jules's character clearly established, the film begins fleshing out Vincent, using thread structure astutely to contrast him with Butch, the prize fighter. Jules and Vincent return to Marsellus's club after a few hours of subsequent harrowing adventures, dressed strangely in shorts and t-shirts, a striking contrast to the black suits and white shirts they sported a moment earlier on screen. Only in retrospect does the viewer realize what has happened in the interim—to their clothes and to their attitude. Vincent in particular has had a very stressful morning. After nearly being killed by the fourth kid in the apartment, he and Jules got into a heated argument about miracles during which Vincent accidently shot their confederate, Marvin, riding in the backseat. That required a panicky cleanup of the resulting mess, with Jules giving Vincent considerable grief. Further, Jules has announced he plans to quit his job with Marsellus and go wherever God sends him, which Vincent finds incomprehensible. Still more baffling, Jules allowed the two petty crooks at the diner to walk out the door unscathed. As a final insult, Vincent is no sooner back in the club than Jules and Paul the bartender begin teasing him about his upcoming date with Mia. He insists he's smart enough not to mess with the boss's wife. Having had as much hassling as he can stand, Vincent is all too happy to give somebody else a hard time, and Butch becomes a convenient target. When Butch leaves Marsellus and comes to the bar, Vincent stares at him coldly and calls him a palooka and "Punchy," before leaving to join Marsellus.

This brief exchange shows Vincent rather adolescent, compensating for his own failings by bullying Butch. His behavior contrasts neatly with Butch's in the immediately preceding moments, sitting without expression as Marsellus (Ving Rhames, off screen) gave him instructions for taking a dive in the upcoming fight (Figure 3.4).[8] Marsellus tells Butch "If you were going to make it, you would have made it

3.4
A film
full of
cinematic
allusions:
Marsellus
as the
Godfather.

before now." Butch's eyes shift slightly during this counseling, but otherwise he is impassive. Before relinquishing an envelope of money, Marsellus asks, "You my nigger?" Quietly, Butch says, "It certainly appears so." Marsellus counsels Butch to ignore the "slight sting" as he takes his fall. "That's pride fucking with you." This condescending treatment is as hurtful as anything Vincent has endured that morning, but Butch never blinks an eye. He is planning to bet all that money on himself, win the fight, and get out of town, so he is careful not to risk a confrontation with Marsellus here or an argument with Vincent afterward. Butch chafes at having to be Marsellus's "nigger," while Vincent basks in his status as one of the favored, able to be rude to those he considers his inferiors. The interwoven stories emphasize the contrast: Butch shows self-control and makes carefully calculated decisions; Vincent simply reacts.

Vincent and Lance

More hints of Vincent's immaturity appear as he stops off at Lance's for a fix in advance of his date with Mia. He gets his potent heroin in a plastic bag rather than the typical balloon, unwittingly ensuring that Mia will mistake it for coke when she finds it later in his coat pocket. But the scene also provides character clues. For one thing, it doesn't seem astute of Vincent to get high before a date in which a misstep could send him out an upper window. Further, he rants at length about the person who keyed his car—a crime that merits immediate execution. The ordinariness of

Vincent's ethical judgments sets him in contrast to Jules, who has seriously questioned the justice of Marsellus's decisions. Particularly notable is the in-your-face portrayal of Vincent's drug use which seems, at first, to be glamorized. Lance the drug dealer is very cool and has an extremely cute wife, Jody (Rosanna Arquette), who wears a tongue stud to improve fellatio. The cartoonish filming continues the sense of unreality, with eight extreme close-ups of Vincent shooting up—Lance weighing the heroin, the needle being screwed on, etc. (Figure 3.5). These shots

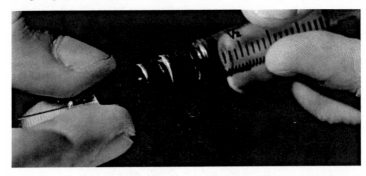

3.5
Drugs for
recreation.

are intercut with a montage sequence of Vincent drifting down the highway in his car with a blissful smile on his face and overlaid with a throbbing music track. (The theme, however, is "Bullwinkle II," a cartoon character not noted for mental agility.)

During the date, there are continual reminders that Vincent is still enjoying his heroin trip. When he arrives at Mia's house, his motions are awkward and his speech slurred as he moves around the living area, waiting for her. As they arrive at Jack Rabbit Slim's, the club she has chosen, the camera does an extended track behind Vincent using a wide-angle lens as he wanders around the restaurant. He stops to look at the miniature slot racers and the camera pans to follow the cars around the track, and then pans further to show the servers (all costumed like famous film actors from the past), to a singer dressed like Ricky Nelson, giant movie posters, and tables full of people. The vertiginous motion of the camera and distortion of the lens accentuate the swirl of images past Vincent's foggy vision. So disoriented does he become that Mia has to yell to get his attention from her table. Vincent's fuzzy state of mind bespeaks his poor judgment in being high when escorting the boss's sexy wife. While casual marijuana use is not uncommon in today's movies, viewers are likely to draw back from a character using hard drugs, a caution reinforced by later events that evening.

Vincent and Mia

Vincent had been certain the date with Mia would be unproblematic, but clues are immediately given as they meet to suggest his judgment is flawed yet again.

Mia (Uma Thurman) is marked as the *femme fatale*: powerful, sexualized and mysterious. She is able to observe Vincent through the security cameras while remaining unseen. The opening shots never show her face, only her bright red lips speaking into the microphone of the intercom system as she directs Vincent to fix himself a drink while she dresses (Figure 3.6). Further, the film hints at a liaison

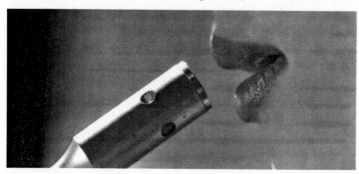

3.6
Mia as
femme
fatale
with
phallic
microphone.

by showing them moving on parallel tracks: matching close-ups have him pouring himself a drink and Mia doing lines of coke. Then, after not hitting it off initially, they become closer as Vincent—instructed to come up with an interesting topic of conversation—raises the issue of Antwan's punishment. Mia is amused to learn that Vincent's compatriots think it occurred because of a foot massage and tells Vincent the only thing the gentleman in question ever touched was her hand at her wedding. Their relationship becomes even closer (the filming switches to shot/reverse shot) when a dance contest is announced and Mia demands that Vincent enter it with her and *win*. (She is the boss's wife, she reminds him.) Later, they appear together, dancing in the door to her house, carrying the trophy. Mia shuts off the security system as they enter, which suggests letting down her guard. She giggles when Vincent dips her, says, "Drinks, music" and runs off to put on "Girl, You'll Be a Woman Soon." The stage seems set for sexual fireworks, with both of them high, enjoying their shared victory, dancing together, and listening to seductive music. Vincent tries to steel himself, but his philosophizing in the bathroom is puerile. Addressing himself in the mirror, he says "this is a moral test" to show "whether or not you can maintain loyalty." Ethical questions are being raised again, but Vincent's attempt to wrestle with this issue is completely fraudulent. He may mouth lofty sentiments about loyalty, but the real issue is all-too-evidently the risk of defenestration.

Adrenaline

Vincent quickly discards his specious ethical musings in favor of self-survival when he exits the bathroom to find that Mia has chanced upon the bag of heroin in his coat pocket, mistaken it for coke, snorted it, and now lies unconscious and bleeding from the nose. Vincent can reasonably assume that Marsellus will not be kindly disposed toward anyone compassing the death of his pretty wife and rushes Mia to Lance's house for help, setting off a scene of comic chaos. Lance races around trying to find his medical book and syringe while Jody keeps up a torrent of abuse. Lance and Vincent try, in bumbling fashion, to figure out how to administer the adrenaline, everyone crowds around as Vincent stabs the syringe into Mia's heart, causing her to jolt upright, the syringe dangling from her chest. Lance blurts, "If you're all right, then say something" to which Mia replies, deadpanned, "Something." The frenzy is intensified by frenetic camerawork and editing. The camera races from point to point in the room following the panicked characters without cutting, then drops to six inches above floor level as Lance and Vincent hover over Mia with the hypodermic. Close-ups show the syringe being filled, air expelled, and Vincent marking the spot he will have to hit. Then as Lance counts "One-two-three" the camera tracks in to Mia's bloody face, cuts to a close-up of the syringe being raised, racking focus to a drop coming off the tip,[9] (Figure 3.7)

3.7
Drugs for "re-creation" (much excitement but less fun).

and then rapid close-ups of the other characters crowding in a tense circle. Vincent strikes down, Mia's eyes fly open, and she flings the men off her. The hysterical situation, outrageous dialogue, and frenetic editing make this scene almost unbearable to watch. The evening ends with Vincent dropping Mia off at her home—they both look like corpses—and agreeing not to say anything to Marsellus.

The sequence is another roller coaster ride, with the viewer as shaken as Vincent by the terrifying events that occur. Only in retrospect does one appreciate Tarantino's astute altering of the time order of his story threads. The scenes that end the film, where Jules is converted by his near-death experience and decides to abandon the life of crime, actually occur *before* this date scene. In Brett's apartment, Vincent stood next to Jules and, like him, was missed by all the bullets fired by the fourth boy who popped out, but he pooh-poohed Jules's idea that their survival was a miracle. Now on this date, occurring just a few hours later, Vincent experiences a second narrow escape and sees Mia almost literally resurrected from the dead. Because this sequence occurs early in the film, viewers initially sympathize with his desire to do no more than "go home now and have a heart attack." After seeing the film's later events, however, one wonders how many hints God has to drop to get Vincent's attention. Viewers reluctant to read a moral message into such an ungodly film might at least allow that Vincent should recognize that the karma is no longer with him in his current line of work and consider more thoughtfully the example Jules sets for him in quitting. Vincent is charming, but his rudeness to Butch, his drug use, his lack of caution on the date, and his failure to gain any perspective on his life call for a careful judgment. Admittedly, in a film which so intensifies the experiences of the moment, neither viewers nor characters have much opportunity for reflection. It is that paradox which makes *Pulp Fiction* such a fascinating artistic construct.

Captain Koons Introduces Butch

Vincent's character and his decisions are thrown into especially sharp relief in contrast to those of Butch Coolidge, whose narrative is interwoven by the thread structure. Besides casting a sympathetic actor in the part of Butch (Bruce Willis), Tarantino's flamboyant scenes are effective in fleshing out Butch quickly, helping overcome the time constraints imposed by the multi-plot structure. One such scene features Captain Koons (Christopher Walken), who provides a weirdly effective back story. Koons appears in a dream flashback to deliver the watch of Butch's father to the young Butch, tracing its history from Butch's great-grandfather through the horrors of life in a Viet Cong prison camp to the present (Figure 3.8). To be sure, Koons's story becomes increasingly crazy as he tells of Butch's

3.8
Captain
Koons
delivering
Butch's
birthright.

dad hiding the watch in his rectum: "He'd be damned if any slopes were gonna put their greasy yellow hands on his boy's birthright." After Butch's father died of dysentery, Koons concealed the watch in similar fashion for two more years. Multivalent as Koons's story is—simultaneously moving and comical and horrifying—it provides pivotal motivation. One understands why Butch has chosen to become a prize fighter, as if seeking to preserve the family's military heritage in some fashion. The viewer may find the watch a dubious birthright, but it is central in Butch's life. When Butch's trainer sticks his head in to announce, "It's time, Butch," it is time not just for Butch's fight but for him to take charge of his life. Following his plan, Butch wins his bout and escapes to rejoin Fabienne, but he unintentionally kills his opponent, Floyd Wilson, creating a debt of guilt. Butch claims not to feel bad because Floyd assumed those risks, but one suspects he is not being honest. He has betrayed a fellow soldier.

In Search of the Watch

The remainder of Butch's story tests his character. In contrast to Vincent's casual wandering through life—nicely epitomized by his hazy floating down the highway after shooting up—Butch seeks to forge an identity for himself. Discovering that Fabienne neglected to pack the all-important watch, Butch receives an exciting opportunity for self-actualization, along with the real possibility of personal termination. He returns to the apartment, enters stealthily, retrieves the watch and then tosses two Pop Tarts into the toaster for a delayed breakfast. At this point something catches his eye: a machine pistol with silencer lying on the kitchen counter. (As the DVD commentary explains, this was left by Marsellus, who has gone to bring back coffee.) Butch picks it up, hears the toilet flush in the bathroom, and raises the pistol to cover the door, from which an unsuspecting Vincent emerges. The two stand facing one another for a moment, when suddenly the Pop Tarts jump up in the toaster (shown in a one-second extreme close-up, accompanied by an exaggerated "pop" on the sound track). The gun in Butch's hands erupts, blasting Vincent back through the bathroom doorway. Butch's bewildered expression makes it evident he pulled the trigger as a reflex rather than as a calculated act, in contrast to Jules's deliberate shooting of the boys in the apartment. The audience's sympathy with Butch has been strengthened throughout by the work of the camera, tracking with him as he sneaks back to the apartment, showing the key slipping into the lock in extreme close-up, and adopting Butch's point of view (POV) throughout, as in his spotting the machine pistol. In fact, he is given more POV shots than any other character,[10] creating close identification for the relatively short course of his story.

Butch drives away, is spotted and pursued by Marsellus, who arises like a demon after being bounced over the roof of Butch's car. Butch ambushes his former boss inside a pawnshop and begins punching him, saying, "You feel that sting, big boy, huh? That's pride fucking with you, see?" He is repeating Marsellus's words to him before the fight, thereby asserting his identity and taking control of his destiny at last.[11] Having grown up without a father, Butch surely felt the need for one[12] and Marsellus has taken on that role to some degree. However, he condescends to Butch and counsels him to forget about his pride, something Butch has far too little of. In fact, he became Butch's nemesis, a controlling force who sapped Butch's confidence and tried to get him to bargain away his soul. This demonic figure, rising from the pavement like a zombie after being tossed over Butch's car, has at last been vanquished . . . except that a moment later, Butch lies unconscious alongside Marsellus, flattened by the butt of the pawnshop owner's shotgun.

The two men awaken to find themselves lodged in some awful circle of Hell. Tied in chairs alongside one another in the pawnshop cellar, they are gagged in ominous fashion—red balls fastened into the mouth with elaborate leather straps encircling the head. The gags are effective and professional: their captors are experienced. A wonderful shot in front of the two men shows Maynard, the pawnshop owner, going into the room behind them. Their eyes move and Marsellus tries to turn his head, but they cannot see and have only the sounds for clues—locks unfastened, a heavy chest lid lifted, an iron grate thrown back. None of this bodes well (Figure 3.9). After bringing in a hooded creature, the Gimp, to guard Butch, Maynard and

3.9
A bad day in the pawnshop cellar: Butch and Marsellus.

his buddy, Zed, drag Marsellus into the next room for some companionable sodomy. Butch frees himself, knocks out the Gimp with one punch, and flees upstairs. He has every reason to be out the door in a flash, rather than aiding the man who has demeaned and sworn to kill him. But instead, he finds a samurai sword among the pawnshop merchandise, and returns to dispatch Maynard, allowing Marsellus to pick up a shotgun and pump a load of buckshot into Zed's private parts. Marsellus permits Butch to exit the premises, telling him to quit L.A. immediately and for good. Butch departs, leaving Marsellus to call in his "pipe-hitting niggers" who will see to it that Zed's remaining moments on earth are exquisitely painful. Outside, Butch swipes Zed's chopper, picks up Fabienne at the motel, and they roar off to catch the train out of town.

This notorious sequence, over-the-top as it is, is critical in delineating Butch's character and also demonstrates Tarantino's adroit use of thread narrative. The film might well have ended with Butch's escape, chronologically the final narrative event.

It is an upbeat moment,[13] as Butch proves himself worthy of his father's watch by becoming a real soldier. (Audiences laugh at Butch's choice of weaponry, but it is completely appropriate, linked to the *bushido* warrior code.) He has responded to Captain Koons, who told him, "When two men are in a situation like me and your dad were . . . you take on certain responsibilities of the other." To be worthy of his father's heritage, Butch must rescue his fellow prisoner in "the pit of Hell," even if that man is his mortal enemy. Like any good hero, he has descended into the underworld, risked his own life and confronted the forces of darkness. In doing so, he has redeemed himself for the deaths of Floyd Wilson and Vincent, for all that both were unintentional. If Tarantino's only intent were to provide visceral moments, the scene in the cellar would be a perfect climax—set in hell, replete with perversity, and ending with redemption by means of a samurai sword. Instead, he returns to the story of Jules and Vincent, making the climax of the film events which occurred *before* Vincent's date with Mia and *before* Butch's fight. The result of this shift is to throw considerable weight on Jules's decision to free Honey Bunny and Pumpkin. Instead of ending with a man saving his honor by walking back into a fight, *Pulp Fiction* ends with a man saving his soul by walking away from one.

Divine Intervention

Tarantino's story of gangster life now ends in the most improbable way imaginable—with a religious conversion. The action cuts back to the scene of the morning's assignment. As the two men are terminating Brett, a fourth kid leaps out and empties a pistol at them at point blank range. All the shots miss. Jules and Vincent check themselves for damage, then raise their weapons and dispatch young gentleman number four. Jules carefully studies all the bullet holes in the wall and decides this was "divine intervention." Vincent says it was luck and they continue to argue as they drive away, with Marvin their confederate in the backseat. The switch in filming emphasizes the serious rift between them. After standing shoulder to shoulder in the apartment, emptying their pistols into the unexpected assailant, now they are never seen in the same frame—a contrast also with the opening two-shots of them driving to their assignment. Vincent insists the incident was merely "freaky," but Jules thinks otherwise and says he plans to retire as of today. Bewildered, Vincent turns to Marvin in the backseat and asks, "Do you think that God came down from Heaven and stopped. . . ?" At that exact moment and on those precise words, Vincent's gun—pointed carelessly backward—suddenly goes off, blowing Marvin's brains all over the backseat and splattering the two men with gore (Figure 3.10). Now they are in serious trouble, far from home territory, their

3.10
Vincent's
carelessness
or more
divine
interven-
tion?

car's interior liberally embellished with cranial contents. Jules quickly calls his friend Jimmie who lives nearby, and pleads to use his garage for a few hours.

Before we turn to the gruesome clean-up scene which ensues, several observations are in order. To begin with, this argument continues the earlier one about the justice of Marsellus's action in throwing Antwan out a window, being a second philosophical discussion about the way the universe operates (or should). Further, after witnessing Mia brought back from the dead, the viewer now has experienced a second "miracle" as all the bullets miss the two men. The possibility that this might have been divine intervention is underlined by having Vincent's gun go off just as he is asking if God could *stop* a bullet, hinting that God could with equal ease *start* a bullet. And because of the shifted time order, the viewer is aware that Vincent is dead, shot by Butch in the preceding story. Gangster films typically observe a form of "morality," with characters bringing about their own destruction. Tony Camonte in *Scarface* (Hawks, 1932) betrays all human relationships, killing his best friend and feeling incestuous desire for his sister. Sonny Corleone in *The Godfather* can be lured into a trap because of his impetuous nature. One is forced to wonder, therefore, if Vincent dies because he betrays some principle or ignores some lesson—perhaps failing to heed the example Jules is setting for him. Alleva comments that Vincent's ultimate fate shows that "refusing to see the significance of events, dismissing all circumstance as happenstance, refusing to believe that you are undergoing your own destiny can doom you."[14] Since the final sequences place Jules and his decision to quit the mob very much at the center, one must pay close attention to his thoughts and behaviors going forward, especially as they stand in contrast to Vincent's.

The Clean-up

The moments at Jimmie's house are highly unpleasant. Jules is furious at the mess he's having to clean up, Vincent is unhappy at the grief he's catching, and Jimmie is none too happy at having a dead body in his garage with his wife due home in ninety minutes. Fortunately Marsellus has dispatched Winston Wolf to their aid, a specialist in handling difficult situations. He calms everyone down, gathers cleaning supplies, tells the two men what to do, and soothes Jimmie with a generous down payment on some new furniture. When the clean-up is done, Winston tosses the men's bloody clothes in the trunk with the body, hoses them both down, and outfits them in apparel borrowed from Jimmie. The car is dumped at a junkyard which will dispose of its gruesome contents and the pair takes a taxi to get some breakfast. A key question is why these scenes at Jimmie's house are necessary. Jules could have seen the bullet holes in the wall, decided to abandon the life of crime, and subsequently set Pumpkin and Honey Bunny free. The scenes of Marvin's head being blown off, Jimmie railing at the two men about the body in his garage, and the clean-up of the mess might be Tarantino indulging his penchant for grotesqueries, but other options are worth considering.

One important function is further to sharpen the contrast between Jules and Vincent. Although Jules was very much in charge in the opening scene, the banter between the two men made them seem co-equals and Jules's more serious attitude about the fate of Antwan did not appear significant. On his following date with Mia, Vincent gained considerable sympathy because of the terrible crisis he faced (even though due to his own carelessness), appearing warm and vulnerable as he took leave of Mia. However, in these subsequent scenes, Vincent—whose carelessness caused the mess—comes across as petty and truculent. He complains about Jimmie "freaking out," and when reminded that Jimmie is doing them a favor, he snaps back, "If that favor means that I got to take shit, then he can stick that favor straight up his ass." Vincent is similarly unhappy when Winston doesn't say "please" as he sends them to clean the car. Winston points out that time is of the essence, and adds calmly, "Pretty please, with sugar on top, clean the fucking car." He notes that if Vincent had any instinct for self-preservation, he would be moving as fast as possible rather than arguing so much—a telling comment. Then when Jules complains about having to clean up Vincent's mess, Vincent snaps back that a man can only take so much abuse. Despite being the one at fault, he continues to behave as if he is the aggrieved party. In contrast to Vincent's petulant behavior, Jules—while understandably upset—keeps his feelings under control, tries to be diplomatic with Jimmie, and does as Winston instructs.

The second important element in these scenes is the new light they throw on the lives of these men. This is done partly by the visuals, in particular the priceless image of the two men drinking their coffee in Jimmie's kitchen. No longer are they the cool, professional hit men who drove to their assignment just an hour ago. Their suits are a mess, Vincent's shirt is soaked with blood, and their downcast eyes testify to their need for rescuing. Completely incongruous as they stand in a clean, white, suburban kitchen, these gory, woebegone figures undercut the glamorous image of the gangster. Earlier, Vincent's floating down the road after shooting up made drug use seem sexy, but the sexiness vanished when Mia collapsed on the floor. Similarly, blowing away Brett and his buddies made Jules and Vincent seem omnipotent, but that, too, has changed. The switch in status is underscored by Jimmie turning the tables on Jules, asking him if he had seen a sign on the front lawn advertising "Dead Nigger Storage." When Jules tries to stutter some response, Jimmie plows ahead, asserting that the sign is not there "because storing dead niggers ain't my fucking business!" Some have criticized the blatant use of "nigger" in Jimmie's rant, especially since Jimmie is played by Tarantino, arguing that it shows an attempt to create "coolness" by appropriating elements of black culture.[15] There is truth in this, but one should also consider the thematic parallel. Jimmie's haranguing Jules about "dead nigger storage" is the same psychological pistol whipping that Jules performed on Brett an hour earlier. Jules, powerless to fight back, stutters helplessly just as Brett did. The tough gangster image receives a final blow as the two men end up in their new clothing borrowed from Jimmie: shorts and t-shirts. Vincent's shirt touts the UC Santa Cruz Banana Slugs. No longer ferocious hit men, they are now "dorks" (Figure 3.11).

3.11
A new fan for the Banana Slugs and his fellow dork.

Finally, even though Jules has already announced his intention to quit the life of crime, this scene gives further motivation to his decision. Where gangster movies generally glory in the thrill of violence, this one shows the awful aftermath. They calmly exited from the apartment, leaving three victims behind, but this time there is no walking away: they must clean up a car splattered with blood and brains, their own clothing drenched with gore. This might give Jules second thoughts about his chosen profession. The scene at Jimmie's begins, notably, with the two men washing their hands, a highly symbolic act and surely representative of Jules's decision to change his life. The same overtones can be found at the end as the two men stand naked while Winston hoses them down, cleansing and baptizing them, and stripping off the black suits that symbolize their life of crime. Jules's subsequent behavior shows that he has cast off this life for good, a decision surely strengthened by the experience of cleaning up Marvin. Vincent, we know, will shortly reassume his old uniform and end up dead on Butch's bathroom floor.

Back at the Hawthorne Grill

Bringing the story full circle, Tarantino returns to the Hawthorne Grill in a sequence with three major sections. In the first, Jules and Vincent continue their argument about miracles over breakfast. In the second, fast-paced sequence, Pumpkin and Honey Bunny leap up and begin their robbery just after Vincent has headed off to the bathroom. Pumpkin spots Marsellus's briefcase and forces Jules to surrender it, only to find Jules's nine millimeter lodged under his chin. Honey Bunny in turn finds Vincent back from the bathroom, his weapon pointed at her. In the final section, Jules calms everyone down, gives Pumpkin the contents of his wallet, and sends the two shaken amateurs on their way. Then he and Vincent saunter to the door and exit, ending the film.

The opening section, another philosophical discussion by Jules and Vincent as they have breakfast, first appears to be another of Tarantino's amusing riffs, mimicking the earlier discussion of cheeseburgers in foreign lands. When Jules declines the bacon that Vincent offers—"I don't eat filthy animals"—Vincent laughs. "Bacon tastes good; pork chops taste good." Jules responds, "Hey, a sewer rat may taste like pumpkin pie, but I'd never know 'cause I wouldn't eat the filthy motherfuckers." The discussion continues at length, but on examination this clever banter has serious ramifications. Jules says that pigs are filthy because "Pigs sleep and root in shit." In the preceding sequence, struggling to clean up the gore-splattered car, Jules had cried out in frustration, "This is some fucked-up repugnant shit!" He was, at that moment, a creature repulsed by living in his own filth and has decided to do so no longer. As the discussion returns to the supposed "miracle," Vincent argues that what happened to them does not qualify. Jules says it does because "I felt the touch of God. God got involved." He says he will give up the life of crime and just "walk the earth," which Vincent thinks will make Jules no better than "a bum." This dialogue shows Tarantino operating at his best. Here are two hit men, dressed in dorky t-shirts, having breakfast at a neighborhood coffee shop and engaged in a discussion that is positively Jesuitical. The conversation has ranged from the Old Testament to the New, beginning with a debate over what things are clean and unclean and ending with an analysis of miracles. Notably, the discussion has come back to the very topic first raised by Pumpkin and Honey Bunny: how should a person live his life? So firmly is the film lodged in quotidian reality, not to mention the world of pulp novels, that it seems absurd to believe Tarantino intends his viewers to take Jules's conversion seriously. However, the slow track in to Jules's somber face after Vincent has left the table indicates a strong interest in the changes occurring inside him and his subsequent actions indicate that *he* believes in his conversion.

Jules Sets Pumpkin Free

Now Honey Bunny and Pumpkin leap up, brandish their weapons and race about, yelling obscenities nonstop. (An intercut shot shows Vincent on the stool, reading his novel obliviously, underscoring the idea of his being cut off from a more important reality.) Pumpkin spots the briefcase on Jules's table, asks what's in it, and Jules tells him, "My boss's dirty laundry." Pumpkin says having to do the boss's laundry sounds like "a shit job" and Jules, very seriously, replies, "I was thinking the same thing." A moment later, distracted by the case, Pumpkin finds Jules's pistol under his nose and is forced to sit facing him as Jules talks calmly but seriously to him and Honey Bunny. She, nearly hysterical, is standing on a nearby counter with her pistol pointed at Jules. "Normally," says Jules, "both your asses would be dead as fuckin' fried chicken." But right now, "I'm in a transitional period, . . . and I don't want to kill you. I want to help you." One only has to think back to the opening scene to realize how amazing these words are. There Jules calmly shot one boy on the couch without even glancing at him and cold-bloodedly sampled Brett's cheeseburger and drained his cup of Sprite before pumping him full of lead. One can easily imagine the Jules of that moment taking sincere satisfaction in terminating these two foolish amateurs. Their amateur status is clearly shown as Honey Bunny finds Vincent returned from the washroom, his gun leveled at her, and begins to wobble back and forth, not knowing what direction to point her pistol. She whimpers, "I gotta go pee. I want to go home" (Figure 3.12). Jules

3.12 Honey Bunny: Up-angle as before but no longer in control.

again calms everyone down and gives Pumpkin the $1,500 in his wallet, at which point Vincent nearly explodes. Jules explains that he's not giving away the money: he's buying Pumpkin's life, so he doesn't have to kill him. Jules again recites the verses from Ezekiel he quoted to Brett, and admits "I just thought it was some cold-blooded shit to say to a mother-fucker before I popped a cap in his ass." But he now realizes the words apply to him. "I am the tyranny of evil men," a role he rejects, saying he wants to be the shepherd. With that, he uncocks his pistol, and the couple exits hurriedly, clutching one another. Vincent suggests it would be wise if they did the same, and they saunter to the door, tuck their guns into the waistbands of their shorts, and exit casually to the street. The credits roll.

Conclusion

For Polan, this ending sums up the film nicely. That fact that two hoodlums, although now dressed in shorts and t-shirts, can remain totally cool is what the film is all about—"Style winning out over substance."[16] As noted earlier, Polan refuses to grant any serious meaning to Jules's conversion. The film's importance, he asserts, is "as game, as visuality, as cinema."[17] These elements are inarguably central, as they have continued to be in all Tarantino's films. Thomas Leitch also dismisses Jules's religious experience, arguing that the film is rooted "in a world of such stunning violence and amorality . . . that it is impossible to take Jules's conversion, or either of the resurrections that precede it, at face value."[18] A further problem is that the multi-plot structure has left very little time to investigate Jules's conversion in much depth. Evan Smith admits that, after Jules's transformative experience, the film "omits the necessary processes of absorption, consideration, and decision making" which one would expect, although Samuel L. Jackson's performance helps to make Jules's conversion seem convincing.[19]

Pulp Fiction's virtuoso filmmaking, with events rushing along pell-mell, tends to overshadow elements of subtlety, character portrayal, and philosophical probing. Tarantino juggles generic styles, mixing gangster film, horror film, Blaxploitation, and comedy. He turns the screen into a cartoon frame with extreme camera positions, canted angles, wide-angle lenses, exaggerated close-ups, and splashy colors. He fills the film with references to popular culture—film stars, rock music, and television shows. He tops this all with a dazzling script, crammed with witty exchanges, head-snapping changes in tone, and totally unexpected plot turns. Nevertheless, while appreciating the carnivalesque core of *Pulp Fiction*, one is not constrained to renounce all possibility of serious meanings. For one thing, the story contains scene after scene where characters, however humorously, raise ethical issues. Arguments about foot massages raise the question of when violence is justified and when authority is to be questioned. The outrageous story of the watch, likewise, asserts the importance of being true to one's ideals and not abandoning a fellow soldier. Jules and Vincent arguing about filthy animals, especially when they have so recently been drenched in blood, links to the topic of violence and its consequences. These discussions culminate in Jules's revised exegesis of the passage in Ezekiel, which is nothing less than a reexamination of his own life's meaning.

More important, almost all the central characters are forced to make serious decisions about how to live their lives, starting and ending with Pumpkin and Honey Bunny. Character decisions are the engine driving the typical Hollywood plot, but here they involve life or death choices for others and the way they are made is emphasized by juxtaposition. Thus Vincent saves Mia after her overdose but obviously does so to save his own skin. By contrast, in the immediately following episode, Butch could easily escape with his skin intact but puts himself at risk to rescue Marsellus, his sworn enemy. Likewise, at the beginning of the film, Jules doesn't question his assignment, killing Brett and his two buddies without a second thought—indeed, with considerable relish. This is in striking contrast to his actions at the end where he risks his own life, as the panicked Honey Bunny waves her pistol around wildly, in an effort to set these two lives on a better course. The care with which the story order has been juggled to emphasize these contrasts and to put Jules's decision at the very end suggests that something more serious is afoot. This shifting of plot order, in effect makes Jules "the moral center" of the narrative.[20] While none of this changes the visceral nature of most of the film, it suggests that the idea of more serious themes cannot be so summarily dismissed.

Afterword on Narrative Structure

Tarantino has said, "If you were to walk out of the theater after the first hour of *Pulp Fiction,* you really haven't experienced the movie, because the movie you see an hour later is a much different movie. And the last twenty minutes is much different than that."[21] The reading given here bears out that statement. The first scene in the restaurant between Pumpkin and Honey Bunny is full of stylistic fireworks—fast-paced, screwball banter, underlying sexuality, teasing shifts of tone, scatological language, cartoon close-ups, sudden changes of angle, and a freeze frame that halts the scene just as the real action is about to begin. This is the cinematic excitement that so captured viewers initially and which Polan and others characterize as "a rendering of a viscerality so intense that it substitutes for all concern with deep meaning."[22] The film returns to the restaurant scene at the end and, as Tarantino suggests, the final twenty minutes are completely different. After the attempted robbery, the pace slows dramatically. The scene of Jules talking to Pumpkin lasts seven and a half minutes, with an average shot length of 6.8 seconds compared to 5.1 seconds for the robbery. Especially notable are the thirteen shots where Jules meditates on the meaning of the passage in Ezekiel. Here the shot length is 9.8 seconds, the intensity increased by tight close-ups on Pumpkin and Jules, with Jules's pistol looming in the foreground of each shot (Figure 3.13). (A nine millimeter functions much as the sight of a hangman's noose, marvelously focusing the mind.) Jules is rethinking the meaning of his life at this moment and suggesting that Pumpkin would be wise to do the same.

3.13
Jules's 9 mm.
helps focus
Pumpkin's
mind.

The final sequence may be relatively brief, but the slower pace, the close camera position, and the altered time order which has moved it to the end of the film give it extraordinary emphasis. Films which seek only to excite the viewer and glorify violence typically end with an adrenaline-pumping scene of chases and gunfire and bodies falling everywhere. This film finishes by showing the grisly clean-up of a shooting, with the cool hit men turned into pathetic losers in silly t-shirts. Then, following a discussion of animals that live in their own excrement, it finishes with a scene of one man sitting at a table talking to another, trying very hard to *avoid* violence. After the earlier brutal assassinations, this scene ends without a single shot being fired. Thus, despite all its darkness and violence and drugs, *"Pulp Fiction* proffers a fictional universe where miracles still happen, where love can still make a difference."[23] In this grotesque comedy, with its cartoon violence, comic book colors, and a script larded with outrageous jokes, we find the network narrative spun in a whole new direction. While eight people die in this grisly world, another six manage to escape their purgatory. One man harrows Hell using a samurai sword, two others miraculously escape death, a woman is resurrected, and the ending potentially sets three characters on the path to redemption. The final image, appropriately, is of two men emerging into the light of morning. Unlikely as it seems, among Tarantino's wild pastiche of elements, one finds hints of a *commedia* reminiscent of Dante's.

Notes

1   Peter Brooker and Will Brooker, "Pulpmodernism: Tarantino's Affirmative Action," in *Pulping Fictions: Consuming Culture across the Literature/Media Divide*, Deborah Cartmell, et al., eds. (Chicago: Pluo, 1996), 137, summarizing the views of critics such as James Wood, Finian O'Toole, and Mark Kermode.

2   Robin Wood, "Pulp the Hype on the Q.T.: Slick Shtick," *Artforum* (March 1995): 63.

3   Dana Polan, *Pulp Fiction* (London: BFI, 2000), 76.

4   Tarantino says the film's episodic structure was designed to mimic the experience of reading a pulp fiction novel, picked up at odd moments and read for a few pages. Quentin Tarantino, "Quentin Tarantino on *Pulp Fiction*," *Sight and Sound* 4, no. 5 (May 1994): 10.

5   Tarantino's script specifies this scene is to be done "in rapid-pace His Girl Friday fashion." Pat Dowell, "Pulp Friction," *Cinéaste* 21, no. 3 (1995): 4.

6   George Mott, "Quentin Tarantino and the Pulp of Enjoyment," *The Psychoanalytic Review* 82, no. 3 (1995): 466.

7   Richard Alleva, "Beaten to a Pulp," *Commonweal* 121, no. 20 (18 Nov. 1994): 30.

8   The shot of their conversation is clearly intended as homage to the opening of *The Godfather*. It shows only the back of Marsellus's head, emulating Coppola's strategy of establishing the leader's power by initially denying viewers the sight of his face.

9   This close-up of the hypodermic with adrenaline parallels the earlier close-up of the needle being screwed on for Vincent to shoot up, emphasizing the link between his carefree drug use and his current terrible predicament.

10 Polan, *Pulp Fiction*, 31.

11 Shawn St. Jean argues that Butch cannot achieve manhood by simply fleeing from Marsellus's control or by killing Vincent, who was not a worthy opponent. Manhood implies control of time—hence the watch linked to Butch's father—and to gain it Butch must confront Marsellus, who told him his time was up. "Cases of Myth-Taken Identity in *Pulp Fiction*," *Studies in the Humanities* 24, nos. 1/2 (1997): 77.

12 Alan Barnes and Marcus Hearne note the many infantile markings Butch carries, including his shaved head and wide-eyed gaze, his use of baby talk with Fabienne, his outbursts of temper, and his clinging to childish souvenirs. *Tarantino A to Zed: The Films of Quentin Tarantino* (London: B. T. Batsford, 1996), 34.

13 bell hooks does not find the ending so upbeat, since a central black male undergoes homosexual rape and has to be rescued by a white man. *Reel to Real: Race, Sex and Class at the Movies* (London: Routledge, 1996), 48-49. For all that the scene shows the redemption of Butch, and for all that the action with the samurai sword appealed to Tarantino's geek fans, the strong undertones of racism and homophobia make this whole episode unappealing to many viewers. In this instance, Tarantino's flamboyance ends up revealing very unattractive underlying values.

14 Alleva, "Beaten to a Pulp," 30.

15 Dowell sees this as "the wannabe posturing of a hip white guy" ("Pulp Friction," 4-5) and Sharon Willis thinks Tarantino has tried to provide himself with an "alibi" by making Bonnie black (she is shown for an instant in an imagined moment of her returning home). "She is supposed to exempt him from cultural rules, from ordinary whiteness." *High Contrast: Race and Gender in Contemporary Hollywood Film* (Durham, N.C.: Duke University Press, 1997), 206-7.

16 Polan, *Pulp Fiction*, 86.

17 Polan, *Pulp Fiction*, 83.

18 Thomas M. Leitch, "Know-Nothing Entertainment: What to Say to Your Friends on the Right, and Why It Won't Do Any Good," *Literature/Film Quarterly* 25, no. 1 (1997): 9.

19 Evan Smith, "Thread Structure: Rewriting the Hollywood Formula," *Journal of Film and Video* 51, nos. 3/4 (July/August 1999-2000): 90.

20 Todd F. Davis and Kenneth Womack, "Shepherding the Weak: The Ethics of Redemption in Quentin Tarantino's *Pulp Fiction*," *Literature/Film Quarterly* 26, no. 1 (1998): 65.

21 Gavin Smith, "'When You Know You're in Good Hands': Quentin Tarantino Interviewed by Gavin Smith," *Film Comment* 30, no. 4 (July/August 1994): 42.

22 Polan, *Pulp Fiction*, 77.

23 Davis and Womack, "Shepherding the Weak," 65.

4

Amores Perros

Of Dogs and Rats and Goats

Alejandro González Iñárritu is familiar to American audiences because of *21 Grams* (2003) and *Babel* (2006), but his less well known first feature, *Amores Perros* (2000), deserves a place alongside those later big-budget productions. It is notably inventive in its use of multiple story lines, something that has characterized all his films. Iñárritu began his career at a propitious moment. After a fairly vital period in the 1940s and '50s, the government-controlled Mexican film industry sank into the doldrums. Since all films were financed by—and hence approved by—the government agency IMCINE [Mexican Film Institute], the only ones produced were vaguely styled "art films" that appealed to few viewers. As Iñárritu remarked sarcastically of the agency's policies, "If nobody understands and nobody goes to see a movie, that must mean it's a masterpiece."[1] Many talented Mexican directors went abroad to work rather than submit to this system, so that by the mid-1990s fewer than a dozen films were produced annually.[2] This dispiriting situation changed when the film industry was privatized in 1990, allowing ticket prices to rise, old theaters to be renovated, and new ones built. Attendance at films increased.[3]

After a successful career as a DJ and creating more than eight hundred TV commercials for companies including Ford and Coca-Cola, Iñárritu felt ready to tackle a feature film. He worked for three years on the script for *Amores Perros*, collaborating with well-known novelist Guillermo Arriaga. The resulting work was a stunning success, voted best film during Critic's Week at Cannes, nominated for Best Foreign Film at the Academy Awards, winning prizes at the Edinburgh and Tokyo festivals, and sweeping the awards at the Mexican Film Festival. It was shown widely around the world at a time when few Mexican films could find distributors and earned $10 million in Mexico alone on an initial investment of $2.4 million. That made it the second highest grossing domestic film in Mexican history,[4] especially notable given its avoidance of stereotypic portraits of Mexican life and saccharine story lines found in films such as *Like Water for Chocolate* (Arau, 1992).[5]

Story Summary

The film interweaves three stories. In the first tale, Ramiro and Octavio live with their mother in a poor district along with Ramiro's school-girl wife, Susana, and an infant son. Ramiro supplements his meager income as a supermarket clerk by robbing convenience stores in off hours. Gentle Octavio does his best to protect Susana from her husband's abuse, but then gradually seduces her, using the money he gets from entering Cofi, Ramiro's Rottweiler, in dogfights. Susana eventually agrees to run away with him, but flees with Ramiro and the baby after Ramiro is beaten by a group of thugs who threaten to kill him. (Ironically, Octavio paid for this beating to put Ramiro in his place, but loses Susana as a result.) In a final dogfight, Octavio's bitter rival El Jarocho shoots Cofi, seriously wounding him, and in turn is stabbed by Octavio, setting off the desperate car chase that opens the film and then is re-shown three times.

In the second story, Daniel, a well-to-do magazine editor, leaves his wife and daughters to move into a new apartment with the famous model Valeria. Unfortunately, on that very day her car is struck by Octavio's as he races away from Jarocho's gang. Her right leg—featured on billboards all over the city touting "Enchant" perfume—is badly broken, putting her in a wheelchair and her career on hold. To add to her distress, her little white Lhasa Apso, Richie, falls down a hole and gets lost beneath the apartment floorboards. When Daniel takes no effective action to rescue it, Valeria struggles to do so and re-injures her leg, requiring its amputation. The story ends with the two of them staring teary-eyed out the apartment window at the empty billboard formerly graced with Valeria's leggy image.

The third story concerns El Chivo, "The Goat," an unkempt elderly man who wanders the city with a pushcart full of scavenged items and a pack of mongrel dogs. He is also a some-time hit man. A former teacher, he abandoned his family to become a revolutionary, was imprisoned, and is now estranged from his only daughter, Maru (Maria Eugenia), who believes him dead. El Chivo is hired by a young businessman, Gustavo, to eliminate his partner, Luis. El Chivo witnesses the car crash, helps pull the unconscious Octavio from the vehicle and rescues Cofi. After nursing Cofi back to health, he returns home after a day of stalking Luis to discover that Cofi—a trained killing machine from his months in the dogfighting rings—has dispatched every other member of the pack. This event causes El Chivo to abandon his assassin's career. He leaves Luis and Gustavo to settle their own problems and heads out of town after leaving a message for Maru, hoping for a future reconciliation.

   Amores Perros is a classic—and masterful—**network narrative**, with interwoven stories. Specifically, it is a **hub and spoke** plot, where the characters are thrown together for a single moment and thereafter move in separate directions. That contact is a car crash, an idea picked up by Haggis's film *Crash* four years later and which has become a staple in such films. (As David Bordwell remarks, "It seems that a network movie can't do without a traffic jam, smashup, fender-bender, felled pedestrian, or brake-squealing near-miss."[6]) An encounter so violent insists on "the ways in which lives are interconnected, with the actions of characters dramatically affecting those of the others and changing the course of their lives."[7] In all Iñárritu's films this connection is established through violence, suggesting how it permeates human culture, with careless actions by one person impacting many others. *Babel* carries this idea to its greatest extreme, connecting the lives of people from three different cultures on three different continents, but *Amores Perros* is stronger, benefitting from Iñárritu's intimate knowledge of life in Mexico City. Although the characters come from widely disparate classes and only meet a single time, Iñárritu interweaves scenes from their lives to comment on one another. Thus El Chivo killing a man is juxtaposed with Octavio and Ramiro arguing, underscoring the violence that permeates both their worlds. Most important, all three stories illustrate how *machismo*—the "dog" side of human nature (*perros*)—causes three men to cast aside the ties of family (*amores*), a decision each comes to regret.

The Car Chase

   The opening scene dramatizes the violence human selfishness unleashes on the world, as Octavio and his friend Jorge flee for their lives in a dramatic car chase. In just two minutes and sixteen seconds, the viewer is bombarded with seventy-one shots—an average shot length of less than two seconds. There is a blurred white line, two boys yelling frantically at one another, the rush of cars, a black Rottweiler bleeding in the backseat, a yellow truck zooming forward in pursuit, near collisions, and finally an awful crash. The sense of desperation is increased by the intense sound track: the boys yelling, tires squealing, engines roaring, and horns honking. Tight shots emphasize the fear on the faces of Octavio and Jorge and disorient the viewer, who has no perspective on the action. The camera is constantly changing angles—shooting the boys from all sides, jumping from the car's interior to the exterior, looking out the car windows, and then jumping to a shot in the rearview mirror (Figure 4.1). Further, the film's color has been dramatically altered by cinematographer Rodrigo Prieto, who used a

4.1
Opening
hysteria:
The car
chase.

"pass-bleach" process on the negative that intensifies blacks and whites and the red of the blood, producing "a quasi-hallucinogenic effect."[8] Since the viewer has no idea who these people are or what has motivated this terrifying chase, the scene is disorienting in the extreme. One may feel some sympathy for the two boys, pursued by a larger truck with armed occupants, but there is no time to develop real empathy before their car runs a red light and the crash occurs. The scene ends as precipitously as it began when their car rolls to a stop in flames, with a horn wailing and a quick shot of a blond woman trapped behind another car's window.

This opening thrusts the viewer headlong into a world of senseless brutality from which there will be little respite in the film's remaining two and a half hours. As it encapsulates the lives of the protagonists, it would seem to follow the Hobbesian description of human existence as "nasty, brutish, and short." However, the viewer is also allowed to revel freely in the excitement of the chase, insulated because the characters are unknown. When this chase is replayed, fifty minutes later, the intervening flashback has given the audience greater understanding of the precipitating events and stronger empathy with the two misguided boys. Octavio has been portrayed as initially gentle, trying to protect his sister-in-law Susana, turning over his dogfight winnings to her, seducing her, and then losing her and the money. When he enters Cofi in a final fight, hoping to regain some of his winnings, the brutal Jarocho shoots the dog, angry at all the bouts he has lost to him. The second version of the chase, then, reflects Octavio's point of view, strengthening the audience's link to him. The sound track is distorted—underlain with a droning noise, sometimes giving no words even though the boys' lips are moving, other times giving the words out of synch, and further distorted by sudden bursts of nondiegetic music (that is, music from outside the story world).[9] Time is speeded up—some shots are truncated, others cut out entirely, and the frame speed has been noticeably increased. (The sequence takes only 44 seconds compared to 2:16 in the opening.) In the final five seconds, there is only a roaring sound, quick images of the car racing forward, the traffic signal changing, a car in front, and then the screen goes black. Climaxing in this fashion, the scene is effective on many levels. Subjectively, it replicates the blurred viewpoint of Octavio and Jorge, with everything suddenly going black at the moment of impact. It leaves the viewer stunned, more unsure than ever of the ultimate fate of the car's occupants, fearing that this first story may be ended for good. It emphasizes the uncertainty that characterizes the lives of people in the lower classes.

Wrapped around this second version of the crash, Valeria appears "live" for the first time in the story, having been seen previously on her elevated billboards, gazing like a goddess over Mexico City. She is being interviewed on the TV show "Gentes de Hoy," showing off her supposed boyfriend, the handsome Andrés Salgado (a decoy to conceal her liaison with Daniel) and her Lhasa Apso, Richie, which she introduces as her son. Based on this initial appearance, her life seems to stand in complete contrast to the gritty reality of Octavio and Susana. Treated with deference by the interviewer, Valeria is dressed in chic clothes and glamorously lit. (The cinematographer, Rodrigo Prieto, shot Valeria's story on a different film stock "to make it crisper and cleaner than the other two chapters."[10]) Valeria lives in a protective bubble, represented by the artificial setting in the TV studio. The same is true in the following scene when she exits the studio, still in enclosed spaces, walking beneath huge satellite dishes that roof the parking lot while her screaming fans are held back by an iron fence. Then she enters still another refuge, as Andrés leads her to the new apartment where Daniel is waiting to surprise her. From the opening shots of her behind the glass of the TV screen, the entire sequence—in dramatic contrast with the car chase—has shown Valeria living a pampered existence like her dog Richie, safely enclosed in a sheltering cocoon.

Valeria gets a few more moments in her cocoon, singing along to the song "Corazon" as she drives to the store to get some celebratory champagne. The camera cuts from the music blasting inside the car, to shots outside where it is heard only faintly. The sound track thus reinforces the sense of Valeria gliding along in her own separate world, cut off from reality. There is more narcissism as she looks in the car mirror to apply lipstick while stopped at a red light. Then the light turns green, the camera cuts to an outside shot, and her car rolls forward—only to be struck with an enormous crash by Octavio's Marquis which catapults in from the right side of the frame. Octavio's car becomes a violent vector force, impelling Valeria's and Daniel's lives in a new direction that will test the strength of their commitment to one another. This third version of the crash emphasizes the unexpected connections between people, a frequent theme in network narratives. Equally important, it emulates Valeria's perspective: the viewer is blindsided as much as she is by the car that bursts into her protective bubble. That in turn suggests the precariousness of existence, even for those supposedly dwelling above the cares of life.

The final version of the crash presents a wholly new viewpoint, this time El Chivo's. He is closing in on his next target, the businessman Luis, when the crash explodes in front of him. Replayed for the fourth time, the crash is marked again by brilliant camerawork as it adopts El Chivo's point of view, allying the viewer with him for much of the action. It tracks with him as he runs forward to help wrench open the door of the Marquis, "liberates" Octavio's wallet, and helps lift the bloody youngster out onto the pavement. Equally important, the editing and camerawork make the crash's horror hideously real. The pace is frenetic, with 55 shots in 165 seconds, for a three second average shot length. The hand-held camera is never still—tracking, panning, and zip-panning from one space to another. We see Octavio lifted into an ambulance, the dead Jorge hauled out, and other rescuers trying to extract Valeria. Camera angles change dramatically from one side of the car to the other, from interiors to exteriors. The chaotic motion is reinforced by the strident sound track: a blaring car horn, ambulance sirens, victims crying out, and men yelling as they try to help. This grim scene is entirely antithetical to the glorified portrayal of violence in the typical Hollywood film. What began as flashy *tour de force* car chase, drawing the viewer into its frenzy, now just as brilliantly exhibits the horror that results. The remainder of the film, similarly, will reverse our initial impression of each of the characters.

Dogfights

The film's title makes obvious the importance of dogs. Arriaga's script originally carried the title *Black Dog/White Dog,* and dogs are present in all three stories. Marvin D'Lugo says using the noun *perro* as an adjective suggests "the instinctual, animal nature" of the drives that motivate the central characters.[11] The English title, *Love's a Bitch*, is cute, but a more accurate rendering would be *Bestial Passions.* For his part, Iñárritu says, "Obviously, men have this divine nature and animal nature. Normally, the animal nature is winning all the time—you want to eat, maybe you want to sleep with your best friend's wife, or kill somebody. . . . So all these characters are always fighting between these two possibilities."[12]

Befitting the title, the first scene after the opening crash takes place at the dogfights that serve as the objective correlative of the human passions that tear lives apart. The camera cuts to a tracking shot at knee level alongside a fighting dog being led to a ramshackle arena. The camera pans to a second dog having the blood washed off, a third being dragged away like a gory sack of potatoes, and a fourth locked in a wire cage. The click of the dog's toenails as it prances in, mixed with the din of barking, continues the dense aural texture of the opening chase scene. The camera now tracks forward ahead of the dog, Pancho, and pans up to the face of its owner, the young gang leader, El Jarocho. The connecting pan immediately suggests a symbolic link—the fighting dog as phallic symbol, held between its master's legs (Figure 4.2). Preliminaries commence: the ringmaster

4.2 Canine *machismo*: El Jarocho and Pancho.

announces the stakes, people begin betting, the dogs are "heated up" (encouraged to lunge at one another while still restrained), then loosed. The scene ends on another effective aural device: the "thud" as the two dogs collide fiercely and a sudden sharp whine. The dogfight arena illuminates the characters in the first story, portraying in the most graphic terms the "dog-eat-dog" world they inhabit. For most of them, the only hope of getting ahead lies in illegal activities—dogfighting in Octavio's case or robbing convenience stores, Ramiro's avocation. Everyone is drawn in: we see spectators betting around the ring and children watching, wide-eyed. The way the dogs are so casually injured and killed for the economic advancement of their owners suggests, in turn, the way the lower classes are exploited by an economic system which gives them no control over their destiny. Scenes of dog fighting pop up continually through the first story, an insistent reminder of the underlying violence upon which these lives are built.

The link between the dogfights and the two brothers is manifested as they first appear at the family breakfast table where their rivalry is immediately established. The younger brother, Octavio, walks into the kitchen where Susana is feeding the baby and greets his nephew cheerily: "How's it going, little dude?" As he joins his sister-in-law, the camera ceases its "jittery" movements, holds them in extended two-shots, and uses frequent shot/reverse shots as they talk, signaling the importance of their relationship.[13] Octavio's laughing with Susana is thrown into sharp contrast a moment later as Ramiro comes in to toss his store uniform in Susana's face, complain about her poor washing job, and accuse her of letting Cofi escape again. When Octavio tries to intervene, Ramiro insists, "This is between me and my wife." An intercut shot from behind Ramiro shows the frightened Susana pinched into a narrow space between his waist and arm, emphasizing her entrapment (Figure 4.3). Octavio gets Susana off the hook by saying he was the one who let Cofi

4.3
Susana:
Trapped
in the
male world.

out, Ramiro stomps away, and Doña Concha tells Octavio to stay out of it, leaving no doubt as to which son she sides with. The audience is meant to side with Octavio here, since he is played by the charismatic Gael García Bernal, cheerful, tender with the baby, and protective of the oppressed Susana—all traits that stand in sharp contrast to the brutish Ramiro. But the dogfights that precede and follow this scene serve as commentary on it. Although Octavio is initially made much more sympathetic, he and his brother are "a pair of vicious dogs engaged in a meaningless battle to the death for the right to rule over an already disintegrating family home."[14]

The film continues to interweave the scenes of dogfighting and the family, emphasizing the parallel violence. A subsequent scene shows the two brothers quarreling again at the breakfast table. After Ramiro tells his mother he has no money for diapers, Octavio quietly heckles him about his robbery sideline: "Aren't drugstores good business?" Ramiro flares back: "One word and you're dead." The possibilities for violence escalate as Susana later tells Octavio she's pregnant and cries in his arms, but rejects his suggestion that they run away together. This baby is obviously *not* Octavio's since Susana repulses his advances for the time being. Rather she is in trouble because neither her husband nor her mother-in-law will appreciate having another mouth to feed. Rejected by Susana, Octavio paces in circles and stares through the Venetian blinds as if they were bars. This image of him as a caged beast complements the sense of suppressed passion in the scene, shot almost entirely in extremely tight shot/reverse shot. It also links to the dogfighting arena and the wire cages holding the animals there.

Amores Perros

The overlap between *amores* and *perros* becomes clear when Octavio decides to win Susana away from his brother. He justifies his decision to his friend, Jorge, by saying he liked her first and that his aim is not to make love to her but to get her to leave with him. As he gives these rationalizations, Octavio is washing Cofi, whom he plans to enter in the dogfights and earn the money to take Susana away. Cofi is, in fact, Ramiro's dog, but Octavio claims the dog as his because he feeds it and cares for it. This is essentially the same argument he is making about Susana: she is really his because he loves her and will take care of her better than her doltish husband, even though she is married to Ramiro, has borne his child, and still feels loyal to him. Both arguments are suspect. Using the money earned at the dogfights to tempt Susana, Octavio in effect is buying her affections, prostituting her. This makes him no better than Ramiro, who brings Susana a Walkman, undoubtedly the fruit from one of his robberies. Hence, although Octavio initially appears the more positive character, a similar bestial nature appears in both brothers.

It becomes increasingly apparent that Octavio's interest in Susana is motivated as much by rivalry with his brother as affection for her. He checks out in Ramiro's lane at the grocery store, complaining that he couldn't find any condoms big enough to fit him. Besides this sexual challenge, Octavio is buying the diapers which his brother failed to provide, thus announcing himself as the man of the house. As he is leaving, he head-butts Ramiro, giving him a bloody nose (emphasized by an explosive crash on the sound track), knowing Ramiro cannot retaliate while at work. Octavio then hurries home and gives the diapers and money to Susana, smugly showing himself the better provider. In turn, Ramiro later catches Octavio in the shower and beats him savagely, emphasizing their rivalry and their similarity—each taking advantage of the other in a vulnerable situation. This rivalry is transplanted to the dog arena, where Cofi kills Jarocho's new dog. Jarocho becomes a convenient stand-in for Ramiro, and in defeating him repeatedly Octavio triumphs symbolically over his brother. He is also changing personally, for he was not present at the dogfights previously—only Jorge had been seen—but now they become his life.

The transmogrification of Octavio into the mirror of his brother is made evident in the film's two brilliant cross-cut montage sequences. Like the famous baptism scene in *Godfather I*, parallel actions are played against one another for ironic effect. In the first one, Octavio embarks on his dogfighting career in scenes juxtaposed against Ramiro and his partner holding up a convenience store, the images brilliantly paralleling the two brothers. Ramiro and his partner, stocking caps over their heads, whirl and point their pistols in all directions in movements that mirror the aggressively lunging dogs in the fighting ring. Octavio counts his winnings, followed by the store's cash drawer being yanked open. Octavio brings his money to Susana, while Ramiro is seen shagging a female employee in the stock room—two versions of seduction. This, in turn, is juxtaposed with two fighting dogs lunging at one another, emphasizing the overlap of violence and sexuality. Octavio is seen reflected in the glass tabletop at Marucio's, the dog promoter's house, exactly as the robbers are reflected in the store's curved security mirrors (Figures 4.4 and 4.5). The dogfight ends; the robbery does also, and the robbers run from the store

4.4
Octavio
reflected as
his money
is counted
out.

4.5
Ramiro
reflected as
he prepares
to collect
his money.

with passing cars squealing to a stop to avoid hitting them. Moments later, Octavio squeals the tires of his newly purchased Grand Marquis as he drives out of a used car lot. The scenes are further connected by the pulsing rap song that underlays the entire sequence, "Sí Señor" by Control Machete. While Octavio regards himself as Susana's savior, the sequence makes evident how much the brothers resemble one another.

The triumph of Octavio's animal nature is made even clearer in the second montage, after he has finally seduced Susana and is planning to run away with her.

Thanks to his connections at the dog ring, Octavio can now get revenge on his older brother. He arranges to have Ramiro beaten up by thugs in a scene cross-cut with one where Octavio makes love to Susana. As Ramiro exits from the supermarket, he is grabbed and stuffed into the backseat of a car, taken to a deserted spot, thrown to the ground and savagely kicked by three men. Intercut with this, Susana starts to wash clothes, is embraced by Octavio coming up behind her, and the two of them make love on top of the washing machine. There is little romance in the scene, thanks to the constant insertion of the brutal beating of Ramiro. Neither Octavio nor Susana seem to be able to lose themselves in emotion either, for separate close-ups show them each looking troubled, undoubtedly bothered by conscience. There is also something unsettling about their making love on top of a machine: One shot disembodies them, showing only their dangling feet. This montage, like the first, makes evident that the story of Octavio and Susana is not a romance as it first appears, but a sad tale of sibling rivalry and loss of humanity.

Thematic Interweaving

These ironic montages show Iñárritu utilizing the network narrative's key strength brilliantly, juxtaposing scenes to emphasize his themes. He also weaves in brief scenes from the second story of Daniel and Valeria, so that their lives comment on the situation of Octavio and Susana. Thus, early in Octavio's story as he is squabbling with his brother and beginning to lust after Susana, Daniel is shown riding in the car with his wife and daughters and then arriving at home. Lasting barely a minute, the scene suggests family tensions that mirror those in the Concha household. In the car, Daniel is isolated from his family, shown in a separate shot as his two daughters squabble in the backseat and his wife snaps at them tensely. He doesn't interact with them; his eyes go instead to a giant billboard featuring Valeria promoting Enchant perfume. The intense red of the billboard and her provocative pose contrast strikingly with the car's gray interior and the family's bickering, emphasizing Valeria's status as fantasy object (Figure 4.6). The family returns home to find the phone ringing, but the party hangs up when the daughters answer. The same thing happens when Daniel's wife answers as it rings a second time. Her bitter smile and sarcastic comment to Daniel make it obvious she suspects who is calling: the overlap of billboard seductress and ringing phone suggest Daniel's extracurricular activities. In exactly one minute Iñárritu sketches a second family being pulled apart by the same force that destroys the Concha family: the man's desire to show himself the alpha male by possessing the most desirable female.

4.6
Valeria:
The
goddess of
Mexico
City..

Other parallels link the two stories. Octavio calls Susana from her bedroom, pretending there is a phone call from her mother (interrupting Ramiro's making love to her), and Daniel gets a phone call from his "brother" and moves to another room to set up a rendezvous with Valeria. Still later, Daniel tiptoes into the bedroom of his sleeping daughters to kiss them good night—and good-bye. This scene occurs immediately after that of Octavio and Susana making love the first time, an action that will break up the family just as surely as Daniel's walking out of his house. As Daniel kisses his daughters good-bye, Santaolalla's "Love Theme" comes in for the first time, the same theme that will be heard as Octavio stares out the window after learning that Susana has fled with Ramiro. In both cases the music speaks of love being thrown away. Octavio and Daniel sacrifice family ties for *machismo* and passion, decisions the film strongly questions.

The foolishness of disregarding family is shown most strongly as El Chivo's strand is interwoven with the other stories, continuing the themes of dogs, violence, love, and family. In many ways, it serves as a capstone for the first two stories. A college teacher who abandoned his wife and daughter to become a guerilla, his resulting isolation is emphasized in his opening appearance. He is shown loading junk onto his cart, surrounded by the mangy pack of dogs that share his bed at night. The telephoto lens used in the shot sets him at a distance from all other human beings. Cars race by in a blur in the foreground and the sound track is filled with the roar of automobile engines and the toll of a distant bell. Here, as in the majority of his sequences, he is entirely silent and interacts with no one. His iron gray hair and matted beard suggest the appropriateness of his nickname, "The Goat." His isolation, his degraded appearance, and his assassin's avocation present us with an image of humanity at its most bestial.

His story comes to the fore in the film's final section, but he appears no fewer than nine times in earlier scenes, his actions commenting on the lives of the other characters. For example, his isolation in that first scene echoes the loneliness

Susana must feel in the preceding scene, returning from school to be snubbed by her mother-in-law who refuses to babysit the next day, saying, "I raised my children. Now you raise yours." Three subsequent scenes in the Concha household portray the growing conflict between Octavio and Ramiro while interwoven scenes show El Chivo studying the picture of his next target while loading a pistol, dispatching his victim with one shot through the window of a fancy Japanese restaurant, and then sardonically drawing glasses and a moustache on the man's photo in the newspaper story announcing the murder. El Chivo is another symbol of violence, tied to the conflicts in the Concha family just as the dogfights are. The association is made clear because the restaurant shooting comes immediately after the scene of Octavio and Ramiro arguing at the kitchen table. Eating is involved in both cases and the link between them is underscored by specific visual parallels: the restaurant scene begins with a close-up of food cooking on the grill—the same grill across which the businessman's blood will run, sizzling, at the end. This echoes the opening close-up of Octavio's plate at breakfast and the earlier one of Doña Concha's skillet (Figure 4.7).

4.7 Visual rhymes: The Japanese grill and Octavio's plate.

El Chivo's thread is particularly important for introducing the countervailing theme—the importance of family—which Octavio and Daniel ignore to their sorrow. In the same newspaper where he reads the account of his crime, El Chivo comes across the obituary for his former wife, remarried after he left her and now lost to him forever. The eyes of this cold-blooded killer fill with tears as he sits alone at his tiny table, framed in the narrow pane of his kitchen window, emphasizing his isolation (Figure 4.8). When his sister-in-law sees him standing at the edge of the cemetery during his ex-wife's burial, she sends Maru off and warns him to stay away, that he is dead to his daughter. We see the pain on his face as he gazes after the beautiful young woman he abandoned. El Chivo's decision to join the revolution, however noble it seemed at the time, has cost him his family. Octavio, however noble his pretensions of saving Susana, likewise pays a high price for sundering family ties and Daniel fails to foresee the loss he will feel in leaving his daughters behind. These interwoven scenes of El Chivo during the earlier stories thus provide a somber commentary on the short-sighted decisions being made.

Nemesis

The Greeks saw Nemesis operating like a natural law: if a mortal or a god violated a moral principle, it was like pushing a pendulum away—inevitably, the pendulum would swing back. This happens to all the characters. Having accumulated enough money so he and Susana can run off, Octavio delays their flight to allow one last dogfight, and then finds out that Ramiro has fled to parts unknown, taking Susana and the baby with him. (The money is gone, too.) The wonderful irony is that Ramiro fled thanks to the terrible beating he received, courtesy of his younger brother. Not content simply to steal his brother's wife, Octavio could not rest until he had established himself as the big dog in the yard. His hubris now has its reward. He loses Susana and, shortly thereafter, has Cofi shot by El Jarocho and ends up killing his one and only friend, Jorge, in the car crash.

The film's judgment of Octavio is shown when he appears at his brother's funeral. Ramiro had tried to move into the big time by forgoing convenience stores in favor of banks and quickly ended up shot dead. When Octavio appears, he is hobbling on crutches after his car crash and has his head shaved. He is the precise double of his brother, whose dead face seen in the window of the coffin is still bruised from the beating he received. The similarity is emphasized since Octavio's head—disconcertingly corpse-like under the bluish fluorescent lights—is also framed behind a glass window in the funeral home and also bruised (Figure 4.9). Octavio also mimics Ramiro's behavior, showing up at his brother's funeral to insist that Susana, newly widowed, run away with him. Not considering her feelings of loss at this moment, he thinks only of his own desires. At the same time, he may well be clinging to her because of his own desperation, having lost Jorge and Cofi and his money. She rejects this offer and we may admire her for feeling guilt at betraying her husband and wanting to honor his memory. But on the other hand, Ramiro abused her and cheated on her; Susana seems headed for

4.9 Visual rhymes: Octavio as his brother's double.

an empty widowhood, foreshadowed by her bitter mother-in-law and her own drunken mother. Her decision to name the new baby after her brutish husband shows both a nobility of spirit and a sad resignation to her fate in a world that gives so little social support to its women.[15] In the end, everyone has lost.

Daniel and Valeria

The story of Daniel and Valeria shows obvious parallels with that of Octavio and Susana, with the man again trying to show himself the alpha dog by possessing the most attractive female and sundering family ties in the process. Sadly, for all their higher status, Daniel and Valeria reveal that they lack the personal resources needed to deal with the misfortunes that befall them. After Valeria's release from the hospital, she sits alone in the apartment while Daniel is at work, having little to do but throw a ball for Richie. In the first story, the fate of master and animal were linked, with Cofi turned from pet into fighting machine just as Octavio was transmogrified from cheerful younger brother to vengeful sibling. Similarly, Richie becomes lost in the same way that Valeria's life loses direction. He chases the ball into a hole in the floor and cannot find his way back out. The next day, after learning that her contract with Enchant has been canceled, Valeria catches sight of rats beneath the floor and calls Daniel in a panic. Her fear that Richie will be devoured by rats clearly represents her panic over the forces chewing up her life and career. After she re-injures her leg attempting to rescue Richie, Daniel tears up the floorboards in a fury and pulls the dog to safety, but it is a hollow victory. Valeria returns from the hospital in a motorized wheelchair, her photogenic leg amputated.

Iñárritu has argued in interviews that Valeria is not necessarily doomed by this downbeat ending, saying that she "acquires an inner beauty."[16] At least one critic is persuaded, saying that when she cannot continue her modeling career, Valeria "is forced to acquire a new, less superficial, identity," which happens when "she is seen looking at childhood photographs and reconnecting with her premodel reality."[17] This interpretation is problematic because when Valeria is home alone, she does nothing—throws the ball for Richie, pages despondently through fashion magazines, and lies on the bed flipping through TV channels with the remote. There is no sense of her settling into some new satisfying identity; rather, she seems restless and unhappy. Daniel comes off no better. It is true that he stands by her after the accident, paying her bills and comforting her in the hospital when she awakens in terror at night. However, in a film that scrutinizes the relationship of animals and their owners, he is notably ineffectual in dealing with Richie's predicament. He assures Valeria everything will be all right, puts some chocolates in a dish to tempt Richie out of the hole, and goes to make himself an omelet. His lack of real interest or incisive action is telling. Similarly, when Valeria insists that he pull up the floor he refuses, saying he cannot afford to repair the damage. Despite Daniel's ineptitude, Iñárritu says that, by the end, Daniel is firmly committed to Valeria. The final shot of him standing beside her in the wheelchair shows that he "assumes his responsibilities with dignity" and what was a fragile, physical relationship has now "a spiritual, emotional and physical dimension."[18] Again, Deborah Shaw agrees, saying that Valeria has gotten a "happy ending" since "Daniel has decided to stay with her."[19] Peter Chumo is encouraged by "the fact that their last scene has him literally standing behind her and holding onto her, as if this were a reflection of the loyalty he will show her."[20]

This upbeat view of the ending is questionable. Daniel was first seen looking up at the billboard image of Valeria from his car and later gazed at her giant ad several times from the apartment window, which suggests that his attraction has always been to her image and to her status as a famous model. With those both gone, one questions how strong his love will be. There is little specific evidence that Daniel is now emotionally committed to Valeria. Notably, at one point he phones his wife and then hangs up, unable to talk to her, which certainly suggests some inclination to return home. Further, the cinematography throughout calls the strength of their relationship into question. They are often filmed in separate shots, as during their consultation with Valeria's doctor. Scenes in the apartment frequently have the camera at low angle and at a distance, emphasizing its emptiness and the gaping holes in the floor, obviously symbolic.

The final scene in particular contains many negative elements. Valeria is crying in her motorized wheelchair as she stares out the window at the billboard that formerly displayed her picture. It is now empty and listed as "available," a grim suggestion of how completely Valeria herself has disappeared,[21] with the empty billboard a cruel "reminder of the space where her leg had been."[22] She stares out through the Venetian blinds that embody the trap she is now in, her career ended. Arroyo speculates that "Her new life will strangle her to death."[23] Daniel does come up behind her and put his arms around her, but in the final shot, the camera cuts away from this tender medium close-up to a more distant shot behind them that makes the two of them look small against the window and emphasizes the

4.10 Desolate isolation: Daniel and Valeria.

apartment's torn up floor (Figure 4.10). This is not a positive image, especially since their story began with coming together at the apartment, making it symbolic of their relationship. The setting throughout has seemed sterile—a glass-topped table, austere chairs, a small coffee table—and the walls are mostly bare, hinting at empty lives. The music played over this image is equally sad: the same guitar heard as Octavio stared out the window after Susana ran off and when Valeria had cried at night by the window. This music has been used throughout to emphasize loss and broken dreams, not hope. Ultimately we must wonder if Valeria will have the inner resources to create a satisfying life for herself and if Daniel will have the commitment to remain with her. Things have certainly not turned out as he would have hoped: he no longer has the trophy girlfriend he wanted, he is saddled with serious expenses, and he has given up his daughters. Although the story of Daniel and Valeria is left unresolved, its future does not appear bright.

Nemesis Again

Octavio has tasted the bitter fruits of his selfishness and Daniel stands facing the sterile future he has chosen. El Chivo, in turn, finds the pendulum of Nemesis slicing into his life. After nursing the injured Cofi back to health, he returns home after missing a chance to kill Luis and is met at the door by a blood-covered Cofi. In El Chivo's absence, he has dispatched all the other dogs. Of course he has; that's what he's been trained to do. Weeping, El Chivo burns all the corpses, with the faithful Cofi standing patiently by his side. "Cofi, the dog who kills dogs, finds his natural owner in the man who kills men." By killing the other dogs, Cofi "teaches El Chivo the implications of his own actions."[24] Now lying alone on his bare mattress, with the picture of Maru over his head, El Chivo first turns on the light and then, in an obviously symbolic gesture, puts on his cracked and taped glasses. He who remarked so cavalierly that if God wanted him to see blurry, he'd see blurry, now must start taking a closer look at his life and the implication of his actions.

After this loss of his canine family, El Chivo's story moves in an entirely new direction, both from the paths taken by the other stories and from his own past. Rather than shooting Luis, he kidnaps him and handcuffs him to a pole in the shack. On learning that Gustavo, the man who paid to have Luis killed, is his half-brother, El Chivo laughs and calls Luis "Abel." (This reinforces the theme of sibling rivalry, seen with Octavio and Ramiro.) He also asks Luis for help in naming his new dog (Luis only swears), saying, "Dogs take after their masters, you know." This is an admission that Cofi, the killer dog, mirrors him, an example of self-realization that sets him apart from the other characters. Octavio failed to consider how, by turning Cofi into a fighting dog, he was, in effect, loosing his own instinctual nature, entering a bestial world with terrible consequences for everyone around him. Daniel's lack of real concern for Richie's imprisonment mirrored his lack of empathy for Valeria's despair at the disintegration of her life and career. Octavio and Daniel remain paralyzed in the face of disaster. Octavio still clings blindly to his hope of possessing Susana: toward the end of the film he appears for the last time at the bus depot, waiting in vain for her to appear. Similarly, in their final shot Daniel and Valeria stand frozen, looking at the blank billboard that manifests the collapse of their dreams of a happy life together. All three stories portray people trapped in various ways, and only El Chivo shows the introspection and determination to try and break out of his psychic prison.

Escape is only possible, the film suggests, by renouncing violence and its associated *machismo*. El Chivo lures Gustavo to his place, shows him the tied up Luis, and shoves a pistol in his hand so he can do the killing himself. Gustavo is dismayed: "That was your job! I paid you to do it." The viewer may have been appalled at the casual violence permeating the lives of Octavio, Ramiro, and El Chivo, but Gustavo's words reveal the deeper social truth. The lower classes are consigned to this brutal world by the wealthy, who want to keep their hands clean. It's easier to assuage one's conscience when someone else pulls the trigger. El Chivo decides that brothers may go on killing brothers, but he will no longer be the middle man. In his earlier role as revolutionary, he convinced himself that it was acceptable to kill for one's ideals. Later, those ideals crushed, he decided that in a corrupt society the best one could hope for was survival. In this scene, he calls Gustavo "Cain," invoking the biblical injunction: these half-brothers should be one another's keepers. The next morning, as El Chivo is leaving the house for the last time, he unlocks the handcuffs of his two captives, saying he hopes they can work things out between them. "On the other hand, if talking doesn't work, . . . "

he says, and places a pistol on the floor between them before strolling out with Cofi. The two men stare at one another and then begin lunging frantically to reach the pistol—an image that neatly recapitulates the dog fight scenes.[25] It is fitting that the two men now inhabit the house of the assassin, a den for animals, outside civilization. El Chivo is vacating this inhuman space, wanting to return to a realm where human beings are connected, to the world his daughter inhabits, to his family. The fate of the two men is left undetermined. (The script specified that two shots were to ring out, but that moment was cut to allow some hope for the half-brothers.[26]) Nonetheless, like the futures of Octavio, Susana, Daniel, and Valeria, theirs does not seem promising.

Photos

All three stories have emphasized familial breakdown and this theme is echoed in the motif of photographs. They appear notably at the moment when Octavio finally succeeds in seducing Susana in a scene which, for all its tenderness, is filled with darkly portentous images. He comes in with toys for the baby and more money for her, and asks her once again to come away with him. This time she agrees, and they roll backward onto the floor in an embrace. The joy of this conjunction is strongly undercut by disquieting elements, such as their lovemaking on the floor alongside the baby. Besides the perversity in this action, it suggests they are babies also, emphasized by the camera panning from the baby to the two of them. Susana's pose mimics that of her child: she lies flat on her back with arms and legs in the air. The earlier shot of Octavio's hand moving between her thighs had shown her schoolgirl skirt in close-up, a further reminder of their immaturity. Most important, the camera cuts at the end to them reflected in the room's mirror, on which are pasted pictures of Ramiro and Susana; Ramiro, Susana and the baby; and Ramiro and Octavio. The camera reframes slightly to emphasize this image, centering the lovemaking within the group of photos. Octavio's seduction of his brother's wife will break the family links they show.

Photos tell a story in the case of Daniel and Valeria also, with two competing sets. On the one hand there are the images of Valeria and on the other the pictures of Daniel's family. At first Valeria's images dominate. Daniel's eyes are drawn to her billboard as he drives with his family and in the apartment her image is the most notable feature, seen on the billboard outside the window and in the contact prints of her photo shoot blown up into a huge wall montage. After her accident, she thumbs listlessly through black and white photos of herself as a girl, pallid in comparison to her erotically charged, hugely magnified image. She herself seems disinterested in them. Then in Daniel's office, the camera trails across pictures on his desk of his daughters, left behind. At the very end of the film, workmen are seen lowering one of Valeria's huge posters, which crumples to the ground exactly as her career has collapsed and as her relationship with Daniel may founder.

Pictures are used most obviously in El Chivo's story. In one scene, he sits alone in his kitchen, looking at a photo album with pictures of him and his baby girl. Most of the pictures of Maru show her as a child, suggesting that she represents not only his lost daughter but his lost idealism. Earlier, he had quietly broken into her apartment while she was away and stolen a photograph of her graduation. It showed her stepfather standing happily between wife and daughter, the position El Chivo might have occupied. Now he half cries as he compares a grizzled photo of himself with his younger professorial self and pastes his bearded image over the stepfather's face, trying to share the moment. At the end of the story as he prepares to embark on his new life, he takes particular care in packing his photo album and his picture of Maru, signaling his renewed allegiance to the family he abandoned. After cleaning up, he takes a picture of his transformed self at a Photomat and pastes it into the stolen graduation photograph, as if trying to reinsert himself into Maru's life. Breaking into her empty apartment one final time—its walls covered with family photographs—he reinserts the picture into its frame and leaves a message on her answering machine. He announces himself as her father, apologizes for having left her, and says he will come back when he has the courage to look her in the eyes. Emphasizing the importance of photographs, the graduation picture is seen prominently in the rear during his painful confession, emphasizing his determination to become part of Maria Eugenia's life again (Figure 4.11). Scriptwriter Arriaga commented that the film's three stories might be read as that of the same man at three stages in his life. If so, then El Chivo's act of trying to become part of Maru's life again is all the more poignant, prefiguring as it does "Daniel's future suffering at the abandonment of his daughters."[27]

4.11
Martin
trying to
paste
himself
back into
Maru's life.

Conclusion

El Chivo's life seems to be headed in a more positive direction at the end, emphasized by final interweaving of the stories. Notably, he is juxtaposed with Octavio at the bus terminal, who waits in vain for Susana and then hobbles away in tears. With his shaved head, filmed under nighttime fluorescent lights, Octavio appears even more corpse-like than at Ramiro's funeral. The shock is palpable, then, when the camera cuts from Octavio at night to El Chivo in the morning, panning from a black wall to reveal him taking a shower. The camera move allows him to emerge dramatically from the darkness into which Octavio was seen disappearing, suggesting that if Octavio is dying, El Chivo is coming to life. His skin tones are warm in the morning light and he cleanses himself in a baptismal act. His ablutions are accompanied by guitar music and there are only faint hints of diegetic (story) sound—water splashing, scissors clipping—as he continues his transformation. The shoulder-length hair is trimmed short, the scraggly beard shaved off, the face washed, the horny nails clipped, and the professorial glasses put on. Attired in suit, blue dress shirt, and leather shoes, the former professor reappears. No longer El Chivo, he is now Martin de Ezquerra again. After freeing Luis and Gustavo to sort out their destinies, he leaves his isolated dwelling forever. Where Octavio, limping into the night, seemed headed into oblivion, Martin moves into a new morning.

Nevertheless, for all the courage Martin has shown, the ending leaves his ultimate fate as open as that of the foregoing characters. He heads out of town with Cofi and pauses as a point-of-view shot pans across the volcanic landscape before him. The scene is notably dark, all the more so in contrast to Maru's bright apartment in the preceding scene. Martin and Cofi are black outlines against an empty sky, seen in an extremely low camera angle rather than a crane shot which would have given more sense of expansiveness and perspective.[28] The low angle emphasizes the black, cracked surface, a veritable moonscape (Figure 4.12).

4.12
El Chivo/
Martin
heads into
an unknown
future.

This hostile, inhuman scene may represent the harsh reality in which all the characters live, stripped of human trappings. It suggests the brute reality lying outside civilization, which we defend against by huddling together within our cave walls. Given the harshness of this world, we are foolish to abandon the ties of family and society, our main bulwark against it, a lesson that all the characters have ignored at their peril. Despite these dark visuals, there are hopeful signs as well. Martin is honest enough to realize that, given his long isolation, he must learn how to become part of mankind again. He will travel across this barren landscape in search of his humanity. And when a junkyard man asks the dog's name, Martin decides on "Blackie." Dogs reflect their owners he has said, and Cofi is the embodiment of the blackness that lies within him (as it lies within all men). A point-of-view shot emphasizes Martin's gaze into the dark terrain ahead of him. He faces the bleakness ahead of him with eyes open, just as he has gazed honestly into his own heart. This awareness sets him apart from the other characters and so does his courage in stepping forward, where they seem frozen in place. Most important, Martin will no longer raise his hand against his fellow man, for money or for ideology. We cannot know where he will arrive, but at least he is walking away from who he has been.

Afterword on Narrative Structure

The key feature of the network narrative is its ability to foreground essential themes by contraposing story lines and Arriaga's script takes splendid advantage of this trait. The intercut stories constantly comment on one another. Thus El Chivo's shooting of the man in the restaurant follows immediately after the argument of Octavio and Ramiro at the breakfast table just as the dogfight scenes mirror their fraternal conflict. More important, however, are the themes that emerge in all three stories. Besides violence, there are the themes of childishness and selfishness. Daniel and Valeria are narcissistic, superficial characters—she represented by her giant billboard, he indulging himself in a glamorous model for a girlfriend. As a couple, they suggest children "playing house" rather than seriously committed adults. This, in turn, reflects on Octavio and Susana, who are more literally children. Octavio, like Daniel, gives too little thought to what it will mean to tear his family apart. For both men, love is more about possessing a desirable female than establishing a sincere relationship. Both buy their love object, Daniel with an apartment and Octavio with diapers. Both relationships show *perros* triumphing over *amores*.

Similarly, El Chivo's repeated appearances serve as a representative of the violence that underlies all the lives. This is the violence of the dogfights, with people struggling instinctively to assert themselves over their rivals by any means possible. Brothers will turn against brothers. That, in turn, is reflected in the dog-eat-dog economic system which traps the lower class and where rivals will think nothing of contracting to beat or kill one another. But further, if El Chivo represents, as Arriaga asserts, the eldest incarnation of the same man, he provides a look into the future of the other characters. All his scenes show his isolation—the telephoto shots, the almost total lack of conversation, and his living among a pack of mangy dogs in lieu of a family. His killing other human beings without remorse only makes his alienation that much more apparent. But Daniel, too, is isolated, pictured in separate shots from his family in the car and not interacting with them. Octavio seems more firmly ensconced in the family, but he ends by ignoring his mother's warning, seducing his sister-in-law, having his brother beaten, endangering his beloved dog, and encompassing the death of his only friend. The emotional and physical isolation embodied in El Chivo, on the fringes of society seems to presage the future for Octavio and Daniel. The film shows three families destroyed, not the least of these being El Chivo's loyal pack.

All three stories reflect the conflict encapsulated in the title. On the one hand there are the dogs, the instinctive, animalistic side of human beings. The dogfights which open the film and reappear throughout the first story establish the parameters of this world. Especially notable is the initial camera position that gives literally a dog's-eye view of its bloody violence. The dogs themselves are suggestive in many ways, turned from quiet house pets into killing machines, as occurs simultaneously with Cofi and with Octavio. Notably, too, the preliminary fighting pose of the dogs, jutting out from between their owner's legs as they are "heated up," makes them phallic extensions, equating canine combat and sexual *machismo*. As Iñárritu suggests, the animal side of men is always struggling for expression. But love is not just bestial passion. For all the sibling rivalry in Octavio's seduction of Susana, there is also some genuine affection for her, seen in his attempts to protect her from Ramiro's anger and to help care for the baby. Daniel's tender good-night kiss for his daughters and his broken off phone call to his wife suggest his realization, too late, of what he has given up. The photographs which fill the film emphasize the importance of family ties for emotional survival. Only El Chivo finally hearkens to this message, abandoning his old life in an attempt to reconnect with his daughter. Even then, sadly, he must content himself with a picture of her and her voice on the answering machine, leaving, in turn, only his picture and his recorded voice. One may hope that father and daughter may meet again in real time and in the flesh when he returns from the uncertain future he heads into. In these deftly interwoven stories one senses Iñárritu's wish that parental love may eventually triumph over bestial passions.

Notes

1   Cited in Edward Lawrenson and Bernardo Perez Soler, "Pup Fiction," *Sight and Sound* 11, no. 5 (May 2001): 29.
2   Deborah Shaw, *Contemporary Cinema of Latin America: Ten Key Films* (New York: Continuum, 2003), 52.
3   Shaw, *Contemporary Cinema of Latin America*, 53.
4   Paul Julian Smith, *Amores Perros* (London: BFI, 2002), 12-13.
5   Shaw, *Contemporary Cinema of Latin America*, 51.
6   David Bordwell, *Poetics of Cinema* (London: Routledge, 2008), 204-5.
7   Shaw, *Contemporary Cinema of Latin America*, 56.
8   Stephen M. Hart, *A Companion to Latin American Film* (New York: Boydell and Brewer, 2004), 193.
9   Smith, *Amores Perros*, 63.
10 Jean Oppenheimer, "A Dog's Life [Interview with Rodrigo Prieto]," *American Cinematographer* 82 (April 2001): 24.
11 Marvin D'Lugo, "Amores Perros," in *The Cinema of Latin America*, Alberto Elena and Marina Díaz López, eds. (New York: Wallflower, 2003), 225.
12 Tom Lyons, "Amores Perros," *Eye Weekly* (26 April 2001), www.eyeweekly.com/archived/article/51755 (15 September 2006).
13 Smith, *Amores Perros*, 43.
14 Laura Podalsky, "Affecting Legacies: Historical Memory and Contemporary Structures of Feeling in *Madagascar* and *Amores Perros*," *Screen* 44, no. 3 (Autumn 2003): 282.
15 Smith, *Amores Perros*, 44-45.
16 Hubert Niogret, "Entretien avec Alejandro González Iñárritu: Aller au fonds des choses," *Positif* no. 477 (November 2000): 26.
17 Shaw, *Contemporary Cinema of Latin America*, 66.
18 Niogret, "Entretien avec Alejandro González Iñárritu," 26.
19 Shaw, *Contemporary Cinema of Latin America*, 66.
20 Peter N. Chumo, II, "Script Review: *Amores Perros*," *Creative Screenwriting* 8, no. 2 (2001): 12.
21 Smith, *Amores Perros*, 48.
22 Chris Chang, "Amores Perros," *Film Comment* 37 (March/April 2001): 72.
23 José Arroyo, "*Amores Perros* ('Love's a Bitch')," *Sight and Sound* 11, no. 5 (May 2001): 40.
24 Shaw, *Contemporary Cinema of Latin America*, 58.
25 Lawrenson and Soler, "Pup Fiction," 28.
26 Hart, *A Companion to Latin American Film*, 192.
27 Shaw, *Contemporary Cinema of Latin America*, 61.
28 Smith, *Amores Perros*, 79.

5

Code Unknown

Cinematic Cryptogram

From the first, Michael Haneke's films have treated dark subjects, particularly violence and societal breakdown. His notorious *Funny Games* (1997) shows an innocent family being slowly tortured and killed by two well-brought-up young men, curious to see what murder is like. While the characters in his 2000 feature *Code Unknown* do not partake of the pathological elements found in *Funny Games, Benny's Video* (1992), and *The Piano Teacher* (2001), the film is designedly opaque. Haneke pushes the **network narrative** to an extreme, using the **hub and spoke** pattern to show lives spinning away from one another. People cannot relate to those closest to them and are reluctant to take decisive moral action. At the same time, Haneke eschews black-and-white moral judgments, portraying multifaceted human beings. As in all his films, he brings viewers up sharply against the intractability of evil and avoids simplistic resolutions. The juxtapositioning permitted by complex narrative structure is particularly effective for his purposes. He portrays the disintegration of three families and one couple, which might easily have been told sequentially. However, by intercutting their scenes, he makes the painful outcomes less easy to attribute to the erroneous actions of individuals.

Story Summary

The film takes place for the most part in Paris and has four major stories, although the scenes from each are so brief and disconnected that nothing resembling the usual story arc appears in any of them. The first deals with Anne Laurent (Juliette Binoche), a successful actress in small films and plays, and her current boyfriend, Georges (Thierry Neuvic), a photojournalist who travels on far-flung assignments. Although more scenes are devoted to them than to any other characters, they only appear together in four of them, suggesting the tenuousness of their relationship. Georges's teenage brother, Jean-Pierre (commonly addressed as "Jean"), lives on a farm with their father, Sepp, and the second story shows Jean's dissatisfaction with the stultifying life there, from which he eventually flees. The third story centers on a Malian family living in Paris that includes a young man, Amadou, his parents, Youssouf and Aminate, and three younger siblings. The final story tells of Maria, who has left her husband and family in Romania to seek employment abroad, but can find nothing better than panhandling on the streets of Paris. The lack of clear cause-and-effect plot in any of the stories forces the viewer to assemble the pieces from all four into an overall picture—coming close to *Nashville*'s **mosaic** structure—to make sense of the film. With plot minimized, thematic patterns become particularly important as seen in the film's brief prologue where a small deaf girl in the front of a classroom pantomimes something for her classmates that they are unable to decipher (Figure 5.1). The scene is

5.1
Cut off and
fearful:
Françoise (?).

entirely silent, with the students using sign language to guess what is being acted out, but one feels obvious tension. The girl is not pantomiming something playful (she huddles fearfully against the wall), and seems intense, needing urgently to get her message across. This announces the film's central theme—that human communication is simultaneously critically important and difficult to achieve.

The "precipitating encounter" (the hub moment) in the film's second scene is a *tour de force* single take that runs eight minutes and ten seconds. Anne, the actress, is accosted by Jean-Pierre as she rushes out of her apartment. Not wanting to take over his father's farm, he has fled—for good, he insists. He is hoping his brother will help, but Anne tells him Georges is in Kosovo and she has no idea when he'll return. Hurrying to a meeting, she cannot stop to hear him out, and so hastily buys him a pastry, tells him her apartment code—warning him he can't plan on staying long—and rushes off. Jean wanders back toward her apartment, pauses to listen to some street musicians, then strides away angrily, tossing his pastry wrapper in the lap of a middle-aged woman (Maria) sitting and begging in an alleyway. Jean has taken only a few steps when Amadou, the young black man from Mali, catches up to him and suggests that Jean needs to go back and apologize to the woman. A mild scuffle ensues, Anne rushes back to Jean's aid, and the police arrive (Figure 5.2). Maria tries to slip away, but is nabbed by the

5.2
The scuffle:
Anne, Jean,
Amadou.

police, since she has no ID. Amadou agrees to go peacefully with the police, but when they grab his arms (Jean, being white, has been allowed to leave), he resists and the scene cuts on their struggle.

In the scenes that follow, Haneke keeps his audience removed from the characters even more radically than Altman. The hub and spoke structure means that the characters move in separate directions after this initial encounter. The sense of disconnection is further increased by starkly disjunctive editing: the film is broken into forty-four discrete scenes, separated by unvarying three-second blackouts. The blackouts destroy any sense of connection between the story lines and of causal plot movement—the story probably ranges over several months but it is difficult to tell. The segments proceed in straightforward chronological order, but this is not easily deduced, since there are none of the dialogue hooks or filler scenes normally used to create continuity. Further, as the film jumps from scene to scene, the viewer is constantly thrown into new settings—a taxi cab, a farm kitchen, an empty blood-red room, a dusty quarry—as if to emphasize the disparate worlds in which these characters dwell. A Hollywood film implies human connection by its spatial coherence; in direct contrast, *Code Unknown* uses spatial fragmentation as a constant reminder of the different cultural spaces we inhabit. Further distancing is produced because, rather than using close shots and continuity editing, all but three of the forty-four scenes are done as single long takes, ranging from thirty-six seconds to eight minutes and ten seconds, with an average length of 2:25. The events portrayed are notably mundane: friends eating at a restaurant, a farmer and his son cleaning the barn, or a father talking to his son about a problem at school. The meaning behind these quotidian scenes is elusive and the individual characters remain notably opaque.

This obfuscation is deliberate. As Haneke comments, film and television, despite being the most recent art forms to emerge, are the most retrograde in their depiction of reality. Much twentieth century literature, for example, has abandoned the attempt to capture "reality," settling instead for fragmentary, uncertain moments. By contrast, says Haneke, Hollywood films offer "the comforting illusion of being able to completely describe and thus explain the world." They offer the viewer a prepackaged view of reality, making him a passive participant, "a simple consumer."[1] Haneke specifically refuses to provide such a clearly explicable world. He says, "As soon as the spectator finds himself out on his own, confronted with questions that are raised by the narrative, yet without instantly given instructions for interpretation, he feels harassed and begins to fight against it—a productive conflict, in my opinion. The more radically answers are denied to him, the more likely is he to find his own."[2] Nonetheless, some answers will emerge, provided the viewer can find a way to assemble the scattered potsherds of Haneke's loosely networked narrative into incomplete but recognizable forms, using the thematic patterns scratched upon them.

Multivalent Characters

Haneke's difficult narrative patterns are necessary because he is dealing with evil, that most intractable of human problems. Where Hollywood films typically present clearly defined heroes and villains, Haneke rejects such simplistic stereotypes and instead presents multivalent characters with both good and bad sides. This makes responding to them more complex, but more accurately portrays human nature. A first example of this nonstereotypic portrayal can be found in scene six. Jean-Pierre's father, Sepp, sits in the cramped farmhouse kitchen eating supper and reading his newspaper. There is a white bowl in front of him, a loaf of bread lying on the plain blue table cloth, a bottle, a glass, and an ash tray. The bare walls are painted with cheap green paint. At the sound of a door opening he glances up, responds "Bon soir," to Jean (off screen) and returns to eating. When his son comes to sit at the table, Sepp rises to fill a bowl at the stove and push it to him. "Beets. That's all there is." He passes the boy a spoon and goes back to eating (Figure 5.3). Sepp's face is expressionless; Jean stares at the table; the only sound is the clink of spoons. Finishing up, Sepp goes to the sink to rinse his bowl and spoon, then walks to the bathroom. He closes the door behind him and sits in

5.3
Sepp and
Jean:
No eye
contact.

the semi-darkness staring straight ahead. After a moment, he lowers his head and turns to flush the toilet. Cut to black.

This scene lasts 3:06 and has just seven words of dialogue. The only other two scenes of Jean and Sepp last 1:57 and 0:49 respectively and have no dialogue whatsoever. But Haneke brilliantly encapsulates the relationship of father and son, while remaining carefully neutral in his portrayal. From Jean's petulant outburst to Anne, we know he hates life on the farm. Since the film's scenes unfold in chronological order, we can infer that we are seeing Jean's return from Paris, having temporarily abandoned his plans to run away. (He is wearing the same green jacket he wore when he accosted Anne.) Perhaps a day or two have gone by, so Sepp's lifting his head when the door opens reveals his relief that Jean is back. Rather than going to him, however, Sepp hunkers down over his bowl, possibly feeling anger or rejection. But his face registers no emotion—he simply looks at his son for a moment and then dishes up his supper. His matter-of-fact behavior suggests that life will go on as before, just as the cramped kitchen and the meager supper suggest how spartan that life will be. Sadly, father and son seem to share no connection, indicated by the lack of eye contact and conversation. We can empathize with Jean's desire to flee this claustrophobic, deadening environment.

At the same time, Sepp is not portrayed as an abusive father, railing at his son and demanding to know where he has been. Rather, he dishes up the boy's supper—something Jean is certainly capable of doing for himself—and slides the bowl toward him. He does not, one notes, slam it down angrily on the table. It seems likely that the only way Sepp knows how to express his love is through food. (When Georges and Anne visit him later, he offers them a bite to eat after their trip out from Paris. As someone whose livelihood consists of raising food, he is, in effect, offering something of himself.) That Sepp cares for his son is made evident in scene fourteen, when he drives his battered van into the farmyard, removes the bungee cord securing its rusted rear door, and wheels out a spanking new red motor scooter. He disappears into the barn and a moment later, Jean emerges, hurries to the scooter and buzzes quickly out of sight. Clearly, Sepp intuits Jean's dissatisfaction and is indulging his son in a luxury that—given the farm's run-down condition—he can ill afford.

But Haneke does not make Sepp the stereotypic curmudgeon, who needs only the ministrations of a Heidi to uncover the warm heart beneath the crusty surface. Rather, he is a sadly stunted man, unable to express his feelings—indeed, afraid to do so. Thus at the end of the supper table scene, he retreats to the bathroom, closes the door and flushes the toilet—all to conceal the fact that he is crying with relief at his son's return. (Haneke cooperates in this concealment: the bathroom is extremely dark and Sepp turns his face *away* from the camera, allowing only a glimpse of his pained look and the faintest sound of a sob.) In a later scene, reading the note from Jean announcing his final departure from the farm, Sepp keeps his face turned from the camera and continues preparing his supper, showing no apparent response. Unable to express his own feelings, Sepp seems equally uncomfortable sharing the emotions of others, for example, not following Jean out to the courtyard to share in his pleasure at the new motor scooter. During the later scene when he talks with Anne and Georges about Jean's leaving, Sepp continuously shoves some grains of tobacco around on the tablecloth, expressing his inner pain in typically constricted fashion. And when Anne reaches out to touch his arm in sympathy, Sepp leaps up as if burned, says he left the pump running, and rushes out of the room, obviously fearing his emotions will break through. Anne and Georges were brought to the farm by a neighbor's report that Sepp has shot all his cattle, and indeed we see him in a brief scene walking past their corpses in the barn, closing the door, turning out the lights, and calmly lighting a cigarette. To murder the animals he has cared for so lovingly and around which his life revolves is unbelievably horrifying. The irrationality of this act testifies to his violent frustration at Jean's abandoning the farm and his inability to deal with this emotion in any constructive way.

The final feeling from these half dozen short scenes is one of sadness, first at the loss of this way of life. Sepp is last seen driving his tractor over a sunny field, plowing his hay crop under and then disappearing off screen. This moment parallels Jean's roaring out of sight on his new motor scooter, full of adolescent impatience. The two vehicles head off in opposite directions, both passing beyond the camera's view so we cannot know where these two equally unhappy individuals will end up. People that should care for one another are locked determinedly into their own needs, a pattern that will recur. The viewer grieves for these wasted lives but, true to his artistic tenets, Haneke offers no simplistic judgments of right and wrong, merely showing the pain human beings inflict on one another.

Amadou and His Family

Haneke is equally skillful in using the nine disparate segments from the lives of Amadou and his family to paint a complex picture. In the precipitating scene, Amadou is low-key as he taps Jean on the shoulder and, with hands in pockets, asks, "Was that a good thing to do?" To be sure, his behavior is puzzling: people generally do not accost strangers on a city sidewalk and ask them to apologize to street beggars. We note, however, that Amadou is not belligerent: he does not raise his voice or act in a threatening manner. It is Jean who curses repeatedly and strikes out at him. Amadou's responding to such a minor indignity as a tossed piece of paper suggests that this dark-skinned young man is sensitive to discrimination based on personal history. Continuing the complex portrait, a wholly charming Amadou appears several scenes later at a restaurant with his date, a white girl. He accepts with good grace the waiter's explanation that they did not get a window table as requested because of their late arrival and calmly asks for a menu. So although sensitive to discrimination, he does not erupt at the slightest provocation. Amadou's gentle flirtation with his date, his relaxed manner, and his excellent French suggest a pleasant young man, totally acclimated to French life, and not someone who walks around with a chip on his shoulder.

Not only does Amadou seem a well-balanced young man, but the scenes of his family suggest close ties. His cab-driver father, Youssouf, immediately heads off to help on learning of Amadou's arrest and in a later scene his mother, Aminate, insists to the local marabout (a religious teacher), that "He's a good boy!" The strongest scene of family unity occurs in the family's living room when Youssouf questions Demba, Amadou's younger brother, accused by a classmate of using drugs. With all the family present, including Aminate's sister and her daughter, Youssouf listens to the accusation and then leads Demba gently to the adjoining room. There he sits down facing him at the dining room table (Figure 5.4) and, sternly but quietly,

5.4
Youssouf
and Demba:
Sympathetic
parenting.

asks to hear the true story. The fact that Youssouf doesn't threaten Demba, wants to believe him, speaks to him quietly, and sits at his eye level all bespeak a loving parent. So does his thoughtful attention as Demba stammers out his story, accentuated by the close, unmoving camera. It turns out that Demba was accused of drug use by a white boy in revenge because Demba refused to steal money to ransom back his own jacket, stolen by the boy. Demba's story, told in a whisper through his tears, is utterly believable and a confirmation of the experiences that have made Amadou so sensitive to racial slights. The power of this scene is increased by contrast with the early scene between Jean and Sepp, which also took place at a dining table. The lack of eye contact and absence of communication between father and son there make the connection between Youssouf and Demba all the more powerful. While deliberately fragmenting his narrative, Haneke plays his fragments against one another very effectively.

But loving as this family is, the pressures of trying to survive in a foreign culture are taking their toll. Just four scenes later, at the same table where Youssouf had his heartfelt talk with Demba, the four children sit at breakfast while Aminate works in the kitchen behind them. Salimata, Amadou's deaf sister, is asking him when their father will return. Amadou, trying to seem casual, says to her in sign language that he doesn't know. Salimata says she misses him and Rokia throws in cynically, "He doesn't miss us," adding for her mother's benefit, "He'll take a new wife half my age." Aminate demands that Rokia show respect for her father, but Rokia reminds her that their uncle never returned. Salimata wonders if Youssouf won't be lonely, but Amadou says his brother and family are there. He explains that Papa is old and wants to go home to Africa. Salimata asks, "Where is Africa?" and the scene ends.

In its low-keyed way, this scene is devastating. Amadou's family is shown to have strong ties and great emotional warmth, but the strains of immigrant life threaten to dissolve it. Apparently wearied by the constant struggle to adapt, Youssouf has returned to Africa and left the family on its own. (In scene thirty-eight, he drives his car off the boat in Mali.) This means the boyish Amadou is now the head of the household, signaled by his being in the foreground of the shot. The dynamics of the scene foreshadow the coming problems, with Rokia throwing in cynical comments and arguing with her mother at the same time that Amadou is trying to talk to Salimata. It speaks volumes that Salimata has to ask where Africa is—her question accentuated by coming the instant before the screen goes dark. Already cut off from the world to a degree by her deafness, Salimata's question suggests she is cut off from her cultural heritage as well. Again, the contrast with Sepp and Jean adds resonance to the scene. The family dynamics appear entirely different, but a sad parallel appears: after seeing a father abandoned by his son, we now see children abandoned by their father.

Maria

As the film continues to unfold, the breakdown already seen with Sepp's and Amadou's families continue in Maria's story. Maria is initially invisible. In the precipitating second scene, she is not sitting outside the bakery door as Anne first runs in to get pastries, but when Jean wanders back, the camera pans left just far enough to reveal Maria now sitting against the wall (Figure 5.5). Nonetheless,

5.5
Invisible
people:
Maria
begging.

the viewer is unlikely to take note of her. Her drab olive coat matches the wall almost perfectly and she sits unmoving, looking down, her hands cupped in her lap for a possible coin. After Jean throws the wrapper and Amadou raises a fuss, Maria tries to slip away, but Amadou stops her and then the police arrest her. In the whole scene, she doesn't say a word, seeming just a homeless street person. After a quick scene of her deportation, she appears next walking through clouds of dust holding her grandson's hand and shouting to be heard above the roar of machines. This bleak environment—a quarry or mine—neatly encapsulates the harsh struggle for the inhabitants in this small Romanian village. We also see the ties that bind her to this place as her husband, Dragos, comes to stand in front of her and she runs her hands tenderly over his chest and shoulders before being enfolded in his embrace.

However, characteristic of Haneke's multivalent storytelling, the rifts in Maria's family life soon appear. When she tours the house that Dragos is building for their engaged daughter, Nuta, she is clearly delighted to be back among her family, and admires the house, even though the walls are bare brick and the lights only dangling bulbs. But Nuta suggests that, since the house is not completed, she will probably accept her fiancé's offer to live with his parents. This echoes the situation with Sepp and Jean, since Sepp also had been constructing a house for Jean to live in when he took over the farm, an offer Jean refused far less diplomatically. The snide remarks of Maria's oldest daughter, Florica, about her father's drunkenness, likewise, remind us of Rokia's cynical comments about her father. This is the third family, then, experiencing conflicts without and within, the parallels emerging as the scattered shards of the narrative fall into patterns.

The financial problems of these Romanian families are embodied in the stark visuals—the Stygian quarry scene, Nuta's rough home-to-be, and a street full of half-completed houses that Maria later rides down with a neighbor. So dire are the pressures that, some time later, Maria agrees to be smuggled back into France. She cannot hope to send much money home, given that her plan is to sell newspapers; the best she can do is not be a drain on the family finances. Even that plan comes to naught when she learns that another woman has purchased the license promised to her, giving her no choice but to return to begging. Back in Paris later, Maria breaks down as she tells another woman how, the previous winter, a man had thrown a twenty-franc note into her lap rather than putting it into her hand, "as if I nauseated him." She had hidden herself and cried her eyes out the entire day. Jean's thoughtless action of tossing the pastry wrapper in her lap two months earlier must doubtless have reawakened this memory of denigration. As always, the narrative's pieces continue to play against one another in meaningful ways.

The ending of Maria's story is as desolate as Sepp plowing his field under and Youssouf returning to Africa. As she searches for a suitable begging spot on the street in Paris where she first appeared, she finds a new woman occupying her former place by the bakery. No sooner does she locate another likely spot than two men appear and make it clear that this is their territory and she is not welcome. She hurriedly picks up her plastic bag of belongings and moves down the street, with the men following to ensure her departure. This is the last time she is seen, another parent separated from her family like Sepp and Youssouf, like them struggling to make a living, and like them unable to find a place where her humanity is affirmed. Although the three families portrayed have no direct connection, their difficulties seem related. By telling their stories simultaneously, Haneke suggests that the evil of the world is built into the very societal patterns which these characters, existing on the margins of that society, have little power to change. The fractured narration mirrors a cultural environment with few bridges between people; the absence of a clear narrative arc suggests the difficulty individuals have bringing about change.

Anne and Georges

The glimpses of these other families, living for the most part on the fringes of society, provide an effective background for the two central characters. Anne and Georges appear in nearly 40 percent of the film's scenes and are apparently successful in their chosen professions, actress and photojournalist. Yet they, too, have difficulty making human connections as is hinted at in the scene where they dine with two other couples in a restaurant. Anne describes the film she's making as she debones Georges's fish for him. Anne passes the fish to Georges, who gives her a quick kiss in thanks and one of the other men suggests to his wife, Francine, that she could benefit from this example of service. Then talk turns to Georges's adventures. Asked what it's like returning to civilization, Georges replies, "Over there, it's simple. Here, life is complicated." At this point, Anne breaks in to ask one woman if she brought the address of her dentist: Anne needs to see one. Next the group discusses an absent friend whose wife has moved out and taken the kids, interrupted when another friend arrives to introduce his girlfriend.

Typical of so many scenes in the film, nothing extraordinary happens and yet Haneke is richly suggestive. For one thing, there is no strong sense of connection between Anne and Georges, although he has just returned from Kosovo and we might expect to see them hanging upon one another after a long separation. As she tells about the picture she is making he seems uninvolved, making no comment and giving no encouragement. Correspondingly, when Georges is questioned about his work, Anne does not urge him to share details of his experiences and interrupts to ask about the dentist. Neither seems to enter into what the other is passionate about. The sense of distance is emphasized by their joking references to one another as "monsieur" and "mademoiselle," the same form of address they used four scenes earlier when Anne returned to her apartment to find Georges back. In that scene, rather than flying into one another's arms, they stood on opposite sides of the room to talk and only at the end did Anne finally walk forward and stroke his face, saying "Hello, you." It is also revealing that the two of them are only seen together in four of the film's forty-four scenes and do not appear on screen as a couple until the film is one-fourth over.

Sharpening the sense of disconnection between Anne and Georges, Amadou and his date appear in the same restaurant scene, with Amadou relating the story of his father's entering France. The contrast between the two juxtaposed parties could not be more striking. Amadou is very animated as he tells his story and every time they are interrupted by the waiter the girl prods him to pick up the story again—precisely what did not occur with Anne and Georges. The sides of the booth enfold the young couple, and the sense of intimacy is enhanced as the camera moves in closer, dropping to eye level, and blocking out most of the restaurant (Figure 5.6). This contrasts strikingly with its higher angle and more distanced shot of the French group, surrounded by other diners and blocked out four times by people passing between them and the camera. Where Amadou and his date smile and look into one another's eyes, the French group primarily attend to their eating (Figure 5.7). The contrast—close connection versus bored interaction—is subtle but distinct.

5.6
Amadou
and his
date:
Cozy
chatting.

The stories told at the two tables show the same contrast. Amadou tells how another Malian aided his father's arrival by running with Youssouf's passport to secure a job for him—a story of human solidarity. By contrast, human discord is a recurring theme at the French table, seen in the laughter at the story of the wife leaving her husband and in Francine's teasing by her husband. The scene ends strongly on this theme, with Francine hectoring Georges about his photographs. She says, "[You think] that you have to photograph death and destruction so I know what war is?" Georges takes this calmly and Anne, smiling, notes Francine is back on her favorite argument, to which Francine responds, "Why not? If I can't attack my friends, who's left?" Her husband jumps in: "Me, darling. I'm your punching bag." She laughs and shoves at him playfully. This scene again shows Haneke using an apparently random "slice-of-life" moment to point up clear differences: human connection at one table; casual assemblage at the other. The inconsequential argument at the French table does not suggest abiding animosity between the friends, but the scenic momentum heads relentlessly toward Francine's final remark—admittedly stated as a joke—that the function of one's friends is to serve as targets of attack. The film as a whole deals with the difficulty of coming to know others and Haneke here portrays sincere emotional connection displaced by trivial banter and empty disputation.

Georges

Failed emotional connection is made Georges's salient trait from the first. He is introduced in the third scene speaking in voiceover (possibly voicing a letter to Anne) but is not seen. Instead, the screen is filled with a succession of horrifying images from Kosovo: snipers, a burning house, refugees, injured people being helped to safety, a young girl crying over the corpse of her dog, and repeated scenes of dead civilians and half-buried corpses. Rather than commenting on these images, Georges recites matter-of-fact details about his movements around the country. There is no sense that he connects with these scenes of horror, which are notably random and fail to present any coherent picture of events.[3] This sense of disconnectedness extends to Georges's personal life, as he mentions hoping to be back to take his son out on his fifth birthday. "Eve promised I'd have him for the day." He seems separated from Anne, apologizing for missing the opening of her play and adding, "Sorry for my behavior on our last day." He is also absent when Jean comes to Paris seeking help. Georges's failure to "be there" for others is emphasized by the contrast with the immediately following scene where Youssouf gets a call in his cab that Amadou is in trouble and unhesitatingly drops his fare off so he can help his son—more of Haneke's careful juxtapositioning.

Introduced by this striking disjunction between image and sound—the horrors of Kosovo versus a banal travelogue—Georges clearly personifies the failure to connect with others, embodied in the camera he uses to hold people at a distance. Alone in Anne's apartment in scene twenty-five, Georges modifies his camera so he can hang it casually around his neck and secretly click the shutter using a cable hidden in his pocket. He is later seen on the Paris Metro slyly taking pictures of passengers seated across from him. Their images then appear in a sequence paralleling the one from Kosovo, with another dramatic contrast between Georges's voiceover story of near-execution at the hands of the Taliban in Afghanistan and the black-and-white close-up images of Parisians on the Metro staring off into space (Figure 5.8). Georges reduces people and their experiences to images, objectifying them rather than relating to their humanity.

The Afghanistan sequence also serves to cap the earlier scene where Anne and Georges visited Sepp to talk about Jean running off and the reports of Sepp having slaughtered his cattle. As that sequence ended, the two of them sat at the table—Sepp having fled the scene—and Anne demanded of Georges, "And just what are you going to do?" Georges sat without answering and the scene ended

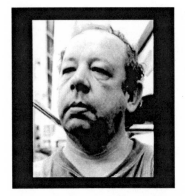 

5.8
Detached
Metro
riders
photo-
graphed
by a
detached
Georges.

with that question hanging in the air. The sequence with the subway photos gives the answer: Georges will not hang around to make sure his father will be all right or track down his juvenile brother to keep him out of trouble. Instead, he will accept a still more distant assignment. In his voiceover, he remarks, "I don't think I'm fit for a peaceful life," using contact with the exotic to substitute for his lack of connection with others. At the same time—and with Haneke there is always an "at the same time"—Georges is not doing conscious evil and is risking his life to document the violence in the world. Perhaps one cannot look continually at such violence without some protective detachment, but the film's position seems clear: the violence will not end until people find a greater sense of connection to others, a sense Georges obviously lacks.

Anne

Belying the apparent randomness of his narration, after the initial precipitating encounter Haneke subsequently presents each of the main characters in a scene that encapsulates his/her nature and simultaneously introduces key themes. Thus Sepp and Jean's scene eating beets succinctly reveals Sepp's emotional morbidity and the breakdown of communication between father and son. Amadou's appearance in the restaurant shows his personal warmth while reminding of his status as a social outsider. The theme of noncommunication is particularly evident with Maria, who doesn't speak at all in the precipitating scene and continues to be silent in the striking shot of her deportation. Brought to the plane ramp by two large policemen, her handcuffs are unsnapped, she is taken inside, and the plane doors close definitively behind her. The scene is terribly cold—the colors are all blue, the engine noise drowns out human voices, and the camera sits frozen in place—making Maria's expulsion brutally mechanical. Georges's emotional detachment is suggested by his failure to connect with his own photos while the pictures themselves dramatically emphasize the all-important theme of societal violence.

Not surprisingly, then, the expository scene for Anne Laurent is revelatory. She is clearly at the heart of *Code Unknown*, appearing in fourteen of its forty-four scenes and the closest thing to a central character.[4] The film's various stories are set in motion with Anne's emergence from her apartment door in the second scene, and everything ends when she flees back inside that door in scene forty-two, locking Georges out and ending their relationship. In the precipitating scene, her character remains unclear. When Jean-Pierre shows up unannounced, she listens with a mixture of sympathy and amusement to his all-too-familiar story of teenage rebellion. Although he's not really family—her boyfriend's kid brother—she buys him a quick pastry and gives him the code to her apartment so he'll have a place to stay for the moment. At the same time, she is primarily driven by her own agenda, talking on the fly rather than really stopping to focus on his issues.

Then in her second scene critical aspects come into focus. In it, she auditions for a role in *The Collector*, a film about a man who poses as a real estate broker, lures women to his home, locks them in a room, and then observes them as they die from the gas he pipes in. Binoche's performance in this scene is extraordinary. Playing the part of the trapped woman while the director (off camera) reads the collector's lines, she moves from puzzlement to disbelief to terror. By the end of the scene she is in tears, pleading to get out, and demanding what he wants. His response is puzzling and chilling: *"Show me your true face."* Dumb struck, she stares at him, tears running down her cheeks, and bleats, "What!" In this scene, Haneke forges a strong connection between the audience and Anne, holding her in an increasingly tight camera position to accentuate her entrapment (Figure 5.9). The idea of entrapment is key in the film, found in both the immediately following scenes—Jean returning to the barren farm kitchen and

5.9 Anne trapped by the collector.

Maria being taken into the plane—and returning repeatedly thereafter. It is seen as Sepp and Jean move like automatons, cleaning the constrictive cow barn and when Jean races off on his motor scooter, desperate to escape. It appears again when Maria is crammed into a compartment above a truck cab to be smuggled back into France, trapped by economic forces that drive her away from her family. Interesting, then, that Anne, a privileged member of this society, should find herself in a similar situation, locked in a bare, blood-red room, facing irrational forces of destruction. In fact, Haneke says his films are traps. "I'm playing with the public," he says, "and I make them fall into all kinds of traps and I show them they've fallen into the trap."[5] By linking the audience to Anne emotionally, Haneke has lured us in.

A second key element in the audition scene is that Anne appears before the viewer in her role as actress, and a very talented one. That role is emphasized as she is seen acting in three more segments, later filming a scene from *The Collector*, then auditioning for the role of Maria in *Twelfth Night*, and finally dubbing the sound for *The Collector*, where she keeps breaking up and flubbing the takes. The line she is supposed to speak to her "husband" is "I love you," and when Anne can't stop her giggling the director asks, "Anne? Is it so hard to tell him 'I love you'?" The scene ends at that exact moment, suggesting that this may be a critical question for Anne to answer. Notably, all three of these later scenes are shot in ways that distance the audience from Anne. In contrast to her audition scene for *The Collector*, where the tight camera position made her performance immediate and powerful, the later scene of filming shows the Steadicam operator and sound man preceding Anne and the realtor into the room where he will trap her, reminding us of the scene's artificiality. Similarly in Anne's audition for *Twelfth Night*, the bare stage, the hollow sound, the camera's distance from Anne (it films from the balcony) and her use of the larger gestures required in stage performance—stomping around as she laughs uproariously at Malvolio's discomfort—keep the viewer removed. Her stagey laughter is particularly jarring because it comes immediately after the chilling scene of Sepp murdering his cattle—another neat juxtaposition by Haneke. Finally, the dubbing scene begins normally enough with Anne and her "husband" seen embracing in a swimming pool, but then the camera pulls back to reveal the studio with the film image projected on a large screen in the front. As the scene is replayed and rewound and replayed and rewound, with Anne constantly breaking up, it becomes increasingly artificial. These scenes remind us that she is an actress, living in an artificial environment and capable of playing many roles. In this sense, she mirrors everyone's typical social behavior, where it is often difficult to find the "true face" behind the persona.

The Child Next Door

After the various acting scenes, Anne is next found alone in her apartment at night, ironing as she watches television. After a full minute of ironing (in a scene as mechanical as Sepp and Jean raking the barn), suddenly a faint child's scream from another apartment is heard. Anne quickly grabs the remote to mute the TV. She stands listening, frozen, as the child continues screaming and angry adult voices are heard (Figure 5.10). A particularly piercing scream makes her turn her head away. When silence finally falls again, Anne slowly returns to her work. She folds a garment, takes a wine glass from the table behind her, drains it, and picks up the next garment. Then noting the TV still playing silently, she takes the remote, un-mutes it, and returns to her ironing as the scene ends.

5.10
Anne
ironing,
frozen in
place.

The heightened sound track of this scene, amplifying every gurgle of the iron, accentuates the horror of what we are hearing. Not only does Anne hear it, but evidently has heard it before. She does not stand puzzled, wondering what is going on, but immediately grabs the remote and stands listening intently, as if thinking, "Oh, no, there they go again." Her pained breathing, the way she turns her head away, and her gulping down the wine all suggest she is struggling with how to respond. It is not an easy decision. She may not know the neighboring family at all and urbanites tend to respect the anonymity of others. The very ordinariness of this scene, with Anne ironing and watching TV, makes the incident seem almost unreal. On the other hand, Anne has shown her ability to put herself in the situation of someone who is trapped and helpless. So why does her empathy fail here? Haneke holds the camera on Anne for a full minute after she goes back to ironing. As we have learned, the final shot and final line of dialogue in each sequence are always especially meaningful. Here the camera seems to be waiting for her to act, but she does not. Normally films derive their meaning from what characters *do*, but Haneke reverses things, ending his scene by focusing intently on a character who is choosing *not* to act.

In the Grocery Store

At first it seems as if the issue of the crying child may go away, just as Amadou's arrest apparently came to nothing, but then in scene nineteen, Anne comes home to find a note under her door. She puzzles over it for some moments and then tries to call Georges, but he is out. She downs a glass of wine and hurries across the hall to query Mrs. Becker. Without even reading the note, Mrs. Becker announces firmly that she writes no such things and disappears into her apartment, leaving Anne standing in the doorway. Later, as Anne and Georges talk in a grocery store, the contents of the note are made clear and, more critically, their characters are brought sharply into focus. The pivotal nature of this scene is suggested by its placement in the exact center of the film. With the camera preceding them, Georges pushes the cart down the aisle as Anne argues that if the note really came from a ten-year-old girl it wouldn't be signed, "a defenseless child." Georges thinks it's probably the neighbor who wrote it and advises Anne to call the cops or forget it. Or she could question the child's parents, but Anne points out what an impossible conversation that would be: "Do you hit your child? Torture her ever?" She accuses Georges of not caring and he responds that she got the letter, not him, adding, "I can't decide for you." He points out that he knows no one in the building, has never heard the girl crying, and repeats, "Not my problem." She hisses back at him, "It's never your problem. When there's trouble, you're gone." A few moments later he remarks, "Why don't you grow up and stop letting others decide for you?" As he moves ahead, she demands, "Have you ever made someone happy?" When she insists that he answer, he stops, head down, and says quietly, "No." At that point, she runs to him and kisses him passionately. Then, straightening themselves, they go on down the aisle, Anne teary-eyed. Just before the scene cuts to black, Georges asks, in a momentously trivial line, "Didn't you want some rice?"

Moral debates in classical Hollywood films are typically simplified. One person is clearly right and the other either realizes that truth and amends his behavior or persists in a pattern of error leading to disaster. This scene is far more complex: both characters are simultaneously revealing their own shortcomings and pinpointing the other's failures with devastating accuracy. For her part, Anne is perfectly correct that Georges seems never to be around when others need him. He is not there for Jean-Pierre in the beginning nor for the opening of Anne's play, may not get back for his son's birthday, and flees to Afghanistan rather than support his devastated father. While he's correct in saying that Anne got the note, he is living in Anne's apartment so it's his building, too. Most important, he says the problem isn't his since he doesn't know the people personally—an argument that makes nonsense of his career of documenting the violence in other countries. (The key event in the precipitating scene is Amadou's feeling impelled to defend Maria's dignity as a fellow human being, even though he doesn't know her at all.) Georges's desire to avoid involvement is nicely encapsulated by his determined pushing the cart forward throughout the scene, as if anxious to leave the argument behind.

By the same token, Georges's suggestion to Anne that she grow up and make her own decisions is exactly on target. In the precipitating scene, Anne remarked to Jean, "Go easy now on my poor little soul." It seems a casual remark, but might be a hint that she's still a little girl or that her soul is not fully developed. A further hint is given in the scene of sound-dubbing when she gets the giggles and the director calls out in exasperation, "Recess is over." Anne has shown amazing powers of empathy, but little evidence of taking action. Thus, in the ironing scene she listens without acting, and when she receives the note, her response is first to call Georges for advice and then go talk to Mrs. Becker. When Mrs. Becker politely closes the door, the camera holds on Anne, doubly framed in the two doorways as if to emphasize her paralysis (Figure 5.11). Her taking a stiff drink in both scenes also suggests a desire to escape the problem.

5.11
Anne,
framed in
two door-
ways,
unsure
what to do.

Of course it is natural to seek advice from others, but as Jean-Paul Sartre pointed out in his existential treatise *Being and Nothingness*, this exemplifies *mauvaise foi*, bad faith. Sartre argues that most people never make *authentic* moral choices but simply follow social norms. An authentic choice requires weighing the alternatives carefully and accepting the consequences of one's actions. A common strategy to avoid the agony of solitary decision-making is to ask someone for advice: now the responsibility is shared. Furthermore, we generally choose a person who will give the answer we wish to hear. That is precisely what Anne does in turning to Georges, whose history of detachment makes it totally predictable that he will suggest calling the cops or forgetting it. His determination to continue shopping neatly parallels her earlier insistence on rushing to her meeting when Jean-Pierre had asked for help, telling him, "We'll talk it through later, now is not the time." Each wishes to postpone dealing with a problem that stands squarely before them.

The scene's impact is enhanced by the brilliant staging. The argument might have played out differently had they been face-to-face in Anne's quiet living room and the abused child perhaps only a few hundred feet away. Instead, during the four-minute scene they push through the supermarket—a maze of shelves and freezer cases, lit by cold fluorescent lights. Their argument is constantly interrupted by other shoppers pushing past or by pauses to dump bottles of wine and bags of chips into the cart (Figure 5.12). The commercial

5.12
Trapped
by every-
day life:
Anne and
Georges.

setting, the clack and squeal of the cart wheels, the need to push forward, and the constricted aisles all testify to the difficulty of dealing with ethical issues amid the pressures of contemporary life. These same pressures were evident in many previous scenes—the street bustle in the precipitating encounter, the whining airplane engines as Maria was deported, the chaos of the Romanian quarry, the people passing in the restaurant, the TV that played as Anne ironed, and so on. With these repeated patterns, Haneke emphasizes how the press of everyday life becomes a convenient distraction, allowing us to avert our gaze from critical moral issues.

At the same time, neither Anne nor Georges is a monster. They cannot be sure what to do—consider Amadou standing up nobly for Maria's dignity which resulted in his arrest and her deportation. Even when one makes a decision one hopes is for the best, the results are never predictable. (Sartre illustrated this in his classic short story "The Wall" in which a captured resistance fighter is offered a reprieve from execution if he will reveal his leader's location. As a gallows joke he sends the police on a wild goose chase to a random address, only to discover that the leader happened to be at that location.) Georges's sad confession that he has never made anyone happy reveals the underlying failure of his life and the essential loneliness of his existence. Anne's desperate embrace following that testifies to her own need for an authentic relationship—and for someone to hold on to. The "true face" of each has been revealed, and we see ordinary people, failing to connect with their fellow human beings and unable to come to grips with the serious problem facing them.

The results of that failure appear eleven scenes later, as a small group stands at a graveside on a sunny day hearing a final prayer for little Françoise, a name never uttered previously. Among those who step forward to throw flowers and a spoonful of earth into the grave are Mrs. Becker and Anne. They shake hands with the family members and walk together past white headstones for a long time. Neither says a word nor looks at the other; Anne clutches her coat about her as if cold. Their appearance at the funeral could be a simple gesture of neighborly support, or taken as a silent admission of responsibility. But where a Hollywood film would make the judgment clear by having the two trade guilty looks or stammer excuses to one another, Haneke only follows them relentlessly with his camera for a full minute, just as he held it on Anne when she went back to ironing. Notably, Françoise is never seen, another anonymous victim. (One fascinating thought is that the thin-faced little girl doing the pantomime in the very first scene, cowering against the wall in apparent fear, was Françoise.) What is the responsibility of human beings for one another?—a question raised from the initial precipitating scene. There Anne was reluctant to do much to help Jean and when Amadou tried to defend Maria's dignity it only caused trouble for both of them. Georges's pictures from Kosovo, likewise, implicitly ask what responsibility other countries in Europe have to halt the carnage there. It is notable that when Sepp killed his cattle, a neighbor alerted Georges. Likewise, Maria's neighbor in Romania gives her a lift when he sees the heavy load she is carrying. This sense of neighbors taking responsibility for one another is too often lost in the anonymous urban setting, as shown by the refusal of Anne and Georges to become involved.

On the Subway

The issue of protecting others comes home with a vengeance at the end as Anne rides on the Metro. A young Arab at the far end of the car begins to harass a woman sitting with her back to the camera. It is Anne, but Haneke withholds that information initially. As with keeping Françoise off screen, this reminds us that we should empathize with any human being who is maltreated, not just those we know. The terrorizing here repeats the scene of *The Collector*, but now in a public, very real environment rather than an isolated, fictional space. The Arab plunks down beside Anne and asks, "How can you be so beautiful yet so arrogant?" When she moves to the other end of the car, he follows, and leans over her: "Do I smell? I'm just a little Arab looking for a little affection." He drops into the seat beside Anne, who has been steadily trying to avoid eye contact, and when the train stops, he spits full into her face and rushes out the door. As he runs past, an elderly Arab directs a kick at him, causing the young Arab to jump back in and confront him. The older man hands his glasses to Anne and stands up to face the punk. "Shame on you!" he snaps. The young man sits down and the train starts up again. Anne hands the older man his glasses back, wipes off her face, and wraps her arms around herself, fighting back tears. At the next stop, the young Arab exits, but yells loudly from off screen, causing everyone to jump and Anne to cover her face, crying. She controls herself long enough to thank the older Arab, then breaks into sobs. After this encounter, she hurries home and when Georges arrives some time later he finds the door code changed and is last seen trying to flag down a cab in the rain. Various pressures have torn at the fabric of the other three families, and now they have finally sundered the relationship of Anne and Georges.

Conclusion

The subway scene replays the opening precipitating encounter. Just as Jean's throwing the wrapper reflected his Oedipal frustration and Amadou's intervention reflected his memory of racial slights, so the young Arab's actions obviously have little to do with Anne. In part, he may be taken as a representative of France's long troubled history with Algeria. (The street riots by Muslim youth in the spring of 2006 serve as a confirmation of the truth of Haneke's 2000 film.) Anne runs away from problems in the final scene as she did in the opening one. Her retreating to her apartment and changing her code is emblematic of the European refusal to grapple with the issues of their increasingly multicultural society. Anne, the beautiful, successful actress, becomes the current incarnation of Marie Antoinette, symbol of the societal elite that wishes to ignore the problems in its midst. Seen another way, the Arab youth is the ghost of the dead Françoise, returned in demonic guise to torment Anne for her failure of engagement.

As always, the setting ties in brilliantly. The cold chrome of the Metro car, like the fluorescent-lit supermarket, emphasizes the lack of warmth in human relations, especially in an urban setting. The train races along from stop to stop, continuing the theme of frenetic rushing that began with Anne's hurrying out her door to a meeting. This hurtling steel capsule is another entrapment, allowing Anne no escape from those riding along with her. The other occupants of the car, typical city dwellers, try to stay uninvolved in the ugly situation occurring before their eyes. They stare off into space like the passengers in Georges's photos, replicating Anne's avoidance of the problems occurring next door. Again, it is an outsider to the culture, like Amadou initially, who has the courage to intervene and protect another person's dignity.

Afterword on Narrative Structure

Faced with the intractability of human evil, audiences have generally been happy to accept the fantasy solutions offered by Hollywood. Evil is embodied in some character who is totally *other* and then eradicated by the stalwart hero. This time-honored solution offers the particular advantage to theaters that, since evil is never truly extirpated, audiences must return every week and buy more tickets to witness its re-eradication. Haneke satirizes this approach in the scene of Anne's filming of *The Collector*. In it, she and her "husband" kiss and splash in a rooftop pool. In the midst of their play, Anne screams as she sees their small son climbing up on the wall outside the pool, its height emphasized by a dramatic zoom down from the child's point of view. In rapidly edited shots, they swim frantically to the edge, run to the wall, and pull him to safety. After embracing her son and breaking into tears, Anne insists to her husband that they must move. "I can't live on the twentieth floor, always worrying he'll fall." At this point the director's voice interrupts the scene, the camera pulls back and the two actors walk to the microphones to overdub the lines. With splendid irony, it is a shot of Juliette Binoche in the swimming pool—one of the most uncharacteristic shots in the film—which adorns the cover of the DVD (Figure 5.13).

5.13
Standard melodrama: Anne in the pool.

In contrast to the single takes in the rest of the film, this scene is filmed in "standard" Hollywood fashion, with twenty-four shots, many of them shot/reverse shot. It also provides "the accessible and trivial mix of emotion expected from Hollywood film: attractive people, sexual titillation, danger, resolution and emotional catharsis. Anne's actual life is far more complex and ambiguous."[6] Indeed. The sunny setting and love play that begin the scene and its facile resolution seem hopelessly trite in comparison to the real lives portrayed. The child so easily rescued here reminds of other children with futures far more in doubt: Jean-Pierre, who has run off; deaf Salimata and her little brother whom Amadou will have to support; Maria's daughters growing into womanhood without her; the children of Kosovo caught in a world of terror; and Françoise, who is dead.

Because Haneke's view of societal evil is more complex he rejects the simplistic Hollywood model and a devises a particularly dark variation of the **network narrative** to portray the world he sees. Rather than building *toward* the hub event, which would tend to emphasize the ironic operations of fate that bring people together, his **hub and spoke** plot puts the scene of congruence at the beginning. It presents a casual agglomeration of diverse individuals, nicely representative of today's multicultural Europe. Their lives necessarily connect, but that precipitating scene succinctly illustrates why those connections break down, presenting motifs repeated in subsequent scenes: self-centered lives, failure to communicate, family breakdown, isolation, entrapment, discrimination, and refusal to honor the dignity of fellow human beings. Particularly important is the theme of violence that begins subtly with Jean's pitching his pastry wrapper at Maria and then recurs with increased intensity: the police's rough treatment of Maria and Amadou, Georges's images of Kosovo, the maniacal collector, Sepp murdering his cattle, the Arab harassing Anne, and the death of Françoise.

Besides the repeating (and escalating) motifs, Haneke's second key structural element is the narrative's fragmentary nature, which tosses together bits and pieces of the various stories without apparent connection. (The film's subtitle is *Incomplete Tales of Several Journeys*.) Telling the stories one at a time would have encouraged a focus on how the actions of the characters have led to the difficult situations in which they find themselves. Instead, the repeated scenes of breakdown and noncommunication, of isolation and entrapment, of discrimination and violence, suggest patterns woven into the fabric of society rather than the result of one individual's decisions. This is accentuated by Haneke's rejection of the typical forward-driving narrative arc. Such an arc supports the view that our actions shape our destinies: by choosing to remain in Tombstone to avenge his brother's murder, Wyatt Earp helps bring civilization to the West—in John Ford's view (*My Darling Clementine*, 1946). The lack of such an arc, tellingly, suggests human paralysis.

Examining evil, Haneke shows that it tends to be invisible. People avert their eyes from Maria begging at the alley and the economic strictures which put her there. Even when they do see it, as Georges does in his photographs of Kosovo, they do not connect with it emotionally, reflected in the trivial discussion at the French café. Others, like Anne, have great powers of empathy but no moral commitment. Her profession of actress is emblematic of her ability to slide smoothly from one social role to another, but without developing an *authentic* being, to use Sartre's terminology. Hence she looks to society around her for answers to the problems she encounters, turning to Georges and Mrs. Becker for advice. She hopes to avoid the problem by moving to the other end of the car, but it only follows her.

Although Haneke most clearly indicts Anne and Georges for their failure to live authentic lives, there are no simple villains in the film. Obvious villains would allow the viewer to feel comfortable that the "evil" in the world is located elsewhere and not have to examine her own heart. The multifaceted nature of the portraits and the complexity of the storytelling underline how difficult it is to understand societal problems. It is equally unclear what choices should be made. Amadou's defense of Maria's dignity only makes her situation worse. The old Arab's protecting Anne cannot prevent the emotional trauma that causes her to retreat to her apartment, breaking off contact with the world and with Georges. If Anne and Georges had intervened, could they really have saved Françoise? We cannot know. Haneke offers no simple explanations for the injustices portrayed: they are doors hard to unlock, codes difficult to decipher. He himself has argued, "Every kind of explanation is just something that's there to make you feel better, and at the same time it's a lie. It's a lie to calm you, because the real explanation would be so complex." It is not his job to explain people, he argues, but to raise important questions for the audience to ponder.[7] In his shattered narrative structure Haneke has found the ideal mode for encapsulating the dark reality he perceives.

Notes

1   Amos Vogel, "Of Nonexisting Continents: The Cinema of Michael Haneke," *Film Comment* 32, no. 4 (1996): 75.
2   Vogel, "Of Nonexisting Continents," 75.
3   Fatima Naqvi argues that Georges's disconnected Kosovo photos suggest Haneke's critique of the constant bombardment of media images. "Although images are meant to inform or impel into action against violence, maybe even generating a counterviolence, they can also dull our responses." "The Politics of Contempt and the Ecology of Images: Michael Haneke's *Code inconnu*," in *The Cosmopolitan Screen: German Cinema and the Global Imaginary, 1945 to the Present*, Stephan K. Schindler and Lutz Koepnick, eds. (Ann Arbor: University of Michigan Press, 2007), 246.
4   Anne Laurent is also the name of the central character in *Le Temps du loup*, suggesting that Haneke intends the name as a designation for typical European.
5   Nick James, "Code Uncracked," *Sight and Sound* 11, no. 6 (2001): 8.
6   Robert van Dassanowsky, *Austrian Cinema: A History* (Jefferson, N.C.: McFarland, 2005), 255-56.
7   Leonard Quart, "Code Unknown," *Cinéaste* 27, no. 2 (Spring 2002): 35.

6

The Edge of Heaven

Parallel Paths

Fatih Akin's Turkish parents came to Germany in the 1960s as part of the guest worker program and Akin was born in Hamburg, the city where he lives and works to this day. His fourth feature, *Head-On* (*Gegen die Wand*, 2004), catapulted him into the international spotlight. Premiering at the Berlin International Film Festival, it won the Golden Bear Award—the first German film to do so in eighteen years. It went on to win Best Film and Best Director at the European Film Awards and garnered many subsequent honors including the 2006 American National Society of Film Critics Award for best foreign language film.[1] The vitality of the films by Akin and his German-Turkish compatriots led one critic to ask if the "New German Cinema" is Turkish.[2] "As this reference to New German Cinema suggests, German filmmakers of Turkish origin, such as Thomas Arslan, Yüksel Yavuz, Ayse Polat and Fatih Akin, are perceived as the next wave of *auteurs*" who may raise German cinema to "the level of international acclaim that was hitherto associated with the likes of Rainer Werner Fassbinder, Wim Wenders and Alexander Kluge."[3] Akin's films are notable because, rather than dealing with 'immigrant problems,' he shows people (who happen to be immigrants) trying to resolve their personal difficulties. As "the first filmmaker to put forward images that truly imagine the possibility of life as a transnational inhabitant,"[4] his films befit a world increasingly globalized and interconnected.

Akin's touch became even more assured in his 2007 feature, *The Edge of Heaven*. Its German title, *Auf der anderen Seite,* translates literally as "On the other side." On the DVD commentary, Akin says that he began with a more elaborate title—"On the other side of life"—but decided it was too pretentious.

Clearly, he intends to create a story where characters must look at lives unlike their own and at other sides of their own life. The title also conveys a political message, suggesting the "incomprehension that the Germans and Turks have of each other and the preconceived ideas they have of the other party; the whole idea of having sides seems to conveniently overlook the fact they are all humans."[5] The film's narrative moves freely back and forth between Germany and Turkey, illustrating just how interconnected these two cultures have become. But while showing the interaction of Turks and Germans, the political and social issues serve only as background to the problems people have in dealing with their personal prejudices and with members of their own family.

Story Summary

The story deals with six of these "transnational inhabitants," three sets of parents and children. Ali (Tuncel Kurtiz) is a Turkish widower, retired and living in Bremen, while his German-born son, Nejat (Baki Davrak), is a professor of German literature in Hamburg. Ali patronizes Yeter (Nursel Köse), who works in the brothel district to support Ayten (Nurgül Yesilçay), her grown daughter back in Istanbul. Lotte Staub (Patrycia Ziolkowska) attends the university in Hamburg and lives with her mother, Susanne (Hanna Schygulla). In the film's first section, "Yeter's Death," Yeter accepts Ali's offer to become his live-in woman after two radical Muslims threaten harm if she continues her brothel career. Although Nejat is initially dismayed by his father's new companion, he warms to Yeter as he sees her sorrow at having lost contact with Ayten. Sadly, Ali assaults Yeter in a drunken rage, thinking (mistakenly) that she slept with his son, and accidentally kills her. He is deported to Turkey and disowned by Nejat who heads to Turkey to look for Ayten, hoping somehow to make amends. While putting up posters of Yeter around Istanbul, he finds a German bookstore for sale that seems a more congenial locale than his lecture hall.

The film's second section, "Lotte's Death," reveals that Ayten previously fled to Germany under an assumed name. Part of a revolutionary Turkish group, she captured and hid a policeman's pistol during a May Day demonstration, but fled when her comrades were arrested. Lotte befriends Ayten at the university in Hamburg and takes her home when she discovers the young woman has no place to stay. Susanne is not pleased to have this revolutionary in her bourgeois home, even less so when the two girls become lovers. When Ayten is apprehended and deported, Lotte follows her to Istanbul, hoping to secure her release from prison. She rents a room from Nejat, now owner of the bookstore. When Lotte announces she will remain in Istanbul as long as it takes to free Ayten, her mother withdraws all support. Susanne comes to rue that decision when, some months later, Lotte is killed by street urchins with the very pistol Ayten had hidden.

After all this tragedy, the film ends on a hopeful note in the third section, "Edge of Heaven" ["On the Other Side"]. Susanne arrives in Istanbul and rents Lotte's old room from Nejat. She visits Ayten in prison and promises to help her. Ayten, in turn, uses her "Right to Repent" to renounce her revolutionary ties; she is freed from prison and taken in by Susanne. Simultaneously, Susanne helps Nejat decide to reconcile with Ali, who has returned to Trabzon, his home village on the Black Sea.

Parallel Lives

Like many **network narratives**, *The Edge of Heaven* builds connections. It intertwines the various stories to emphasize the links that bind us to our fellow humans who live in a different reality but one not entirely dissimilar from our own. Constant narrative and stylistic parallels create the sense of linkage, a common device in network narratives, but one which Akin uses with particular effectiveness. First, the film weaves its narrative around the idea of the journey, one that leads to unexpected encounters. Ayten travels from Istanbul to Hamburg, hoping to find Yeter; Nejat travels from Hamburg to Istanbul, hoping to find Ayten. Second, the film emphasizes commonalities by focusing on the most basic human relationship—the link between parent and child. A father-son relationship is sundered in the first section and the same fate befalls a mother-daughter relationship in the second. In both cases, the rupture occurs because a person from outside enters and unwittingly pushes parent and child apart. Third, the film creates a sense of human connection through frequent parallel scenes, with characters undergoing similar experiences, sometimes one of them walking in the precise footsteps of another. Finally, after actions that have riven family ties, the film ends with people finding new homes and establishing new relationships, emphasizing how central these elements are in our lives.

At the same time, while emphasizing human commonalities, the film reminds us that other people's lives are not simple mirrors of our own. We cannot expect to connect with other people if we will not stretch ourselves to accept their differences. Even the scenes set entirely in Germany reveal contrasting worlds that exist side-by-side. When Nejat visits his father, Ali cooks a fish dinner for them, reminiscent of his years on the Black Sea coast, and they partake of raki, the national drink of Turkey. Much of their time is spent out on the patio, where Ali waters his tomatoes, a fruit central in Turkish culture. The horse race they attend together is also culturally relevant: "Horses were sacred and indispensable for Turks; they were born, grown up, fight, and die on the horse [sic.]."[6] Susanne's kitchen shows a completely different, totally German world—neat, geometric, and efficient. Even the color schemes differ, with the warm yellows of Ali's patio contrasting with the gray and blue tones of the Staub household.

However, the fact that very different worlds can exist within the same country, even the same city, suggests that the major differences separating people are as much personal as historical and political. Bridging them requires looking into our own hearts. Akin employs the network narrative superbly to present a nuanced portrait of the commonalities and diversity of human societies.

Opening: The Journey

One way *The Edge of Heaven* emphasizes interconnections is by portraying life as a journey that necessarily brings us into contact with our fellow travelers. The theme begins with the film's brief prologue. With the screen still black, the sound of waves is heard, a reminder of the eternal ocean. The shot opens on a completely unremarkable scene: a village dirt road, a small hut, some trees, and a mongrel dog nosing lazily around. Slowly the camera tracks right to a tired look-ing gas station in white and ochre. A man's voice sings plaintively: a recording of Kazim Koyuncu, a popular Turkish singer. A nondescript car drives into the frame and stops, neatly posed between two pumps (Figure 6.1). The driver emerges, a

6.1
The journey begins: Nejat's car appears.

young man in jeans, t-shirt, and open shirt, his hair rumpled. He tells the owner's son to fill it up, returns the greeting of "Happy Bayram," greets the station owner, orders a cheese toast at the grill counter, and strolls among the snack shelves selecting sustenance for his journey. He pays and then is back on the tunneled road, the music pulsing on the sound track. When his car disappears into the sec-ond tunnel, the screen goes black again. This opening presents a character "on the road," a familiar trope inviting us on a life journey. The nondescript appearance of this unknown voyager belies the fact that he is a former Hamburg University professor. His casual stroll, likewise, is deceptive, for his journey has a serious purpose. This is Nejat Aksu on his way to Trabzon, Ali's village, to reconcile with the father he disowned. The prologue, revealing so little of Nejat's character or motivations, reminds us to be cautious in our first judgments of people.

Further, this opening announces that we are going to be looking at life "on the other side," (as the German title suggests), looking at people who move through worlds unlike our own. Setting, music, and language would be unfamiliar to most Westerners and the scene lacks any clear tonality, either hostile or welcoming. It is most notable for being unremarkable: rural, quiet, nondescript. In fact, it is the antithesis of almost all the other settings in the film, the majority of which occur in the metropolises of Bremen, Hamburg, and Istanbul. Even the color scheme is antithetical: the brown tones contrast sharply with the blues, grays, and bright yellows of the German landscapes, just as the ramshackle structures are unlike Germany's geometric architecture. We are in the modern world—the power lines overhead show that—but in a very quiet corner of it. A slow pace of life is suggested by the leisurely track to meet Nejat's car driving up, his fatigued shamble through the gas station, and the relaxed tempo of the two long takes. This is a world where human contact is important: all three gas station workers wish Nejat "Happy Bayram" and the owner stands to shake the stranger's hand. The owner mentions that the singer, Koyuncu, comes from Artvin, suggesting a rural world where people are forever linked to family and place of birth. Nejat's failure to recognize this popular artist marks him as a stranger. Born and raised in Germany, this is not his world. He travels through this landscape to connect with his father again. As the film will show, people must be willing to leave familiar landscapes and discover new places, physically and psychologically.

This journey, so critical in Nejat's life, is shown again at the close of the first section. Visiting his cousin after seeing the lovely bookstore he eventually will buy, Nejat announces he may give up teaching and stay in Istanbul. He will not, however, have anything ever to do with his father. "A murderer is not my father." Immediately on those words, the film jumps forward in time to refute his words, again showing him on the road to Trabzon. The trip's importance is emphasized by a stunning visual, as the camera races down a side road at high speed, angling in to meet and track with Nejat's car as it rushes along to the music of Koyuncu. Besides being "bravura filmmaking,"[7] the shot embodies the narrative trajectories: tangential paths unexpectedly flow together. This brief moment of travel, lasting just 1:15, separates the first section ("Yeter's Death") from the second ("Lotte's Death"). The forward rush of the vehicle, floating through the musical landscape, provides a momentary escape from the scenes of pain before and after it. The eagerness of the camera to join Nejat's journey signals its endorsement of the forgiveness that now impels him. The forward movement ultimately implies life; perhaps if we can connect with others who may seem foreign to us, some hope is to be found.

Parents and Children

Another way *The Edge of Heaven* suggests our commonality is by focusing on a key human relationship, that between parents and children. The opening section has Nejat traveling from Hamburg to visit his retired father in Bremen. The two share a meal and go to the track the next day, and when Ali's horse wins he treats his son to ice cream. As Nejat is leaving to take the train home, Ali asks him who he's screwing at the moment, but Nejat lightly says gentlemen don't discuss such things and departs. In most regards, the casual interaction suggests the father-son relationship is good. Nejat kisses his father affectionately when he arrives and leaves and has brought him a book in Turkish to read. Their meal is relaxed, and on the porch after supper the scene's warm light conveys a sense of family togetherness as Ali waters his tomato plants and Nejat reads the paper. At the same time, undercurrents can be seen, as in the novel Nejat brings his father. *Demircinin Kizi* (*The Blacksmith's Daughter*), by Selim Özdogan, a German-Turkish author, tells of a girl who lives most of her life in a small village in Turkey, but follows her husband to Germany and, at the end of the tale, prays she will not die in the cold winters there. Dealing with the plight of immigrants, one can see this as Nejat's effort to find reading material that might provide a topic of conversation with his father. However, it is also a reminder of the educational divide between father and son. Nejat is an intellectual, a university professor, while his father is an ordinary guy. Ali comments as they eat their ice cream, "It's impossible to talk to you about anything." He shows no interest in the book, saying merely "Yeah, yeah" when Nejat urges him to read it.

Ali's behavior reveals the strains faced by a cultural outsider which, in turn, complicate his relationship with his son. The film does not have to show scenes of overt discrimination against Ali: the tensions caused by Turks living in Germany are well known. Outsiders like Ali have their identity continually eroded. He has come from a culture with a strong and secure masculine role, but that world is 1,800 miles away. A retired widower, he has no family within which to assert his authority and his sense of self-worth is further undermined now that he is no longer an active breadwinner. His first act in the film is to patronize a brothel, suggesting his need to assure his masculinity (Figure 6.2). Unfortunately, his interaction with Yeter also undercuts him. She calls him "Uncle," and then, in another slap to his masculinity, asks, "Can you still get it up at your age?" In their second session she urges him, "Come on now, old man!" as he huffs and puffs, to which he replies, "I'm not fourteen any more. I don't come that quickly." These early references to his age and failing potency set the stage for Ali's later Oedipal conflicts with his son. Although Nejat can fend perfectly well for himself in the new culture, Ali controls everything at home and at the racetrack. His query about

6.2
Yeter
at the
brothel:
Ali's
refuge.

who Nejat is screwing, in particular, is a crude assertion of sexual dominance. Ali's situation as an immigrant exacerbates these tensions, but at base one sees a universal problem—the difficulty of an aging father to reconcile himself with his declining potency.

Parallel Scenes: The Trolley

The film is filled with parallel scenes that suggest people traveling the same road. Two such scenes occurring on the trolley help explain why Nejat comes to bond with Yeter. In the first, Yeter is riding away from the brothel district on Helenenstraße when she is accosted by two religious extremists who spotted her there and heard her speaking Turkish. She pretends not to understand when the men plunk down into the seats next to her and say, "*Selamün Aleyküm.*" She replies, "*Nicht verstehen,*" but they are not fooled. "You're both a Moslem and a Turk." One says quietly but intensely, "You are on the false path. Repent!" and his companion echoes, "Repent!" She stares at them for a moment, then says quietly, "I repent." The first man says, "Don't let me catch you there again" and the second adds, "It would be a shame about you." They say nothing further, but simply ride with her, leaving at the next stop. As they depart, they again say "*Selamün Aleyküm*" to which she replies, "*wa-Aleyküma selam.*" Alone, she stares bleakly out the window, her face showing concern. The seriousness of this threat is emphasized by the tight shots which give Yeter no place to escape—the heads of the men completely fill the frame. The scene's dark blue coloring, the cold fluorescent lighting, and the mechanical sounds of the trolley increase the sense of hostility (Figure 6.3). The threat conveyed in this scene impels Yeter to accept Ali's offer to become his live-in woman.

The contrasting scene takes place after she and Nejat have rushed Ali to the hospital after a heart attack. Riding back with Yeter on the trolley, Nejat tentatively

6.3
Yeter
boxed in
and
blocked out.

asks her if she has children, and learns she has a daughter who is twenty-seven. Yeter adds, "I'd do anything for her. I didn't want her to be uneducated. I wanted her to study and become like you." This last is said in Turkish: Yeter switches naturally to her mother tongue to express more personal feelings. In this case, their shared language suggests communion rather than threat as it did with the two men. Although this scene takes place at night like the earlier one, the mood is entirely different. Nejat does not loom over her like the men but sits rather shyly along-side her. Where the men made aggressive eye contact, Nejat only glances in her direction, cautious about invading her space. The camera angle is lower, placing them in a comfortable two-shot rather than squeezing her into the corner (Figure 6.4). Nejat's question about children is obviously an attempt to relate to her more

6.4
Nejat and
Yeter
beginning
to bond.

personally (and also suggests how he may be drawn to her in the role of mother). His asking if her daughter knows what she does for a living suggests his sympathy for Yeter's plight, prostituting herself to provide a better life for her child. Rather than judging Yeter, Nejat appreciates the sacrifices she has made. Yeter, in turn, respects him and what he has achieved. Her very first question when they are alone during dinner at Ali's is, "Are you really a professor?" He has attained the success she dreams of for her daughter. At the end of this trolley scene, the two of them ride along quietly, not looking at one another. This is the night of their initial meeting, but already in this short time a bond has been established.

It may seem strange that Nejat comes to feel so strongly about Yeter, a woman of ill-repute whom he encounters only briefly. A key reason is his having lost his own mother at the age of six months, so that he and Yeter fall into something like a mother-son relationship. When he meets her over dinner at his father's place, she first comes across as courageous more than motherly, explaining that she lost her husband in the 1978 Maras massacre.[8] Then after he has put his drunken father to bed and asks her how the two of them met, he is quietly shocked when she tells him unabashedly she is a hooker, but his feelings grow more positive as he learns about Yeter's dreams for her daughter. Her desire to find her lost child mirrors his wish to find the mother he never knew. Their relationship is solidified in a pair of small gestures. Watering his father's tomatoes on the patio while Ali recuperates in the hospital, Nejat passes a ripe tomato to Yeter. She breaks into tears as she tastes it, sorrowing over Ayten with whom she has lost contact and he puts a comforting arm around her shoulders. When Ali returns from the hospital and accuses his son of sleeping with Yeter, Nejat angrily quits the house. Yeter hurries after him with some börek for his trip home, which he gratefully eats later in his study in Hamburg. This is the gift of sustenance, the root of the mother-child relationship and a primal human gesture of support. Every culture honors this, but in the Middle East the obligation to offer food and shelter to guests is felt with particular strength. Yeter and Nejat are linked as surrogate mother and son and also as givers of nourishment. On top of that, Nejat is a scholar of the Enlightenment—he lectures on Goethe—and so obviously feels an obligation to atone for his father's wrong in killing Yeter. What better to do than help provide for the daughter's education, the thing Yeter had hoped for so fervently? Hence his decision to follow her coffin to Turkey and search for her lost daughter.

Parallel Scenes: May Day

More parallel scenes occur at the beginning of the first two major sections, each a May Day demonstration. In the first section, after the melancholy title "Yeter's Death," the scene fades into a street march where the mood seems more festive than confrontational. Set in the charming market square in Bremen, the opening shots show the fifteenth-century statue of Roland, the city's protector, holding aloft his sword Durendart, and his shield bearing the double-headed imperial eagle. We see the Gothic era Rathaus, Gerhard Marck's bronze sculpture of the four animal musicians of Bremen, and the Cathedral of St. Peter.

Although the crowds carry red protest banners—"Proletarians of All Countries, Unite!"—no police are in evidence. People on the sidewalks are smiling and a marching band accompanies the parade with snare drums and a melodious lyre. There are no chants or shouts; one group sings a revolutionary ditty that strongly resembles a jolly drinking song. The demonstration seems mostly a lively distraction, a sense increased as the camera picks up Ali heading jauntily toward the brothel district.

The second major section, "Lotte's Death," that presents Ayten's story, also begins with a May Day parade, but not the sprightly festival found in Bremen. The opening aural landscape is ominous: the angry buzz of helicopter rotors is overlaid with the tumult of chanting crowds, marching feet, whistles, and sirens. The action this time takes place in Istanbul, but the locale is less clearly established, leaving the viewer disoriented. Many varied groups are taking part; one group of women chants "Öcalan, we are with you," marking them as Kurdish protesters.[9] These marchers are more serious—chanting slogans, many of them wearing scarves over their faces. The chaos and implicit violence in the scene is emphasized by the visual discontinuities, with rapid cuts, sharp differences in lighting, and constantly changing camera angles. From aerial shots of crowds below, the camera jumps to ground level shots of police in riot gear and upward views of the circling helicopters, all intercut with a jumble of marchers hurrying past with their placards. This time, instead of breaking off to track a recreational trip into a brothel, the camera shows a descent into mob rule, as the marchers assault a suspected plain clothes policeman, kicking and beating him with clubs in a fury.[10] The first images of Ayten herself are as disturbing as the rally—an androgynous figure, face concealed in a black ski mask, who grabs the policeman's pistol from the ground and flees, pursued by packs of officers (Figure 6.5). Ayten does not participate in beating the policeman, but by picking up the pistol she incorporates the possibility of violence into the fabric of her life and will discover in time the consequences of that action.

6.5
Ayten
fleeing
with the
policeman's
gun.

Parallel Scenes: The Classroom

A particularly poignant example of parallel scenes portrays the same exact moment in two story segments. In the first section, Nejat is seen lecturing with a dark-haired girl sleeping in the rear of the classroom. This shot appears again in the second section, for the girl is Ayten, the very person Nejat will later leave Germany in the hopes of finding. Forced to flee Istanbul when her fellow conspirators are rounded up, she arrives in Hamburg. Members of a cell there provide temporary lodging and suggest that she hang out at the university where she can take showers and get cheap food in the cafeteria. She quickly falls out with her revolutionary family members who want to use her for cheap labor and is left on her own, sleeping in the corners of buildings and panhandling for food. Knowing Ayten's backstory, the viewer is intrigued by the quote Nejat reads from Goethe as she dozes. "Who wants to see a rose bloom in the depths of winter? Everything to its own time. Leaves, buds, flowers. Only a fool could want this untimely intoxication."

Goethe is arguing against revolution, asserting that nature's order seems a sensible one, best not tampered with. His classicism, arguing that human society should emulate the natural order, seems quaintly anachronistic. Yet humans have begun to discover the price to be paid for riding roughshod over the world rather than living in harmony with it. Goethe's image of the rose is particularly interesting because the pseudonym on Ayten's passport is Gül Korkmaz, and *gül* means "rose" in Turkish. Ayten certainly seems the rose in winter, stranded in the cold German landscape like the woman in *The Blacksmith's Daughter*. However, we also recall that the rose in winter, despite Goethe's negative view, is ultimately an image of hope, linked to the coming of the Christ Child, as embodied in the famous Praetorian carol "Es ist ein Ros' entsprungen." This may hint that these two sad souls—the professor lecturing dryly to his bored students and the exhausted girl lost in a friendless world—may yet find a rebirth. In each case, however, doing so will require a sincere change of heart, and in Ayten's case this will mean heeding Goethe's warning about revolution.

Parallel Scenes: The Argument

Panhandling at the university, Ayten meets Lotte, who buys her a meal at the student cafeteria and then takes her home when she discovers Ayten has no place to stay. In another pair of parallel scenes, Susanne, Lotte's mother, argues first with Lotte and then with Ayten, expressing her disapproval of their life choices. Both arguments occur in Susanne's kitchen, the first immediately after Lotte has brought Ayten home, loaned her some clothes, and then encounters her mother in the kitchen while Ayten is showering. Susanne sits drinking her tea and says dryly, "Very generous of you, letting a stranger come and stay with us." The two argue with quiet intensity, Lotte insisting that Ayten needs shelter and Susanne saying she should apply for asylum if she needs protection. The tension between mother and daughter is emphasized by the mise-en-scène. Susanne sits with her back to Lotte, only glancing at her momentarily, her rigid body posture reflecting her disapproval. The camera's position is equally rigid, panning slightly as Lotte enters the kitchen but thereafter locked on the two women, with Lotte pinned in the rear corner. The kitchen is neatly ordered, every utensil in place, and marked by strong blue tones and sharp geometric lines: it perfectly reflects Susanne's cool, unwelcoming stance (Figure 6.6).

6.6 Maternal disapproval: Susanne's geometric kitchen.

The parallel argument occurs the following morning after the two girls have come home drunk from a nightclub. From her upper window, Susanne watched them stagger out of the taxi, giggling and embracing. Her coldness toward the relationship was again reflected visually through her white pajamas, white desk lamp, white laptop, and geometric room. When Ayten calls out "Good morning" as she enters the kitchen later that morning, Susanne—her back turned as before—replies, "It's already noon." Her displeasure is clear. She asks about Ayten's political cause and receives a lecture on the fight for freedom, to which she replies condescendingly, "Maybe things will get better once you get into the European Union." Ayten pounces on that idea, using sharply vulgar language to characterize the colonial powers controlling the European Union. Susanne asks her not to use such language in her house, causing Ayten to run upstairs, strip off her borrowed clothes in favor of her own, and wait outside for Lotte's return. Susanne wishes to break the bond between the girls but her action strengthens it. Hoping to drive out the stranger, she will drive out her own daughter as well. Just as the parallel kitchen scenes link the girls symbolically, so does Susanne's treatment: they are both now her daughters. This is foreshadowed a moment later when Lotte drives up and finds a tearful Ayten asking, "Can you help me find my mother?" On those words, the camera cuts to Susanne watching in the upper window, the woman who will later come to Ayten's rescue and help replace the mother she has lost.

Parallel Destruction

The two parent-child relationships in the film are broken by the same powerful force: sexuality. In the scene where Yeter meets Nejat for the first time at dinner, her position at the table between the two men signals that she will come between them. When Ali returns from the hospital after his heart attack, he misinterprets the closer relationship between Nejat and Yeter and accuses his son of sleeping with her. This is an obvious Freudian scenario, reflecting Ali's feeling of physical decline, further exacerbated by the heart attack. The sexual threat he feels is groundless. While he is in the hospital, the two of them are shown sleeping separately, Nejat on the couch and Yeter in the bed. So powerful are Ali's fears, however, that he cannot abide any thwarting. When he demands sexual favors of Yeter after Nejat leaves, she refuses and starts to pack her things. Her announced departure constitutes a terrible threat, repeating the loss of Ali's wife and undercutting the virility he sought to ensure by purchasing Yeter's exclusive favors. The drunken blow he directs at her is in the outpouring of patriarchal anger by a man whose masculinity has been eroded by age and his outsider status in the culture.

In similar fashion, sexuality invades the Staub household in the form of the mysterious and passionate Ayten. Her name, Ayten, means "moon-skin" as she explains to Lotte, someone with skin as fair and pale as the moon. In actuality, her skin appears dusky next to Lotte's but her link to the moon, symbol of romance, is appropriate. Her power is shown at the nightclub where she and Lotte drink, dance, share a toke, join in a passionate kiss, and return home to fall into bed together. Ayten's irresistibility is emphasized by the strongly contrasted filming of Lotte's preceding argument with Susanne in the kitchen and the two girls at the club. Instead of two characters speaking angrily, backs turned, there are two people dancing intimately, face to face, in close shot. The kitchen was static, cold, blue, with the entire argument done in a single take lasting thirty-five seconds during which the camera's medium long shot held the viewer at a distance. The nightclub is intensely erotic and draws the viewer in. Pulsing Turkish music on the sound track blots out all other sound; the lighting is saturated reds and yellows; the camera is constantly moving as the girls dance and the focus slightly blurred, suggesting their alcoholic haze; most shots are close and four of the shot transitions are quick dissolves, increasing the sense of the girls blending. The first nine shots last just five seconds on average, increasing the frenzy as the girls gyrate and toss their hair with abandon, sweat gleaming on their faces (Figure 6.7). Then the cam-

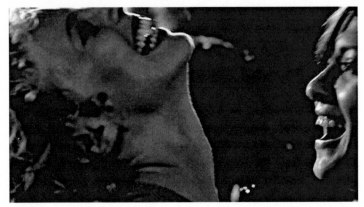

6.7
Lotte and Ayten dancing: Passion overcomes reason.

era does a forty-two second slow track in as they sink into a kiss, its inexorable movement suggesting the powerful passion that draws them together. On the one hand, the connection between the women seems positive in contrast to the other scenes of brutality, suspicion, and callous prostitution. On the other, Lotte is being carried away by her sexual feelings, oblivious to the violence with which Ayten is associated. Much later, after Ayten has been picked up by the police, tried, and repatriated to a prison in Istanbul, Lotte races around her home in a fury, certain that her mother has hidden her passport. As she does so, Susanne plucks it from the bureau where it lies in plain sight and says quietly, "*Schau mal wie blind du bist*" ("See how blind you are"). Indeed, like Ali, Lotte's passion has clouded her vision and her judgment.

Near Misses

The idea that human lives are webbed together is repeatedly suggested in moments when characters brush by one another but fail to connect. One example is Ayten sleeping in Nejat's classroom and another is Susanne and Ali arriving simultaneously at the Istanbul airport but never seeing one another. A third occurs when Lotte appears in Nejat's bookstore, researching the Turkish justice system, and tells Nejat she is helping a friend, Gül Korkmaz. Unwittingly, her use of Ayten's alias prevents Nejat from realizing the girl in question is the very person he has come to Istanbul to find. Most poignant of all is the moment when Lotte and Ayten drive to Bremen in search of Yeter. As they drive, the camera tracks right with them accompanied by the same melancholy guitar theme heard during Ayten's flight to Germany, a journey that was as much about finding her mother as fleeing Istanbul. Then as their car pulls forward out of frame, the camera tilts up and racks focus to show Nejat and Yeter riding in the same direction on a train directly behind them. The camera tracks with them for a short time, the same music continuing to play, and then they, similarly, pull ahead and out of frame. Here are mother and daughter in the same shot, never glimpsing one another. Neither of them is talking to their companion and we are free to imagine each is thinking about the very person gliding by just a few feet away. Their nearness is emphasized by the visual parallels: the white car and white train, the black-framed windows, the frozen poses, and the slow glide off the right edge of the frame. Mother and daughter will never see one another again, magnifying the moment's poignancy. The shot marvelously conveys the sense that people's lives often move mysteriously in parallel, though they may be unaware of it. This, in turn, reinforces the film's message about our responsibility for the other human beings who share the journey with us.

Parallel Paths

Particularly toward the end, the film connects people ever more tightly, showing them literally following in one another's steps. Thus Lotte visits Ayten in prison, gets directions for finding the policeman's pistol, and does so with actions that recapitulate Ayten's original flight from the police. Lotte rounds the same street corner, climbs the same stairs, finds the roof door locked just as Ayten did, and asks the same woman for help in opening it. Once on the roof, she is pictured with the exact camera setup used when Ayten was there—only a few items of roof detritus have been rearranged to suggest a different time. In effect, she is now walking in Ayten's footsteps. When she puts the pistol in her purse, she is carrying Ayten's life forward from where it left off in Turkey and in doing so she suffers the fate that may have awaited Ayten in her revolutionary zeal. Her purse is snatched by a gang of urchins, she chases them through disreputable neighborhoods, and finally stumbles upon them in an empty lot, sniffing glue and rifling through her purse. They find the gun, tussle over it and, when Lotte approaches, one stumbles fuzzily to his feet, points the pistol in her direction, closes his eyes, and pulls the trigger. There is a sharp crack and the boys run off, leaving Lotte lying in the debris like some doll dropped by a careless child.

Another parallel moment occurs when Ayten is brought in from her cell for what she assumes is routine questioning and defiantly refuses to talk without her lawyer. She is stunned to learn her interrogators don't care about her revolutionary group but are hoping to defuse the international uproar over a German citizen being murdered in Istanbul, the woman who came to visit her the day before. As they continue to question her about possible motives for the killing, Ayten can only look around vacantly, wide-eyed, unable to comprehend this horror. The men urge her to use her "Right to Repent" and get a light sentence, an ironic reminder of the men who cornered her mother on the trolley and urged her to repent. Yeter, with honest sadness, had replied, "I repent," not so much capitulating to the men as admitting her unhappiness with the life she was leading. At this moment, Ayten surely feels a similar despair. Her repentance is shown when Susanne later comes to visit her and all Ayten can say through her tears is, "I am sorry! Forgive me!" Ultimately she does use her "Right to Repent," renounces her life in the revolution, and leaves prison just as Yeter renounced her life in the brothel and left Helenenstraße. A telling shot shows Ayten riding on the ferry after being freed, looking backward from the stern at the churning water. Like her mother, riding alone and staring out the trolley window, she cannot see clearly where her life is headed and can only repent her mistakes in the past.

Most poignantly, when Susanne arrives in Istanbul after Lotte has been killed, she comes to tread in her daughter's footsteps, knowingly and unknowingly. She contacts Nejat, asks to see the room he rented to her daughter, and then lies on Lotte's bed reading her diary. In it, Lotte expresses her determination to follow her destiny and her surprise that her mother doesn't understand her actions since "She was just like that herself." Lotte adds, "I find myself taking paths very similar to hers." Lotte had told Ayten on their first meeting that she had just returned from India and Susanne, similarly, tells Nejat that she had been in Istanbul thirty years earlier, hitchhiking to India. (As Susanne relates that bit of history to Nejat, their taxi traverses the same street Lotte had walked along when she first arrived in Istanbul, further overlapping the footsteps of mother and daughter.) Their spiritual link is indicated by Susanne laying Lotte's diary on her breast as she goes to sleep on Lotte's bed, taking her daughter back into her heart (Figure 6.8). It is seen again the next morning as she wakens to a momentary vision of her daughter smiling at her. Where Lotte had previously followed in her mother's steps to India, now Susanne follows in hers. She rents Lotte's room from Nejat and tells him she will stay as long as necessary to secure Ayten's release, exactly Lotte's decision—the one that caused Susanne to break off with her daughter and which she obviously regrets. The congruence of mother and daughter is now complete: Susanne's main goal in life is to secure Ayten's freedom, precisely as Lotte had hoped to do.

6.8
Reconciled:
Susanne
sleeping
with Lotte's
diary.

The sense of mother and daughter taking similar paths is most strikingly embodied in the scene where Susanne sets off to visit Ayten in prison. She steps out the door of Nejat's building and the camera pans left as she walks down the street, greeting the two backgammon players on the sidewalk with "*Hallo.*" This camera move and position are precisely the same as when Lotte set out to visit Ayten for the first time and so is the music on the sound track. The only difference is that Lotte greeted the two men in Turkish: "*Selamün Aleyküm.*" These visual parallels indicate how Susanne's only desire is to align herself with her daughter, turning her footsteps in the direction Lotte had chosen. The ultimate congruence occurs when Ayten is freed from prison and comes to find Susanne, who is minding Nejat's bookstore while he travels to Trabzon. The two embrace and Susanne immediately invites Ayten to come stay with her, the same action that brought Lotte and Ayten together initially. As they exit the bookstore, the camera pans left to the bulletin board and holds on the empty space where Yeter's poster used to hang, put there months ago as Nejat searched for Ayten but now discarded. It is a painful reminder of the loss of Yeter and another "near miss," since Ayten would have recognized the face on that poster were it still hanging there. At the same time, there is a balancing consolation, for Susanne is now stepping in to fill that blank space in Ayten's life. The ultimate sadness of all these parallel paths is how much pain and loss is required to turn people's footsteps in a new direction.

Homecoming and Reconciliation

The disparate threads are finally woven together in the ending as the terrible family rifts begin to heal. The scene of Susanne lying in Lotte's bed signaled the reconciliation of mother and daughter, further sealed with the embrace of Susanne and Ayten. Susanne's change in heart is paralleled in the immediately following scene when Ali appears in Istanbul after his repatriation. He sits in a park reading

The Blacksmith's Daughter, the novel which Nejat gave him in Bremen. As he puts it down his eyes are momentarily filled with tears. Here is another parent grieving over a lost child, savoring the link created by the book as Susanne was by Lotte's diary. No longer having to defend his identity and his masculinity in a foreign culture, he may now be on a better road. The tears in his eyes suggest his repentance for the act that cost him his humanity and the love of his son. Knowing Nejat wants no contact with him, he will head back to Trabzon alone.

Although initially unwilling to reconcile himself with his father, Nejat has arrived in a better place for himself. While he seemed well acclimated to German culture with his prestigious university position, two brief shots of him in Hamburg early in the film convey a sense of alienation through the camerawork and mise-en-scène. In the first shot, lasting just eight seconds, he walks down a sidewalk while a train rolls by overhead in the background. Nejat is a very small figure on the left of the frame, almost unnoticed, and the dominant sound is the screech of the train. The camera does not track or pan to register his presence, but stares fixedly down the center of the street, relegating him to the margin. The dominant tonality is grey, found in the street, the sidewalk, the building on the left, and the train above (Figure 6.9). Then the shot cuts to Nejat in the classroom, lecturing on

6.9 Nejat sidelined on the street in Hamburg.

Goethe. There are twenty-five students seated in a lecture hall designed for two hundred, so his course is not a great favorite. Beginning directly behind Nejat, the camera tracks 180 degrees around to end up in front, sealing him into a cinematic bubble, cut off from his class. These scenes hint that he has not found a real place in German society.

Nejat is undoubtedly surprised when his proper place turns out to be a bookstore in Istanbul, discovered during his search for Ayten. The moment he steps

6.10
Nejat in
the cozy
bookstore.

through the door, it is obvious he has found his home (Figure 6.10). The camera tracks smoothly with him for a minute and a half as he strolls through the orderly shelves, perusing the titles. Bach's Minuet in G plays quietly on the sound track, the lighting is warm, and the owner—happy for the company of a German native—immediately offers him chai. Indeed, the shop is very much Nejat's cup of tea and he laughs with the owner about the irony of the situation: "a Turkish professor of German from Germany ends up in a German bookshop in Turkey." It seems clear that Nejat feels more at home here than in the echoing lecture hall. As he admits to his cousin later, "Maybe teaching isn't my calling." Buying the store helps put his life in balance, still close to the German literature he loves but in an intimate setting suited to his gentle temperament. This new location blends Germany and Turkey culturally, the same thing that occurs when Susanne embraces Ayten. It suggests how the concepts of home and family have to widen, including places and peoples from the other side.

Bayram

Once Nejat has found his proper home, he must take a further step and find his proper family. His guide in this journey is Susanne, whose vision has already been sharpened by the tragedy she has undergone. In this case, she directs her curious gaze out the window of Nejat's home, watching as men hurry through the streets below her and the cry of the imams echoes from minarets all over the city. When Nejat joins her at the window, she asks what is going on and he explains it is Bayram, the Feast of Sacrifice (*Eid al-Adha*). It occurs at the end of the Hajj, the annual pilgrimage to Mecca, and commemorates Ibrahim's refusal to sacrifice Ishmael. Muslims sacrifice an animal and donate one-third of it to the needy.

> The act [of sacrifice] symbolizes our willingness to give up things that are of benefit to us or close to our hearts, in order to follow Allah's commands. It also

symbolizes our willingness to give up some of our own bounties, in order to strengthen ties of friendship and help those who are in need. We recognize that all blessings come from Allah, and we should open our hearts and share with others.[11]

It is appropriate that the human fissures in the stories should begin to heal during this festival whose meaning encapsulates the film's vision. The feast emphasizes the bond between parent and child, a topic with immediate poignancy for Nejat and Susanne, but also suggesting the wider human family to which we all belong.

When Nejat describes this feast, Susanne recognizes it immediately as the story of Abraham and Isaac. "We have the same story," she says. It is a reminder of the sacrifice of Susanne's daughter, the most terrible price a parent can pay. It speaks also of wider human bonds, emphasized by the long take of Susanne and Nejat standing side-by-side, surrogate mother and son. At that moment, Nejat remembers asking his father if he would sacrifice him, frightened because he had already lost his mother as a child. Thinking back, Nejat recalls, "He said he would even make God his enemy in order to protect me." At this memory, he stands for a long moment, obviously shaken, and suddenly asks Susanne if she will look after his bookshop for a few days. The scene closes with the two of them gazing warmly at one another, while through the open window before them the faithful are seen walking down the steps toward the mosque. The filial connection of Nejat and Susanne, the symmetry of the shot, the open windows, and the continuing cry of the imams all signal a moment of quiet epiphany (Figure 6.11). Nejat is realizing that he cannot let one foolish act by his father, how-

6.11
Epiphany:
Surrogate
mother
and son.

ever heinous its consequences, sever their relationship. As Susanne has found it in her heart to forgive Ayten, so he must forgive Ali. The cruelty of death must make us all the more charitable toward the living. Hence the film's final scene shows him arriving in Trabzon and sitting down on the beach to await his father's return from fishing.

Conclusion

This ending does not really bring the story to a close, since many details remain unresolved, including Nejat's search for Ayten. Of course this goal may yet be achieved. After all, he is likely to return to his bookshop in a few days and find Susanne and Ayten there—Ayten who can now use her real name. Equally likely, Ayten might well reestablish contact with her family who would surely tell her of her mother's death and of Nejat's search for her. Akin might easily have tied up all the threads in a "happy ending," and it is indicative that he does not. For one thing, this reminds us that lives are always uncertain: Ayten's former comrades might decide to exact revenge for her renouncing them. And while Susanne may seek to fulfill the mother's role and nurture this new daughter, bridging the cultural divides will not be easy. A neat happy ending would also tend to erase the pain of the human loss foregrounded in all the stories. If these characters do succeed in finding happiness now, it comes at a high price.

Nonetheless, the final shot of Nejat sitting at the edge of the sea is a wonderful close. Andreas Michel notes that protagonists in motion constitute "one of the defining features of Fatih Akin's movies,"[12] and Nejat has been associated throughout with movement, opening on his journey to Trabzon. He comes to Bremen on the train, walks to his father's home, walks in Hamburg, rides on the trolley with Yeter, and rides back to Hamburg after quarreling with his father. Searching for Ayten, he arrives in the airport in Istanbul and then wanders the streets putting up posters. Finally, he is shown driving into Trabzon, his father's village. Classic filmmaking often inserts moments of characters arriving or departing to smooth the transition between scenes, but Akin is using them in a strongly thematic way. These constant shots of Nejat in motion suggest a search for something missing in his life. Further, his journeys have always been accompanied by music, as with the song of Kazim Koyuncu in the opening. Now there is nothing but the splash of waves, emphasizing that Nejat has simply stopped, ceasing his forward rush, able to enjoy the beauty spread before him and the prospect of seeing his father (Figure 6.12). The viewer has a similar sense of arrival, brought full circle by the susurrus ocean sounds heard in the beginning. The tranquil scene shown in a long take, the relaxed way Nejat settles himself on the sand, and the gentle lap of the waves create a sense of life coming momentarily to rest. Given the pain that has marked the lives of these characters, one of the film's messages is to treasure such moments. We should be aware of the other sides of life—the people from different cultures, the loved ones we take for granted, and the moments of closeness to nature—all too easily overlooked.

6.12 Reconciled: Nejat awaiting his father.

Afterword on Narrative Structure

Akin has used **network narrative** in its prototypical form, emphasizing the interconnection of people, and has done so with especial brilliance. In contrast to a film like *Babel*, where an overly symbolic rifle ends up linking widely disparate people in relatively improbable ways, here the connections are natural and believable. The characters inhabit the same spaces which, nonetheless, represent significantly different realities. In the course of the story, they, like the viewers, peer into these other worlds, although (as Susanne warns her daughter) they do not always see clearly. Nejat may first be credulous of Yeter's motives in becoming his father's companion, but then discovers the maternal warmth underneath her toughness. Similarly, Lotte may take an overly romanticized view of Ayten and Susanne an overly cynical one. The brutal reality of Ayten's former life comes crashing in on Lotte when she appropriates the gun, and her death in turn upends Susanne's staid view of the world. Akin's characters—three parents and three children—are credible because they exhibit tensions typical of that most intimate relationship. The focus on parent-child relationships intensifies the film's emotional charge and tightens the story's interconnections. It makes the film's ending, with Susanne greeting her adoptive daughter and Nejat waiting to reconcile with his father, particularly satisfying. All the conflicts are resolved during the Feast of Bayram, which says family ties are inviolable and human life is sacred.

Akin also moves very adroitly through time as he interweaves the separate story strands. The viewer is first introduced to Nejat embarked on his journey and wonders what has impelled it and where it will lead. The story then loops back to Ali and Yeter, brings Nejat in again, and after the death of Yeter sends him to Istanbul in search of Ayten. It loops back again to pick up Ayten, brings her to Germany to meet Lotte, and then both girls end up back in Turkey. Finally, Susanne in her turn is brought to Istanbul to find Ayten again, meet Nejat, and—through her question about Bayram—send him off to Trabzon to rebond with his father.[13] By tracing these independent story lines and then weaving them together at the end, the film creates a real hope that even the most shattered lives can be rebuilt. The network narrative is particularly effective because, in very simple interactions, the characters each impact momentously on the others. Yeter's death sends Nejat back to the homeland of his parents in a move that simultaneously starts him on a new career. Lotte's encounter with Ayten kindles her youthful fervor for adventure—a fervor she likely inherited from her mother—but which has tragic consequences. Lotte's death reawakens Susanne's compassion, which in turn helps free Ayten from the prison of her radical beliefs. Susanne's great loss makes Nejat rethink the denial of his father. These tightly interwoven stories argue that we should be aware of the brutal transience of human existence and treasure those closest to us. They also argue that one person's compassion can work miracles, that even people thrown together by chance can help others see more clearly. With his heart opened once more, Nejat can sit on the tranquil beach and keep watch for his father, content to be perched on the edge of heaven.

Notes

1 Polana Petek, "Enabling Collisions: Re-thinking Multiculturalism through Fatih Akin's *Gegen die Wand/Head On*," *Studies in European Cinema* 4, no. 3 (November 2007), 179.

2 Tuncay Kulaoglu, "Der neue 'deutsche' Film ist 'türkisch'? Eine neue Generation bringt Leben in die Filmlandschaft," *Filmforum* 16 (February/March 1999): 8-11.

3 Daniela Berghahn, "No Place Like Home? Or Impossible Homecomings in the Films of Fatih Akin," *New Cinemas: Journal of Contemporary Film* 4, no. 3 (2006): 141.

4 Randall Halle, *German Film after Germany: Toward a Transnational Aesthetic* (Urbana: University of Illinois Press, 2008), 164.

5 Boyd van Hoeij, "Auf der anderen Seite," 25 May 2007, www.european-films.net/content/view/740/118 (3 February 2009).

6 Burak Sansal, "Turkish Jareed (Javelin)," All About Turkey, www.allaboutturkey.com/javelin.htm (15 September 2009).

7 Ann Hornaday, "'Edge of Heaven' Comes Close to Perfection," *Washington Post* (20 June 2008): C01.

8 Maras was another sad moment in Turkish history, when more than a hundred people of the Alevi minority were killed by their Sunni neighbors. Women in the Alevi sect have a much more respected status than in other Moslem branches, which may account for Yeter's greater independence.

9 Abdullah Öcalan was leader of the Kurdistan Workers Party, the PKK, which began armed conflict with Turkey in 1984, trying to create an independent Kurdistan. He was captured in 1999 and has been held since then in solitary confinement on Imrali Island. However, this is just one group of protesters among many and the film is careful not to link Ayten with a particular movement as the DVD commentary makes clear.

10 Fatih Akin comments on the DVD that this recreates a real incident, captured on video, from May Day in 1996 in Istanbul where left-wing extremists nearly beat a policeman to death. The director was horrified that people could be this stupidly brutal, pouncing on an unknown person merely because someone yells out that he's a cop. These images lingered with him for years and ultimately "gave rise to Ayten's [narrative] arc: the politics of a violence-prone activist lead to her lover's death." "The Making of *The Edge of Heaven*," DVD featurette (Corazón International, 2007).

11 "Eid al-Adha," www.islam.about.com/of/hajj/a/adha.htm (23 July 2009).

12 Andreas Michel, "The Two-Fold Outsider as Insider: German Turks in the Movies of Fatih Akin," in *Selected Papers: 2008 Conference. Society for the Interdisciplinary Study of Social Imagery*, Will Wright and Steven Kaplan, eds. (Pueblo: University of Southern Colorado, 2008), 378.

13 One notes a possible cultural bias in the film, with rigidity and rejection linked to Germany and acceptance associated with Turkey.

Database

Narrative

7

Virgin Stripped Bare by Her Bachelors

The End of Idealism

Korea's film industry became increasingly vital in the 1960s, but its films had primarily local appeal and flew under the international critical radar. Then in 1989 Bae Yong-Kyun's film *Why Has Bodhi-Dharma Left for the East?* won the Golden Leopard award at the Locarno Film Festival. As the quality of Korean films became recognized, a spate of new critical studies appeared and the films of directors such as Kim Ki-duk (*Samaritan Girl*, 2004; *3-Iron*, 2004), Bong Joon-ho (*The Host*, 2006), and Kim Jee-woon (*The Good, the Bad, the Weird*, 2008) were able to obtain international distribution. Another notable director is Hong Sangsoo, whose first feature, *The Day a Pig Fell into the Well* (1996), was called "a gunshot that shook Korean film history [sic.]" by *Cine 21*.[1] Hong's opaque style has prevented him from attracting a wide popular following, but critics and cinephiles have taken note. He has released eleven films as of 2011, several of which, including *Woman Is the Future of Man* (2004), *Tale of Cinema* (2005), and *Hahaha* (2010) were invited to the Cannes festival. David Bordwell classifies Hong's work as coming out of the new "Asian minimalists," his films typified by long takes, a distanced camera, "mundane story action and loosely structured plot," that deliberately run counter to the flashy camerawork and spasmodic editing of popular genres. "The plainness of presentation obliges us to concentrate on details of behavior that might reveal what is going on below the surface of the action."[2]

Story Summary

Hong's third feature, *Virgin Stripped Bare by Her Bachelors*[3] (Korean title: *Oh, Soojung!* [2000]) has a relatively simple story. Set in contemporary Seoul, it tells of a young girl, Soojung (Lee Eun-ju), courted by Jaehoon (Jeong Bo-seok), a well-to-do art gallery owner. Jaehoon is the one-time friend of Soojung's boss, Youngsoo (Mun Seong-kun), a minor filmmaker. The story is broken into five distinct sections, with sections I, III, and V set in the present and relatively short in duration. In Section I, Jaehoon is on the phone at a "love hotel" trying to persuade a reluctant Soojung to join him and consummate their affair as she had agreed. In III, her arrival is delayed when a power outage strands her on a cable car. In V, she arrives, surrenders her virginity in a scene terribly painful to witness, and the film ends with them discussing their marriage plans. Sections II and IV are extended flashbacks, giving two versions of the courtship that has led up to their meeting at the hotel, with many scenes that overlap but with differing details. Section II ("Perhaps Coincidence") presents something that may be Jaehoon's version of events, although it is not specifically told from his point of view—there is no voiceover, for example—and he is not present to witness some of the events portrayed. Section IV ("Perhaps Intention") seems to be told more from Soojung's perspective, although again no specific indicators point to her as the narrator. Puzzled by these narrative obfuscations, the viewer is further put off by Hong's sparse film style using long takes, an extremely static camera, abrupt editing, and a dry sound track, with brief bits of incongruous nondiegetic music over the titles and between major sections.

Like *Run Lola Run* and *The Double Life of Véronique*, *Virgin* is a **database** (or **multiple-draft**) narrative, emphasizing the contrasts found in alternate versions of the same story. But it is a more radical variant. In a simple **forking paths** narrative, the same character undertakes two or more clearly separate journeys. In *Virgin*, the paths simultaneously overlap and diverge, are the same and different, and the resulting contradictions leave the viewer unable to construct a coherent view of reality. Hong's film thus is antipodal to the **network narratives** discussed in prior chapters, most of which show lives connected in subtle ways. Even *Code Unknown*, which shows people failing to communicate, is less despairing than *Virgin* which proposes that they live in disconnected realities. And where other multi-plot films generally support the assumption that human lives have significance, *Virgin Stripped Bare* casts severe doubt on that premise. The directionless lives of its protagonists, their lack of self-awareness, and their failure to connect with one another portray human existence as potentially meaningless, a view reinforced by the circular and uncertain narrative structure. Finally, where other multiple-draft narratives arrive ultimately at a "satisfactory" or "best" outcome, in this case the conclusion—the loss of Soojung's virginity—is highly unsatisfactory. Unlike *Groundhog Day*, where the play with alternative realities is comic, here it is sobering.

Narrative Conundrums

Narratives routinely throw in puzzles which maintain viewer interest as they are gradually cleared up. Hong Sangsoo's narrative obfuscations, however, almost rival those of avant-garde filmmakers, refusing to yield a totally comprehensible story. The two long flashback sections are each divided into seven numbered segments that cover seven different days. As Marshall Deutelbaum astutely points out, while some of the days are the same in the two versions, not all seven are. His outline has events taking place over eight days[4] and a closer reading indicates there are actually nine. Rather than providing careful temporal clues, Hong deliberately confuses the viewer. Some of the apparent contradictions in the two versions turn out to be illusory, but others stubbornly resist reconciliation.

The first set of conflicting scenes occurs as Jaehoon joins Youngsoo and Soojung outside his gallery. (Apparently Soojung has just met Jaehoon for the first time, but that scene is never shown.) In Jaehoon's version of this first day, the three talk briefly and then head off to lunch, but in Soojung's version Jaehoon's chauffeur shows up before they leave. Jaehoon says he won't need him anymore, gives him money for lunch, and, as the three protagonists depart, the camera holds on the chauffeur, emphasizing his importance (Figure 7.1). Deutelbaum proposes

7.1
Jaehoon's
chauffeur:
There or
not?

that giving money to the chauffeur is of no importance to Jaehoon so he forgets to include that detail, but Soojung notices. It makes Jaehoon appear casually generous in contrast to Youngsoo's later stinginess with Park, his assistant.[5] Having a chauffeur and handing out money freely also mark him as an eminently suitable marriage prospect. While the presence or absence of the chauffeur can thus be explained by characters focusing on different details, it already establishes the idea that reality differs for each person.

Another subtle difference appears in this same scene. In Jaehoon's version, the three characters have difficulty deciding about lunch. Youngsoo and Soojung can't remember if they've eaten and the three of them talk indecisively before finally walking off. Jaehoon's section is entitled "Perhaps Coincidence," reflecting his view that things happen by chance and this version might embody his sense that he just *happened* to go to lunch with Soojung the first time. In Soojung's version Jaehoon emerges from his gallery, says, "Shall we go?" and they head immediately to the restaurant. Her simpler version might suggest her more focused view of the world but also might reflect some bias, seeing Jaehoon as more decisive than he is in actuality. This opening introduces a problem that will continue throughout the film: each character presents a subjective view of events and of the other characters. Hence it is unclear which version of events is correct, what the differences signify, and how the essence of the characters is to be defined.

Uncertain Portraits

There are two versions of the ensuing meal and Jaehoon's unwittingly reveals that he and Youngsoo are men whose dreams have collapsed. Hong's characters are often failed intellectuals and artists[6] and that seems to be the case here. As he respectfully pours a drink for Youngsoo, Jaehoon says, "You should start painting again," but Youngsoo, picking a speck of some sort from Soojung's hair, does not hear him. When Jaehoon repeats his comment, Youngsoo snorts derisively, and asks Jaehoon, "What about you?" The latter says he goes to his studio once a week, at which point Youngsoo abruptly switches the topic to ask about Jaehoon's brother. This desultory exchange deftly unmasks the two men. Since both are former artists, presumably having met in art school, and since Youngsoo spent the morning touring an exhibit in Jaehoon's gallery, one would expect animated conversation about the paintings, other recent shows, or favorite artists, but there is nothing of the sort. Youngsoo's preoccupation with hair lint, his derisive snort, and his abrupt change of topic make it clear how little interest he has in art. And if Jaehoon only finds time to paint once a week, he has obviously become a dilettante. (He is never shown at the gallery or his studio.)

Viewers might well miss this picture of quiet failure because the two versions of the meal highlight a jarring contradiction. In Jaehoon's version, he rushes away to the washroom, leaving Youngsoo and Soojung to talk. In Soojung's version, it is Youngsoo who rushes away, leaving her to talk with Jaehoon. Deutelbaum reconciles the contradiction by observing that the two scenes take place at different points in the meal. In Jaehoon's version a pair of diners can be seen in the background whereas in Soojung's version the table behind is empty and the dirty dishes are being cleared away (Figures 7.2 and 7.3).[7] The later time is

7.2
First meal
with
Jaehoon
absent.

7.3
Same
meal,
with
Jaehoon
present
(but at a
later time).

also indicated by the sunlight slanting at a sharper angle on the wall. This blatant contrast overshadows a more subtle but very important difference: the differing conversations about Jaehoon's brother. In Jaehoon's version, when Youngsoo asks about him, Jaehoon responds, "He thinks there's only one way to live, just his way. Nobody can get through to him." Despite his quiet voice, one can imagine the frustration felt by a man whose life is controlled by an elder sibling. The bottled-up emotion is signaled by Jaehoon's rushing off to the toilet a moment later, seemingly nauseated. Youngsoo remarks, "It's probably his stomach," hinting that Jaehoon's frustrations may be manifesting themselves physically. As Soojung relates the conversation, however, Youngsoo asks why he doesn't move out of his brother's house and Jaehoon responds, "I respect my brother. He's a good person. There's a lot to learn from him, in a practical way." Even assuming, as Deutelbaum proposes, that this remark occurs later in the evening, Soojung remembers a response that puts Jaehoon in a more favorable light, showing respect for his elder brother and a more secure sense of self-worth.

If Jaehoon's version perhaps exaggerates the frustration he feels, Soojung's may betray her prejudice toward a man who is single and financially well off. Hence the "truth" of Jaehoon's character is difficult to determine.

Soojung's Character

Although viewers are likely to find Soojung attractive, her character also is difficult to pin down. This can be seen in her second meeting with Jaehoon, this time on the grounds of Kyongbokgoong Palace, located across the street from Jaehoon's gallery. As he strolls its grounds, Jaehoon spots a film crew working there and then unexpectedly meets Soojung. To his surprise, she is carrying the gloves he accidentally left on a bench while eating lunch there earlier. Pleased to see her, he exclaims: "What a coincidence!" (Again, he assumes everything happens by chance, as his section title suggests.) Not surprisingly, Jaehoon presents himself as perceptive and in control. In his version, he spots the gloves in Soojung's hand, whereas in her version she pulls them from her pocket and asks if they might be his. Similarly, where his version begins with him remarking, "You must be here with the crew," her version has him asking, "What brings you here?" and her replying, "I'm here with the crew." Her version, then casts doubts upon Jaehoon's self-flattering picture of himself.

More important, however, are the contrasting pictures of Soojung. In Jaehoon's version, she comes across as quite shy, reflecting his view of her throughout as reticent and virginal. As he portrays it, she approaches slowly on the path, eyes down, and stops several paces away. Greeting him, she ducks her head slightly and touches her face and then her hair nervously. She clutches the gloves to her chest in both hands, as if for protection. Although she smiles from time to time, after handing him the gloves she stands quietly but uncomfortably, hands folded, weaving and unweaving her fingers, and only makes eye contact at brief moments as they talk (Figure 7.4). Toward the end of the conversation, she stuffs her hands in her pockets, and hunches her shoulders as if to cover herself further. At the end, she glances off nervously in the direction of the crew, says she has to go, and hurries off after a quick bow. Her speech patterns and body movements suggest a quiet, rather timid girl.

Soojung's version presents a more relaxed, effusive person. She appears initially in a closer screen position, making her less diminutive in the frame, and strolls forward in relaxed fashion, hands in pockets, smiling openly at Jaehoon. Her increased energy and openness are accentuated by the brighter lighting on her coat and the fact that she arrives in front of him in six seconds compared to twelve the first time. She looks directly at Jaehoon throughout the conversation and when he identifies the gloves as his, she laughs happily. She talks in animated fashion, swings her body casually, and looks around brightly (Figure 7.5).

7.4
Jaehoon's
picture of
Soojung
as shy.

She is equally balanced with Jaehoon in the frame in contrast to the first version where she was pushed against the right edge. In that version, the conversation ended with Jaehoon calling after her to say thank-you; here, she teases him: "Don't lose them again, OK?" Also, where the first scene ended with her scurrying off to rejoin the crew, this time she glances in that direction but remains with Jaehoon, suggesting her interest in prolonging the conversation. Throughout, she seems far more self-confident.

7.5
Soojung's
picture of
herself as
outgoing.

Furthermore, Soojung's version of events includes a scene immediately preceding their meeting that throws new light on her character. In it, she is riding in the van with Youngsoo's camera crew looking for a place to film and she persistently argues that the palace grounds would be the best place, even though farther away than other sites being proposed. Then when the two meet, Jaehoon casually remarks, "I think I told you that I come here almost every day to eat lunch." Armed with these facts, the viewer smiles as Soojung exclaims, "What a coincidence!" when the gloves turn out to be Jaehoon's, for she knows full well it was not coincidence at all. She has done her best to ensure they would meet again. This background inclines the viewer to trust Soojung's version of events, at least in this case, for she possesses knowledge that Jaehoon lacks. Equally critical, however, is the fact that the film itself remains assiduously neutral. The camera's treatment of Soojung and her acting performance have been sharply different, but neither version has been marked as being the "correct" one. If Jaehoon's version possibly reflects his desire to see Soojung as an idealized, virginal girl, hers might also be biased, portraying herself as more outgoing and confident than she is in reality. The viewer has no way to know which is the real Soojung.

Youngsoo

In some cases the conflicting narratives do finally combine to create a relatively unified picture of reality. This is particularly true when Soojung's narrative, coming later, fills in critical details lacking in Jaehoon's, as in the palace meeting which she helped to facilitate. As Bordwell points out, in forking paths narratives the final version of events generally carries the most weight. "All paths are not equal; the last one taken, or completed, is the least hypothetical one."[8] While *Virgin* is an atypical forking paths narrative in many ways, it is still true that Soojung's version, coming second, often seems more credible. In some cases, internal evidence clearly favors her version, notably true when Youngsoo quarrels with his assistant, Park. In Jaehoon's version, he and Soojung witness Park rushing up to confront his boss outside the film office. He chastises Youngsoo—who called the crew in but did no shooting—and demands that he buy them all lunch. Youngsoo brushes him aside and hurries off with Jaehoon and Soojung, his stinginess contrasting with Jaehoon's generosity with his chauffeur.[9] Later that day, Jaehoon and Soojung are present in the office when Youngsoo, on the phone, fires Park when he refuses to come in the next day after having wasted this one. Park is heard cursing and telling Youngsoo to stay put at the office.

Some time later, as Jaehoon and Soojung wait in a nearby restaurant, Park storms into the office to confront Youngsoo. The filmmaker gets up, looking embarrassed, and says softly, "I'm sorry. I'm really sorry." He continues to apologize, holding out his hand, but as the scene closes, Park has refused to take it. In a brief coda, Youngsoo joins Jaehoon and Soojung at the restaurant and, when Soojung asks him how it went with Park, says, "I was too thoughtless. . . . It was my mistake." In Jaehoon's version, then, Youngsoo deals rashly with a key member of his production team but smooths things over and redeems himself by admitting his fault. However, this impression is suspect. Although the office scene between Park and Youngsoo is shown to the viewer as "reality," Jaehoon was not present to witness it, so one must assume this version represents his impression of events from what Youngsoo told them later. Notably, Hong does not mark the scene as subjective narration. (A Hollywood film would have been careful to do so, perhaps showing the scene without story sound but with Youngsoo narrating it in voiceover to make it clear that this is *his version* of events.) In Hong's film, *all* narration is subjective and hence suspect to a degree.

In this case, Soojung's version of the event is far more credible since it turns out that, unknown to Youngsoo, she was an unseen witness to the confrontation. Her version shows her ducking out of the restaurant and into the film office, where she listens unobserved in the corridor as the two men argue. Park thoroughly humiliates Youngsoo—cursing him, slapping him repeatedly, and calling him a loser who's gotten his position because he's related to the boss. He finishes by saying that if he catches Youngsoo fooling around with "the fucking bitch" in the editing room he'll kill them both. (This threat is particularly ominous given that Youngsoo had kissed Soojung that very morning as they were editing.) Soojung then tiptoes away, ending the scene. As Deutelbaum notes, in Jaehoon's version she is careful to ask Youngsoo at the restaurant how the meeting with Park went. Her "disturbed look," listening to him lie about what happened, "shows her certain understanding of Youngsoo's ethical character."[10]

Although both versions of the scene have been presented as "real," Soojung's carries more weight since the camera shows her present to observe it. Furthermore, the particular manner of filming emphasizes her presence. In Jaehoon's version, the confrontation begins with the camera looking down the empty office corridor, picking up Park as he storms in the door, and panning right as he rounds the corner to confront Youngsoo (Figure 7.6). It remains in that position until the scene ends. In Soojung's version, the camera begins in the same position, this time showing Soojung tiptoeing in to overhear the argument already in progress (Figure 7.7).

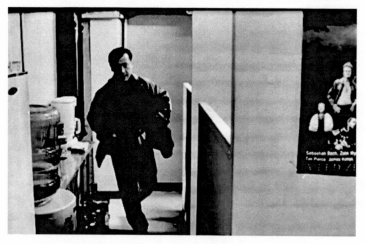

7.6
Park
enters
to confront
Youngsoo.

7.7
Soojung
enters to
overhear
the
confronta-
tion.

The camera pans right to show the majority of the confrontation and then pans left to show Soojung tiptoeing back out. The exact similarity of camera position and especially the panning are notable in a film where the camera seldom moves. Had the camera panned left in Jaehoon's version it would have shown Soojung present. It fails to do so because Youngsoo was unaware she was there, marking this as his point of view, passed on to Jaehoon. Although the viewer feels more confident in resolving the contradictions in this scene, Hong is reminding us that people constantly reshape reality to put themselves in a good light. Since the portrait of each character is filtered through the eyes and memory of another character, all the portraits become suspect. In most stories with an unreliable narrator, enough hints are provided so the truth of events can be determined. In *Virgin*, however, there are *two* unreliable narrators presenting stories frequently at odds, making it difficult to construct an accurate picture of their world and those around them.

Character Opacity

Clearer psychological insight into the three main characters would make it easier to sort out the reality of events, but motives are only hinted at and it seems likely that the people themselves have little conscious understanding of why they act as they do. The character most clearly drawn is Youngsoo whose prevarication about the argument with Park portrays him negatively. He appears just as negative in the scenes of the birthday party to which he drags Soojung, where she finds Jaehoon, whom she has begun secretly dating, already in attendance. In Jaehoon's version, Youngsoo shows up (apparently uninvited) and quickly begins to avail himself of the available food and drink, especially the latter. Later, with several drinks under his belt, Youngsoo deliberately insults Jaehoon and then demands that

Soojung sit beside him. "Pour a drink for your boss, the producer." She has little choice but to comply, Jaehoon leaves the room, and the other party goers fall silent at his rude behavior. In Soojung's version, things are even worse. Very drunk, Youngsoo bonks his head on her shoulder and berates her: "You told me to quit, that I'd be able to find another job." (She may well have suggested such a thing, given his lack of enthusiasm for filmmaking.) Both versions agree on Youngsoo's boorishness, with Soojung's version hinting more strongly at the embarrassment she must have felt—dragged to a party of well-to-do people, all strangers to her, and then humiliated in front of the man she has started dating.

In this instance, Soojung's version throws some light on Youngsoo's behavior because it includes a preceding scene of the two of them at a restaurant. There he had pressured her to confess that she was secretly dating Jaehoon and she had learned that, after promising to finance a film, Jaehoon was no longer returning Youngsoo's calls. Leaving the restaurant, Youngsoo had dragged her down an alley, saying he had something funny to show her, pulled her into a room and stripped her pants off. She had to fight resolutely to stop him from going further. To make matters worse, when she accused him of trying to rape her, he responded scornfully, "Rape, my foot!" even though she had not encouraged him in any way. The scene ended with her comforting him as he cried in her arms—the rapist become a baby. While not excusing Youngsoo's boorish behavior at the party, this background explains his frustration at Jaehoon for welshing on his promise to finance a film and, worse, threatening to steal away the pretty assistant Youngsoo lusts after.

The ultimate picture of Youngsoo is of a shrunken human being. With others present, he makes a great show of his authority by firing Park for insubordination. Then, alone with Park, he allows himself to be humiliated and doesn't respond to his accusations, suggesting their truthfulness. Married with two daughters, he makes repeated attempts to seduce Soojung, beginning with taking time off to squire her to Jaehoon's art gallery. However, his seduction efforts are no more successful than his artistic ones. He clumsily dominates Soojung, picking lint out of her hair at the restaurant and making her sit beside him at the party. Even after she confesses timidly that she once had a crush on him and allows him to kiss her in the editing room, his response is a crude attempt at rape. Youngsoo, in sum, seems mostly persona, his repeated scenes of drunkenness testifying to his own self-loathing. He is not a villain, but rather, like so many of Hong's characters, a quiet failure.

Opacity Continues

If Youngsoo's character is clarified somewhat by the events of the birthday party, those of Jaehoon and Soojung are not. A particular problem is still another restaurant scene, this time with just the two of them. In Soojung's version, this scene precedes the party, but in Jaehoon's it comes afterward. In both versions they neck passionately, but in his version (on the day labeled "5") a fork falls off the table as they embrace. In her version (on the day labeled "4"), they knock a spoon off. As Deutelbaum observes, this discrepancy is easily explained because the events occur on different days (already hinted at by the differing segment numbers): the table setting is not the same and the hostess comments that they are frequent patrons these days.[11] Hong, unhelpful as always, conceals this difference by using precisely the same camera placement, the same booth, and the same costuming in both scenes. Beyond the trivial differences, however, there is a critical discrepancy. Jaehoon's version ends with the two of them necking and nothing more. Soojung's version ends with him saying he wants to go to bed with her and her consenting, saying, "Let's do it somewhere really nice." He proposes going to Cheju Island (a fancy resort area) and she agrees. In her version of events, then, this conversation signals a moment of commitment to one another and occurs *before* the birthday. However, in his version it occurs in the scene at Kojan which, significantly, occurs *after* the birthday party. That, in turn, affects how each of them would view the events at the party.

Since, as Jaehoon remembers it, there is no commitment between them yet—they are only dating casually—his behavior at the birthday party is understandable. Undoubtedly displeased to see Youngsoo barge into the party with the girl he has started seeing, when Youngsoo insults him he simply leaves the table, avoiding a confrontation but signaling his displeasure to Soojung. From Soojung's point of view (although none of this is ever stated) the man who has previously committed himself to her abandons her to suffer through the scene with Youngsoo. To make matters worse, her version of the party contains subsequent moments where, as Youngsoo harangues her, the camera shows Jaehoon necking with the birthday girl in the next room. Soojung thereupon leaves the party. If her version of events is accepted, she has every reason to feel betrayed by the man who previously pledged his love to her. The fact that such an important moment is remembered occurring on two entirely different occasions shows how difficult it is to pin down reality in the film.

Jaehoon

Soojung's view of Jaehoon may be positively biased in some regards—in the first scene she remembers him as generous to the chauffeur and decisive in setting a lunch goal, for example. Nevertheless, enough details emerge to yield a portrait that is far from flattering. Early in their relationship, he (like Youngsoo) pulls Soojung into an alley to see "something funny." Then he grabs her and kisses her forcefully, causing her to shove him away. Possibly regretting his behavior, he takes her to a restaurant and proposes starting "a serious relationship." She refuses at this point, but some days later lets him kiss her in a park and says, "I liked that." This picture of Jaehoon as a gentle suitor continues as he brings her to his apartment. He goes to take a shower, wanting to be clean before they cuddle on the bed, and is shown for a moment, naked on the edge of the bathtub. His sitting there pensively, rather than rushing back to join her, suggests that he is not a suave seducer but someone hesitant and shy. In the petting session that follows, she allows him to put his hand under her sweater but will not let him unfasten her slacks, saying, "I've never done this before," and adds, "I'm a virgin." Jaehoon stops and sits up, saying "Really?" He smiles and reaches out to cup her face tenderly. The scene ends on that protective gesture. Although the petting intensifies in subsequent scenes, Jaehoon's version of the courtship (Section II) ends with him proposing to take her to "the most expensive room in Cheju Island," and then embracing her, saying, "I love you." In his version of events, then, Jaehoon comes across as a shy, smitten swain, the only dark spots on his character being his initial clumsy embrace in the alley and his drunken ranting at her in a park after the birthday party, which can perhaps be excused by his jealousy of Youngsoo.

As always there is another side. Jaehoon's astonishment at Soojung's virginity suggests he is attracted to that attribute rather than to her character. They pet in a number of scenes, but there is never any serious conversation or sense of emotional connection. This is emphasized in yet another restaurant scene where Jaehoon, Youngsoo, and Soojung are drinking together. After asking Soojung for "a big smile," suggesting he is most interested in surface appearance, Jaehoon mumbles a question about Soojung's blood type. She says she's type B and asks, "What's B type supposed to be like?" Jaehoon says he doesn't know, he just wanted to ask. In other words, his query was not intended to reveal anything serious about her, but was simply an idle, drunken question. The superficiality of his affection is suggested most ominously in their later argument in a hotel room at Kojan. While petting there, he unwittingly calls out another woman's name, causing Soojung to flee. When he finds her some time later, he rants, "Is this as if I committed murder? What's so important about a name?" This shows that, when thwarted, his response is to throw a temper tantrum. More seriously, he refuses to acknowledge how much he must have hurt Soojung in calling out another woman's name in the midst of lovemaking. To say that names are not important is to argue that women are interchangeable and hence his professed commitment to Soojung might easily be transferred to someone else.

The ultimate picture of Jaehoon is of someone sadly infantile. His immaturity is shown most dramatically in his journey to Kojan. Eating lunch at the palace restaurant as usual (showing him a creature of habit), he phones Soojung and learns

7.8
Jaehoon:
Lost
without
his
chauffeur.

she is at Kojan (a nearby suburb), and he has no idea where it is or how to get there. She tells him to take the subway and he is seen in the station studying the route maps in total befuddlement (Figure 7.8). As Adam Hartzell notes, "Jae Hoon, forever chauffeured around, is as unfamiliar with a train map as he is with a circuit schematic."[12] On the train, he sits staring glumly ahead, showing not the least curiosity about the passing landscape. Once with Soojung, he shows smug delight in the CD player he has bought her, but is totally unfamiliar with the Western music she is listening to, further suggesting his insularity. As always, he is very conscious of "correct" behavior, pointing out the proper way to hold chopsticks when he takes her to dinner. He does this gently and says Soojung can continue to hold them as she likes "for now," but the suggestion is clear that ultimately she will need to conform to his way of doing things. Finally, the Kojan hotel scene in his version ends, not with an argument, but with the two of them in a tender embrace, having agreed to finally make love in the most expensive room at Cheju. In this episode, Jaehoon tries to present himself as the ideal lover—faithfully following his beloved to distant realms, buying her presents and then, although rebuffed in the hotel, offering to take her to a lovely resort to consummate their love affair—a self-portrait that is entirely too smug. Without his realizing it, his story reveals a shallow mind, a drearily circumscribed life, and an insipid concept of romance.

Soojung's Sexuality

Of the three main characters, Soojung is the most sympathetic—perceptive, sweet, and treated very shabbily by the men. However, her sexuality complicates the image of her. Jaehoon obviously sees her as a shy, virginal young woman, and in his versions of the various lovemaking scenes, she consistently resists his advances, fending off his attempts to put his hand up her skirt or remove her slacks.

Only in the hotel room at Kojan does she finally relent and agree to make love at Cheju. Even in this scene, Jaehoon portrays her as sexually passive, lying on her back quietly as he suckles her breasts. Her only response is to cradle his head and kiss the side of his face, actions more maternal than sexual.

The film's final brutal scene of Soojung's deflowering makes it evident that she is technically a virgin, for it is extremely painful and she bleeds profusely, but earlier events in her version of the story reveal a person not entirely innocent. In a stunning coda to the first day's dinner, Soojung arrives home and climbs into bed, only to be accosted by her older brother who wants her to masturbate him. She tries to resist but he gives her no peace until she relents and gives him a quick, grumpy hand job. Later, when she first goes to Jaehoon's apartment, she secretly strips off her bra while he is showering, making herself more available to him, even though his version stresses her hesitance. The same contrast is found in the two scenes of her necking with Jaehoon at the restaurant. In his version, he is the aggressor, knocking the fork off the table as he kisses her (Figure 7.9), but in her

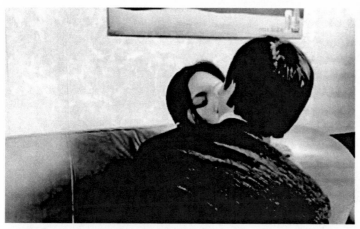

7.9
Restaurant
scene #1:
Jaehoon
takes the
lead.

version she is far more active. The kissing is more passionate, she looks dazed, and when Jaehoon pants, "I want to suck your whole body," she agrees to sleep with him at Cheju. Then she begins the next round of kissing and ends by climbing into his lap, knocking off the spoon in the process (Figure 7.10). The fact that different utensils fall to the floor in the two scenes is far less significant than who is portrayed as the sexual aggressor. Finally, where his version of the Kojan hotel room has her resisting him repeatedly, her version portrays her as far more passionate. She permits Jaehoon's hand to move freely under her skirt—he portrayed her as resisting any incursion into that territory—and is visibly aroused. Rather than lying inert, she pants, closes her eyes, and pulls her sweater up to allow him freer access to her breasts. Her passion is suggested by a closer camera position and she seems on the verge of yielding to him until his blurting out "Junga" ruins everything.

7.10
Restaurant
scene #2:
Soojung
takes the
lead.

Soojung's version presents a much more sexualized woman, an image that may be closer to the truth but may equally well represent her vision of the liberated woman she wishes she could be. The viewer cannot be sure.

In fact, when she had been working with Youngsoo earlier in the editing room and he had leaned over and kissed her, she had allowed the kiss to go on for a long time. Afterward, she had admitted that she went twice to a motel with a close friend to try intercourse as an experiment, but failed: "It hurt so much, and it didn't feel right." This story further complicates the picture of Soojung. While she did not bring on Youngsoo's initial kiss by flirting with him, she does not resist and admits she once had a crush on him. On the other hand, her confession is spoken shyly and hesitantly. When she says, "I like kissing. I really like kissing," the picture that comes across is of a young girl who enjoys romance and tenderness, but is nervous about venturing too far. She seems unsure how to deal with her own sexual feelings or reconcile them with traditional Korean views of female modesty. With Soojung as well as all the characters, the viewer finds it is difficult to construct a clear image, most likely because none of them is entirely sure who he wishes to be.

Kojan

The idea of a unified reality breaks down entirely in the two versions of Soojung's trip to Kojan to visit a friend and Jaehoon's following her there. Many other apparent differences in the two narratives can be resolved, but this incident defies reconciliation. Jaehoon's version tells of his train trip to Kojan, giving Soojung a CD player, eating at a restaurant, and then going to a hotel. When he tries to consummate their affair, she says she's having her period but agrees to rendezvous at Cheju and they end up in an embrace, saying "I love you." Soojung's version is completely different. Instead of the CD player and the restaurant, she recalls him dragging her out onto a frozen lake with ominously cracking ice.

Most critically, in her version of the hotel scene, the lovemaking comes to an abrupt end when he calls out the name of another woman, causing her to shove him away, grab her coat, and march out of the room. Outside, she runs off, and he searches for her in vain, finally sinking onto a bench, his face desolate. At this point she slowly walks in and stands by him, hands in her pockets. He launches into a diatribe, telling her how frantic he was: "I really thought I would go crazy!" When he finally subsides, she gently touches his face and sits down beside him, both of them now smiling.

The startling differences in these versions cannot be reconciled by having occurred at different days or times as in some of the other scenes. There can only have been one encounter at Kojan: the characters wear the same clothing and the hotel room is precisely the same, even to the placement of the glassware on the table. Where most films center on physical and psychological conflicts, *Virgin* proposes conflict at an entirely new level: the narrative itself. In effect, the viewer is presented with two ways this scene might have played out, but without any indication that one of them is the "correct" version. Hong rejects the nineteenth century convention that reality is knowable, showing instead a reality that resists explanation. It is the uncertain world we dwell in today, where events often occur for reasons we cannot fathom and which people perceive differently. The clash of radically different versions of reality is seen frequently in politics and religion, but the discontinuities extend to all areas of experience. The characters in *Virgin* seem to dwell in isolated bubbles that occasionally become tangential to one another but never totally merge.

Submission

In effect, the narrative is presenting contrasting portraits of Soojung's womanhood and no clear "essence" is to be found. However, the ending resolves this ambiguity because Jaehoon's version prevails. Soojung, the healthy, outgoing woman is going to have to conform to Jaehoon's view of her as ethereal virgin, just as she will have to adopt his preferred method of holding chopsticks. This fate is prefigured by the ending of the scene at Kojan, where Jaehoon throws a temper tantrum—an ominous portent of the coming marital relationship—and Soojung quietly says, "Okay. It's my fault." Rather than confronting or abandoning him, she succumbs, emulating Mirabell's willingness at the end of Congreve's *The Way of the World* to "dwindle into a wife." As they talked at one point earlier, he had said, "You know, one can't do everything one wants in life." That resigned outlook, tragically encapsulating Jaehoon's life, was emphasized by a medium shot of her looking at him, one of only two close shots of her in the film. At the end, she seems to be acquiescing to that philosophy. Given her apparent lack of more attractive prospects, it may be best to accept the juvenile Jaehoon, who can at least provide a comfortable life. For all his shallowness, he may even feel some flickers of real affection for her. Hong has cruelly limited Soojung's options—which undoubtedly reflects his view of how Korean society limits those of women generally—and the happy smile she shares with Jaehoon cannot conceal the declivity toward which she heads. In returning to Jaehoon, who sees women as interchangeable, she is agreeing to surrender her individuality and any hope of personal growth.

Soojung's coming life with Jaehoon is foreshadowed by the phone call she gets from Jaehoon when she is alone in the office near the end. The camera cuts to the film's only other medium shot to register her facial expressions with care. Jaehoon proposes postponing their trip to Cheju to some other time and meeting instead in Wooie-dong, a suburb of Seoul. There is a long silence and Soojung's face sags slightly; her expression becomes fixed and her eyes shift downward. When she asks Jaehoon's reason for changing, he simply says, "I want to." She slumps quietly back into the chair, turning her head to stare blankly out the window. At the end, with a bleak face, she agrees to meet the next day (Figure 7.11). In a

7.11 The end of romance: Soojung gives up on Cheju Island.

scene below her window, two men are seen playing badminton. One scores a point and the referee calls out: "Sixteen to ten." Here is the film's picture of romance. After promising to whisk her away to a romantic resort and make love to her in the nicest room there, Jaehoon now asks her to settle for an ordinary hotel nearby and she accedes. The badminton game neatly figures her situation: two players whacking a silly piece of plastic back and forth. She sees the futility of the game, but has decided to play the match out to the end.

Making a Decision

Continuing the opacity of the characters, even after Soojung has apparently committed herself, she seems uncertain. In both the first and third sections, as Jaehoon tries to convince her to join him at the hotel, she is notably reluctant, saying, "I think I'm sick." Jaehoon tells her to take a taxi, but instead she wanders across the city, in no apparent hurry. Most astonishingly, she stops to call Youngsoo, asking if he can meet her—this after he nearly raped her and then insulted her cruelly at the birthday party. When asked about this action, Hong said she made the phone call "because of the anxiety and self-doubt she felt. She was rolling the dice whether to lose her virginity or not. She was passively hoping that Yeong-su could discourage her from moving forward."[13] If Soojung were a scheming fortune hunter, she would rush to the hotel now that Jaehoon is committing himself, but instead she dallies, unsure of what she wants. She is faced with an impossible problem, trying to sort out her own sexual feelings, stifled by social convention, and dealing with men who wish only to pull her clothes off. More mature than either of the men, she seems still as uncertain as they are about the direction her life should take.

In this regard, as many critics have commented, the scene in the cable car in section III is wonderfully expressive of her situation. When the power failure leaves her momentarily stranded, the car is pictured from outside, swaying gently on its cables, nicely capturing her undecided state of mind (Figure 7.12).

7.12
A visual metaphor: The cable car.

While waiting in the car, she holds a crying baby so its mother can change the diaper. David Gray calls this "a beautifully constructed metaphor of her stuck life." All the men in her life "behave in childish, demanding ways toward her, and she is content to hold them as they scream."[14] The claustrophobic space of the cable car is a further reminder of the increasing constriction of her life. Then, after the long section detailing Soojung's version of the preceding events, in section V the cable car starts up again, allowing her to go to the hotel. That final section is entitled "Naught Shall Go Ill When You Find Your Mare," a manifestly ironic maxim, proposing love as a solution to all life's problems. No glorious outcome seems likely for the unfocused lives of these pedestrian characters.

A Sense of Dislocation

Hong has made his film even more powerful by creating a disconnected world to mirror his characters' directionless lives. The sense of anomie begins in the film's opening, showing a street full of tourist busses with a taxi driving by, presumably carrying Jaehoon to the hotel. We don't see its occupant or follow him as he enters the building. Opening shots generally establish a location, provide interesting visual details, and offer faces to lock on to. None of that happens here. The camera pans to follow the passing taxi but in general is quite static; there are only two tracking shots in the entire film. It does not even reframe when the characters move within a shot. This refusal of the camera to track with characters reduces their agency: they do not dominate the frame as in a typical Hollywood film.

The sense of dislocation is increased by the disjunctive editing. In that opening scene, Jaehoon walks down a narrow corridor, enters the open door of a room, and quickly retreats to the corridor when the maid tells him she is not through cleaning. Cut to a down-angle close-up of a man's shoes; they are unzipped, the owner jumps out of frame and the camera holds on the shoes sitting on a white rug. Cut to Jaehoon standing on the bed in his stocking feet, checking out the ceiling ventilator and a wall sconce. Cut to a high down-angle shot from the window, showing a man in a chef's hat far below who strolls away from the camera. Rather than creating a unified space and time, this editing makes everything disjointed. It also slows the pace. Hollywood editing creates a strong forward thrust by cutting shots immediately after the moment of peak interest, allowing just enough time to absorb the critical visual information and then pressing on to the next moment. By contrast, Hong's camera holds on Jaehoon in the corridor waiting for the maid to finish, a moment of no interest whatever but nicely indicative of his personal aimlessness. Similarly, the sequence's final shot holds for a full eight seconds on Jaehoon lying on the bed, listlessly watching television, before the phone rings with the call from Soojung. That sense of waiting for something significant to happen is a hallmark of the film, reflecting the directionless lives of the characters. Editing in most films intensifies screen action and increases the vitality of its characters; Hong's editing drains that vitality away.

Further, the film creates no strong sense of identification with its characters. Shot/reverse shot and point-of-view shots are almost entirely absent; the camera

7.13 Jaehoon: Inactive and denied agency.

remains removed and generally neutral. Jaehoon enters the scene as a figure in shadow walking away from the camera down the corridor, suggesting his general lack of agency (Figure 7.13). His tentative movements and his rebuff by the maid further undercut any sense of strength, as does his disappearing entirely from the frame when he enters the room. This is supposedly a romantic rendezvous, but the narrow corridor, the harsh light from its window, the maid's cart plunked in the foreground, and the drone of the vacuum cleaner suggest an underlying tawdriness. The emphasis is on cleaning up dirt rather than moving toward an embrace. The room, though clean and spacious, is notably sterile. The walls are bare of pictures, the headboard is unadorned, there is no coverlet, the furniture is geometric and the curtains white. The light glaring through the large windows across the back wall reveal only blankness beyond with the faintest hint of winter trees. The room has all the romance of a toilet bowl. The tawdry nature of the hotel is revealed by Jaehoon's careful checking of the ventilator and light fixtures for possible recording devices. The bed sags as he walks on it, rendering his movements awkward and tentative. Then he lies on the bed, looking upward at the ceiling, so the downward shot of the chef is not identified as his point of view, another way the camera denies him agency.

The Desolate World

In the rest of the film, as in the opening, the settings are as lifeless as the characters, drained of energy by the unmoving camera. People stand and talk or sit and talk in spaces of limited visual interest. Flat staging and lighting undercut any

dynamism: characters do not pop out of the background but fade into it, smoth-
ered by a welter of ordinary rooms and buildings. Because the location changes
with nearly every scene, there is no real center to the story: the city of Seoul
remains a collection of unfamiliar settings. Much of the action occurs in public
places, particularly restaurants, increasing the sense of anomie. Soojung's home
is characterized by a brother who assaults her sexually at night and chases her out
of his room by day. The visual drabness is replicated sonically. When Soojung
and Jaehoon make love in the hotel at Kojan, instead of the soothing nondiegetic
music typically found in a moment of romance, there is only the monotonous
drone of cars in the background.

The dreariness of the world is increased by constant reminders of cold—the
trees have no leaves and characters' breath can be seen as they stand outside. Hong
says he chose to shoot the film in black and white to give the sense of Seoul in
winter,[15] with winter drear particularly notable in the scenes at Kojan. As Jaehoon
rides the train, the view is of raw earth, concrete structures, industrial detritus, and
dirty snow. Then, as Soojung admires the new CD player, they are filmed against
an enormous concrete building that emphasizes the utterly un-pastoral setting of
this love tryst. The settings are even more striking in Soojung's version, where she
is seen standing on the balcony of her friend's place staring mutely over the wintry
landscape. Spread before her is a frozen lake surrounded by nondescript industrial buildings (Figure 7.14). Given the preceding scene of the drunken birthday

7.14
The
wintry
world:
Soojung's
future.

party where both her suitors behaved so boorishly, this desolate landscape might
well suggest the future she stares into. That sense is increased a few moments
later when Jaehoon pulls her out onto that lake, reassuring her that the creaking
sounds do not betoken danger. (He will reassure her similarly in the final lovemaking scene that he will be gentle and not hurt her, and continues to say this as she
screams in pain.) The film's only true close-up is not of a person but of a gum

wrapper which Jaehoon finds frozen into the lake with the brand name "Kiss." The two of them squat down to look at it.[16] The shot of them, squatting and kissing on the ice, while one of the genuinely beautiful images in the film, carries ominous overtones, as two small humans hunch down on the perilous ice surrounded by wintry desolation (Figure 7.15). This is the opposite of the green magical world to which Shakespeare's lovers retreat to find their true passion. It seems, rather, the moribund realm of the Fisher King waiting vainly for the renewal of spring.

7.15
Beautiful
desolation:
The
antithesis
of romance.

Conclusion

The final scene, in which Soojung surrenders her virginity, rather than showing a romantic conjunction, only emphasizes the futility of these lives. When Soojung walks down the featureless hotel corridor toward Jaehoon's room, its narrowness embodies her entrapment and every movement reveals her reluctance. She walks slowly and lifts her feet carefully, trying not to make any noise. Reaching the door, she hesitates for a long moment before knocking, and then steps in slowly when Jaehoon opens the door. In the next shot she stands alone in a sterile, white tiled bathroom, removes two hair pins, and picks up a white nightgown. She holds it in front of her, studying her image in the mirror. (The mirror is off camera, so there is no return image, a hint of her oncoming loss of identity.) Her hesitant movements, the stark setting and the hollow buzz on the sound track drain any hint of romance from the scene. Another abrupt cut with the camera at a high angle shows the couple in bed. Only the top of Soojung's head and one arm can be seen; the rest of her is obliterated by Jaehoon's body. He crawls atop her under the covers, coaxing her to open her legs. She cries out as he enters her, and he says, "I'll make sure it doesn't hurt. Really, it won't hurt. . . . I promise." He pushes on, saying "I'll be gentle," and with each thrust she cries. Approaching climax, he asks, "This is Soojung, right?" and between cries, she manages to stammer, "Yes. It's me, Soojung." He continues thrusting, ignoring her cries until the scene cuts. This is a terribly painful moment to watch, with Jaehoon insisting he will not hurt her while she continues to cry out. David Gray says, "Words and actions seem to constantly be at odds in Hong's film, as if the characters are constantly trying to persuade themselves that what they are saying is true."[17] The lovemaking provides no sense of fulfillment, only of pain and loss.

The scene's ending caps the sense of desolation. First, Soojung has to wash her blood out of the sheets—a decidedly nonromantic conclusion—and then as she looks out the window, a high-angle shot shows the hotel chef walking in the driveway. This shot exactly mirrors the one when Jaehoon lay on the bed in the first scene. In that shot, the chef walked away from the camera and here he walks toward it, suggesting that Jaehoon and Soojung see diametrically opposed worlds.[18] Also notable is Soojung's looking out the window, as she did earlier from her friend's balcony and again from the hotel in Kojan. She is looking for something, but by this point in the story it seems unlikely she will find it. After a pause Jaehoon says, "I will correct all the faults I have. I swear on my life that I will." The scene ends as he puts his arms around her and she leans back against him. The viewer is disinclined to accept Jaehoon's promise to change, given his general lack of focus. Notably, too, in the final shot he and Soojung do not make eye contact, but face diagonally away from one another. She no longer looks out the window, but stares up blankly at the ceiling and the shot cuts on that pose. Soojung's only important trait—at least in the eyes of the men—is her virginity, now lost forever. Her individuality, likewise, will be blotted out just as her image was lost in the mirror and her body obscured in bed. Jaehoon's asking her, "This is Soojung, right?" reinforces the tenuousness of her identity. Beauty and innocence are lost; this is a world of mediocrity triumphant.

Afterword on Narrative Structure

Hong's use of the database narrative stands in stark contrast to the other films under discussion here.[19] His film is often described as "*Rashomon*-like," since it tells the same story from different viewpoints.[20] However, while the stories in *Rashomon* vary as each character tries to present herself in the best possible light, each story yields a consistent sense of character. Thus, in his version of events the samurai presents himself as exemplifying the self-control demanded by *bushido* while the bandit touts his bravado. In *Virgin,* by contrast, the viewer finds opaque characters whose motivations are unclear beyond fairly elemental sex drives. Their solipsism is reflected in the very nature of the narrative: separate stories which do not entirely mesh. Both network narratives and database narratives generally emphasize human possibility: people can impact other lives meaningfully or change their own lives for the better. By contrast, the characters in *Virgin* seem incapable of change, do nothing of consequence, and impact no one.

The portrait of the world is as despairing as that of the people, since Hong's opposing narratives strip it of meaning as certainly as the settings strip it of warmth. In place of the standard omniscient narration, there is uncertain narration: facts are left out, contradict one another, and do not always cohere satisfactorily. True, the stories connect somewhat better with careful viewing, but never completely, as in the vastly differing stories of what happened at the Kojan hotel. To make matters worse, the two flashbacks are only indirectly tied to Jaehoon and Soojung. As a result, the viewer is left stranded in a world where truth is increasingly muddied. This does not go as far as a surrealistic film like *Last Year at Marienbad* (Resnais, 1961), but the viewer is left searching in vain for a definitive version of events. We are presented with indeterminate, indecisive characters, floating through life with no clear objective, and the nebulous world Hong portrays reflects their ontological state.

Finally, *Virgin* is notable for its lack of forward movement. While multiple-draft films are necessarily somewhat circular, returning to a starting point to begin things again, they generally move toward some conclusion. *Virgin* offers desultory forward movement at best, filled with aimless conversation and lack of decision. In particular, the repeated scenes of the same event suggest lives that simply recycle themselves rather than advancing. This is the world of *Waiting for Godot*, filled with repeated patterns[21]—items knocked to the floor, people rushing to the bathroom, and questions about drinking. Kyung Hyun Kim notes the important contrast between this film and other multiple-draft narratives. The central premise of a film like *Back to the Future* (Zemeckis, 1985) is that human beings can change their destiny, but in Hong's film, no change is possible.[22] Despite the different paths described by Jaehoon and Soojung, the ending is the same—the loss of innocence. Ultimately, *Virgin*'s disconnected narrative functions ontologically as a critique of Platonic idealism. Plato proposed that human beings can perceive only the shadows of reality, but that an underlying reality exists nonetheless. Postmodern thought has challenged the concept of a unified reality and, in his steady undercutting of narrative certainty, Hong has stripped that comforting illusion bare.

Notes

1   Moonyung Huh, "On the Director," in *Hong Sangsoo*, Moonyung Huh, ed. (Seoul: Korean Film Council, 2007), 3.
2   David Bordwell, "Beyond Asian Minimalism: Hong Sang-soo's Geometry Lesson," in Huh, ed., *Hong Sangsoo*, 20.
3   The English title, apparently chosen with Hong's approval, refers to the assemblage by the same title by Marcel Duchamp.

4   Marshall Deutelbaum, "The Deceptive Design of Hong Sangsoo's *Virgin Stripped Bare by Her Bachelors*," *New Review of Film and Television Studies* 3, no. 2 (November 2005): 191-93.

5   Deutelbaum, "The Deceptive Design," 195-96.

6   Akira Mizuta Lippit, "Hong Sangsoo's Lines of Inquiry, Communication, Defense, and Escape," *Film Quarterly* 57, no. 4 (2004): 23.

7   Deutelbaum, "The Deceptive Design," 194.

8   David Bordwell, "Film Futures," *SubStance* #97 31, no. 1 (2002): 100. (The quoted phrase is boldface in the article.)

9   Deutelbaum, "The Deceptive Design," 195-96.

10   Deutelbaum, "The Deceptive Design," 197.

11   Deutelbaum, "The Deceptive Design," 195.

12   Adam Hartzel, "*Soojung!* Attends the *Monster's Ball*," (27 July 2003). www.korean film.org (23 February 2008).

13   Moonyung Huh, "Interview," in Huh, ed., *Hong Sangsoo* (Seoul: Korean Film Council, 2007), 62.

14   David Gray, "*Virgin Stripped Bare by Her Bachelors*." (21 March 2007). www.hellon friscobay.blogspot.com/2007/03/david-gray-on-virgin-stripped-bare-by.html (24 February 2008).

15   Huh, "Interview," 59.

16   The ironic appeal of that shot—love imprisoned in a world of dirty ice—was so great that Hong admits he staged the shot by freezing gum wrappers all over into the lake. Huh, "Interview," 64.

17   Gray, "*Virgin Stripped Bare by Her Bachelors*."

18   Gray, "*Virgin Stripped Bare by Her Bachelors*."

19   Deutelbaum argues that Hong's deliberately confusing story structure is "a lesson in cognitive therapy," teaching viewers to judge evidence carefully rather than making hasty judgments. This care is exemplified by Soojung's comparing Jaehoon's and Youngsoo's behavior, e.g., Jaehoon's generosity versus Youngsoo's stinginess ("The Deceptive Design," 197-98). This argument would be more convincing if (a) Soojung did not have to overlook so much self-centered behavior by Jaehoon, (b) she were not so uncertain about her final choice, shown by her calling Youngsoo on her way to her rendezvous, and (c) the result of her decision was an uplifting ending rather than a scene of pain and loss with a bleak future ahead.

20   For example, Hye Seung Chung and David Scott Diffrient refer to the "*Rashomon*like narrative strategies" of Hong's films generally, arguing that they reflect a Korean society "in the throes of hypermodernization." "Forgetting to Remember, Remembering to Forget," *Seoul Searching: Culture and Identity in Contemporary Korean Cinema*, Frances Gateward, ed. (Albany: State University of New York Press, 2007), 129.

21   Kyung Hyun Kim, *The Remasculinization of Korean Cinema* (Durham, N.C.: Duke University Press, 2004), 230.

22   Kim, *The Remasculinization of Korean Cinema*, 207.

8

Run Lola Run

Into the Labyrinth of Berlin

Tom Tykwer's 1998 *Run Lola Run* (*Lola rennt*) was an immediate hit, attracting 250,000 viewers on its opening weekend in Germany and equally successful abroad.[1] It drew raves at film festivals, won the 1999 audience award at Sundance, and swept the German film prizes—winning best film, direction, editing, and cinematography. Audiences loved the film's energy, cinematic experimentation— mixing 35mm, video, black and white, stills, and cartoons—and clever plotting, with the story veering in new directions with each run. Critics were generally positive about the film's freshness, but a number undoubtedly agreed with Peter Stack's assessment. "For all its hyperactivity and slam-bang structural experiments . . . the result is an emotional blank." The film "is ultimately vapid. Lola never does develop as a character, and the fuss seems ultimately pointless."[2] On the other hand, in the years since the film's initial release, a flurry of articles has appeared. They discuss the film as a portrayal of the dehumanized urban world (David Clarke), a mixture of German culture and Hollywood devices (Christine Haase), "a kinetic meditation on order and chaos" (Metalluk), an exemplar of the new positive German attitude after the end of the Kohl era (Margit Sinka), and a modern fairy tale (Catherine Wood).[3] Tykwer insists on the film's seriousness: "Some critics . . . said it's just a light piece of cheesecake. For me, it's my most complex and complicated movie, and my most twisted and deepest emotional film."[4] Whatever the director's feelings, a film's ability to connect with the audience is an important indicator of its significance. Naturally, its youthful rebellious heroes, driving music track, and stylistic playfulness make it attractive to young audiences, but its appeal has been broader than that, suggesting deeper meanings.

Story Summary

The plot is simplicity itself. Lola (Franka Potente), a semi-punk twenty-three-year-old with a tummy tattoo and flaming red hair, receives a desperate phone call from her boyfriend Manni (Moritz Bleibtreu), a small-time hoodlum. While undertaking a job for his boss, Ronnie, Manni bungled things by leaving a bag containing DM 100,000 on the subway, subsequently picked up by a bum, Norbert. Manni is slated to meet Ronnie in twenty minutes and is confident of the result should he appear without the money: "All that's left of me will be 100,000 ashes floating down the Spree to the North Sea." Lola must somehow come up with DM 100,000 and get to Manni, standing by his phone booth in the middle of Berlin, in twenty minutes. Moreover, since her moped has just been stolen and Berlin construction makes taxi travel unreliable, she must run. Run she does, accompanied by constant techno music for which Tykwer himself was one of the composers. But things do not turn out well: Lola's banker father rejects her appeal for money and throws her out. Arriving empty-handed, she helps Manni in his robbery of the Bolle supermarket and ends up spread-eagled on the pavement with a policeman's bullet through her heart. Not content with this outcome, Lola resurrects herself, starts her run a second time—delayed slightly when a boy trips her—robs her father's bank, and arrives with her bag of stolen money just in time to see Manni flattened by an ambulance and spread-eagled in his turn. After each of these "death moments," there is a dream-like scene of Lola and Manni in bed together discussing their relationship. Finally, the third time, things work out splendidly. Lola misses her father altogether and wins the money she needs at a casino. Meanwhile, Manni has spotted Norbert, chased him down, and gotten his money back. So when the couple reunites at the end, Manni is back in Ronnie's good graces and Lola has a surprise waiting in the bag she is carrying. In all three versions, Lola traverses the same terrain and encounters the same people—Doris pushing her baby carriage, a group of nuns, a boy who tries to sell her a bicycle, her father's associate Mr. Meier driving his car out of an alley, and a bright red ambulance. Her one weapon is her stunning scream which can shatter glass and, conveniently, drop a roulette ball into the necessary slot.

Lola is another *forking paths narrative*, in which a person's life path splits at some point, and many such films emphasize the vagaries of fate. Thus, if Helen in *Sliding Doors* manages to catch the subway train she runs for, she arrives home in time to catch her boyfriend in bed with another woman and dumps him. If not, she misses that crucial scene, stays with him, and her life goes in a different direction. At first glance, *Lola* seems a foreshortened version of that pattern, with small details—a boy trying to trip Lola as she runs downstairs—creating significantly different outcomes. In fact, however, Tykwer has done something much more creative. The three runs, so obviously alternative paths, can also be read as sequential steps in a single narrative. Tykwer himself encourages such a reading, saying, "At the end the onlooker should have the feeling that Lola has actually been through everything that we've seen, (and not just a part, one-third of it)."[5] For one thing, Lola seems to learn from each run. On the first run Manni shows her how to release the safety catch on a pistol as they are robbing the Bolle supermarket and in the second run Lola deftly undoes the catch on the pistol she points at her father. Tripped by the boy in that second run, Lola in the third run jumps over him and growls at his dog. Beyond that, however, Lola's adventures blend into an archetypal pattern that helps explain its audience appeal: the quest myth. She is the hero undertaking a difficult journey, overcoming obstacles and exhibiting great courage to rescue the kingdom. Like all such quests, the real journey is toward self-actualization and the real issue is not what she does—plead with Papa, hold up his bank, or triumph at a casino—but who she becomes. In the first version, she's choosing to remain a child, dependent on her parent. In the second, she's selfish, taking what she wants at gunpoint. In the third, she gets in touch with karmic forces and finds her own better self. *Lola* resonates with audiences thanks to thematic patterns exemplifying the romance quest; her run across Berlin is a modern telling of the hero's journey.

Lola's Quest

Hero figures have been a staple in every culture, be it Perseus confronting Medusa, Odysseus journeying home, or Ali-Baba outwitting the thieves. In Western literature, this form has coalesced notably in the chivalric tale whose structure has been described by Northrop Frye. The first stage is "the perilous journey and the preliminary minor adventures," followed by "the crucial struggle, usually some kind of battle in which either the hero or his foe, or both, must die," and finally "the exaltation of the hero." The story of St. George is an obvious example, with the hero arriving in a kingdom whose aging ruler and ravaging dragon are manifestations of its sterility. The hero slays the dragon and marries the king's daughter, bringing renewed life.[6] From Beowulf to comic book characters to modern-day action heroes, this formula continues to be successful, as it is with *Lola.*

The mythic elements appear from the first moments of the film, with the opening T. S. Eliot quote emphasizing the importance of the journey. "*We shall not cease from exploration, and the end of all our exploring will be to arrive where we started, and know the place for the first time.*" The quote emphasizes that only when we return to the starting point do we recognize what it represents (and, by implication, who we are). Frye likewise says that the quest involves returning to the starting point. The Children of Israel searching for the Promised Land, for example, exemplifies the hope to find again the place of mankind's origin, the Garden of Eden.

The two spaces "are typologically identical."[7] Joseph Campbell in his epic study *The Hero with a Thousand Faces* tracks the stages of the hero's journey into numinous regions, his adventures there, and his return, bringing his new knowledge to the everyday world. By using Eliot's quote, Tykwer suggests that Lola's journey takes her to another world and back again, in the process coming to new understanding about herself, her relationship with Manni, and to the universe.

The film's second quote—"*After the game is before the game*"—by the famous soccer coach Sepp Herberger (he won the World Cup for Germany in 1954) also relates to the romance quest, since a soccer match involves a struggle between "good" and "evil" forces. A soccer game, further, suggests "play," and brings in the game motif: the film resembles a video adventure game, with constant running, repetitive obstacles, and the possibility of starting over if your character "dies." Herberger's advice for soccer players makes sense for Lola as a romance heroine. You may have lost the previous game, but need to stay focused on the new contest. Lola takes this advice to heart, failing twice but throwing herself into the third run with undiminished vigor. Like any good competitor she profits from her previous mistakes and plays a smarter game by the end. Finally, this comic juxtaposition of quotes by a poet and a soccer coach suggests the film will be comedic in some respects. Comedy and romance share a similar three-part structure: struggle, ritual death, and recognition.[8] Soccer and comedy, then, tie to the concept of the quest—a struggle with a happy outcome.

The film's cartoon-like opening continues to introduce themes from the romance quest. In its first image, a demonic face slices across the screen accompanied by an ominous rumbling sound. It is the golden pendulum of a clock that swings to and fro, wipes the opening titles, and grinds to a halt. The camera cranes up past the clock face with its whirling hands to the snout of a carved wooden beast. With a rumble, the mouth cranks open to reveal a black maw and the camera dives into the darkness (Figure 8.1). The film's heroine has not yet been introduced but already the dragon she must conquer has appeared. This is the monster leviathan, linked

8.1
Plunging
into the
maw of
time.

to death[9] and also to time, which Tykwer identifies as Lola's enemy.[10] The two are joined, since time brings every man to the grave. In the Bible, this beast appears in various guises: as leviathan, behemoth, and the serpent in the Garden of Eden. "If leviathan is the whole fallen world of sin and death . . . it follows that Adam's children are born, live, and die inside his belly."[11] Diving into this darkness, the camera has carried its viewers into the "fallen world," a nebulous void where blurred figures (various characters from the story) hurry hither and yon. Whirling like the lost souls in the second circle of Dante's *Inferno*, they are the creatures in the belly of the beast whom the hero must redeem. From their midst a personage suddenly appears in his official uniform. It is Schuster, the guard at the bank of Lola's father. He smiles and says, "The ball is round. The game lasts ninety minutes. That's a fact. Everything else is pure theory." He kicks a soccer ball into the air, the camera races skyward with it and the ant-like crowd of people below, reduced to dots, flow together into pointillist letters: "LOLA RENNT." The game is on.

Into the Belly of the Beast

In the final section of the titles, our heroine appears in a cartoon figuration of her mythic role. The camera dives from its extreme height down into the letter "O" of the title which becomes a dark blue cartoon tunnel into which a cartoon Lola charges. As she runs, she smashes yellow titles and brushes aside packs of snapping teeth that appear overhead. A first clock appears before her, turning into a face with a gaping mouth which she rushes into, the tunnel now a spiral of teeth. She charges through some yellow spidery things and a giant blue web, creating a purple electric charge and the jagged image of a skeleton—ominous signs. Lola runs forward into the mouth of a second and third clock. Inside the final clock, the tunnel becomes a whirling spiral, a vortex that sucks her into a last fanged mouth (Figure 8.2). Lola's charging into this tunnel is the hero diving into the bowels of the dragon to free the victims previously swallowed. In the Bible, it is represented

8.2
The
fanged
tunnel:
Entering
the belly
of the
beast.

by Jonah entering the belly of the whale and Christ going into the tomb. "Hence the symbolism of the Harrowing of Hell, hell being regularly represented in iconography by the 'toothed gullet of an aged shark',"[12] an image that accords nicely with Lola's toothed tunnel. The monster to be overcome is time, represented by the three fanged clocks which foreshadow the three contests she will wage against it. The number three, magical in fairy tales, is also common in the quest myths.

> A threefold structure is repeated in many features of romance—in the frequency, for instance, with which the successful hero is a third son, or the third to undertake the quest, or successful on his third attempt. It is shown more directly in the three-day rhythm of death, disappearance and revival which is found in the myth of Attis and other dying gods, and has been incorporated in our Easter.[13]

The spiraling vortex at the end suggests the powerful forces—fate and chance—that are beyond the control of any human being. Although Lola's triumph is a testimony to her strength of purpose, it also occurs because she manages to align herself with the karmic flow of the world. The romance is ultimately about a return to Eden, a time and place where human life was perfectly integrated into the surrounding paradise. That sense of oneness—at least in part—is what *Lola* is about.

Manni in Trouble

From an extremely high shot of Berlin, the camera blazes downward with a tremendous roar. It races into the courtyard of Lola's apartment, through a window, down the corridor, around the corner, and into Lola's room, arriving at her bright red telephone in eight seconds flat (Figure 8.3). Terrific onrushing forces from outside the normal sphere of reality are converging on that receiver. This will be no ordinary call. Campbell identifies this as the first step in the hero's quest: the

8.3
The
call to
adventure.

"call to adventure."[14] It occurs in a variety of ways. A dream may move the hero to action, or a frog may appear, offering to bring back the golden ball of the princess from the well, or a monster may arrive—a dragon, a hydra or the Minotaur. A monster is "the representative of that unconscious deep," the dark forces within the world and repressed within the hero himself.[15] The call announces that it is time to face these powers and, in the process, to grow.

> The call rings up the curtain, always, on a mystery of transfiguration—a rite, or moment, of spiritual passage, which, when complete, amounts to a dying and a birth. The familiar life horizon has been outgrown; the old concepts, ideals, and emotional patterns no longer fit; the time for the passing of a threshold is at hand.[16]

Campbell's phrase "passing of a threshold" is à propos, because Lola's action, once she has learned of Manni's problem, is to dash out her door, an action she repeats twice more. Given that she is living with her parents and dependent on them, her decision to leave that safe space signals her acceptance of the quest. Her task is clearly impossible—to get clear across Berlin in just twenty minutes and magically come upon DM 100,000 as she does. Tykwer says as much: "All odds are against Lola."[17] This, however, is the typical situation for the quest hero, who faces "miraculous tests and ordeals."[18] Heroes have to travel impossible distances, defeat terrible monsters, and penetrate into Hell itself. Lola is about to join their ranks.

Having settled on Papa as the person most likely to help, Lola tears out of her room and down the stairs, an action repeated in each of the three runs. It is appropriate that she comes down from above for "attributes of divinity will cling to the hero" who "is analogous to the mythical Messiah or deliverer who comes from an upper world."[19] Since the quest hero is linked to the three-part solar cycle of disappearance and resurrection, he is readily associated with the sun god, making Lola's trademark red hair especially appropriate. (Tykwer describes it as "flame-red" and Stuart Klawans says, "This isn't hair; it's a flickering aura."[20]) Tykwer cleverly photographs her with frequent flashes of red color in the background, suggesting the effulgence she casts over her surroundings. Thus, at the beginning of her run, bright red window frames and a red door pass behind her. A small bridge she crosses has red navigational markers on it and her red hair flashes above the railing like the sun breaking out of clouds. Most notably, at one point she runs past a billboard-sized Japanese sunburst (she is posed against it in one of the film's publicity stills), linking her to the sungoddess, Amaterasu (Figure 8.4). Her blue and green running outfit may represent the terrestrial ball over which her resplendent hair casts its beams.

As she crosses Berlin, Lola traverses two bridges, one being the Oberbaum Bridge which was an important Cold War crossing between East and West Berlin. Critics have seen this as a sign of Lola's ability to unite the formerly divided city, but more importantly it fits with the hero's function of uniting the ordinary

and numinous worlds. Crossing a bridge, likewise, is an age-old symbol of entering a new stage of personal development, exactly what occurs in the quest hero's journey. The Berlin of Lola's run is strangely depopulated, with only a few passersby and occasional cars. Add to this the many shots of construction projects along the run and the scene clearly represents the wasteland to which the hero must restore fertility. It is not unknown for filmmakers to use mythological references consciously—George Lucas found the shape for his *Star Wars* scripts after reading Campbell's *The Hero with a Thousand Faces*—but in Tykwer's case these links to hero figures and solar deities more likely suggest that his artistic structuring fell naturally into archetypal patterns.

Papa and Jutta

Breaking suddenly into Lola's run, two ghostly denizens of this wasteland pop onto the screen in the form of Papa and Jutta Hansen, his mistress. The contrast with Lola could not be more startling. One moment she is charging across the Oberbaum Bridge straight into the camera, red hair flying. The next, the techno beat drops out with a crash, replaced by utter silence, and a completely unfamiliar personage appears. It is Jutta in a tight shot, her back to a curtained window, saying, "It's worst at night." She is pale and blond, unmoving, speaking uncertainly, her hands pressed together in front of her mouth as if in prayer—a ghostly apparition in some painful purgatory (Figure 8.5). This action seems to be taking place in an entirely different world, accentuated by being shot in grainy video with a handheld camera. Tykwer created a deliberate contrast by shooting all the scenes with Lola and Manni in standard 35mm film stock, "because for me, that's the only real world in this film."[21] Scenes with neither of them present were shot in video to appear "artificial and unreal" ("*künstlich und unwirklich*").[22] In another interview he said, "In a sense, the film images are true and the other images are untrue."[23] The first words out of Jutta's mouth speak of night and her fear of the dark.

8.5
Ghostly
denizen
of the
underworld:
Jutta.

This portrayal accords with Frye's description of the conflicting forces: the antagonist "is associated with winter, darkness, confusion, sterility, moribund life, and old age, and the hero with spring, dawn, fertility, vigor, and youth."[24] In this scene, Papa and Jutta appear to be pallid specters, their existence rendered all the more uncertain by the wobbling of the handheld camera and the backlighting which bleaches them out. They seem, indeed, the embodiment of "moribund life."

Since romance stories are built on clearly opposing forces, Papa and Jutta's relationship is made the mirror opposite of Lola and Manni's. Lola is dynamic, charging forward to reach Manni, accompanied by pounding music. In Papa's office there is only passivity and silence with no sense of connection even though he and Jutta are in the same room. They are shown separately in eight of their nine shots, and, when finally seen together, are at opposite corners—Jutta standing by the window, frame right, and Papa sitting on the floor to the left (Figure 8.6). He

initially has his eyes closed, glances at her only once, his face remains expressionless, and he doesn't respond to her fears. Jutta is voicing her anxiety over their illicit relationship, which seems to be going nowhere. The sense of sterility is reflected in the office setting—German efficiency at its worst—with pale walls, furniture constructed of metal and glass, arm chairs upholstered in black leather, and wood floor bare of rugs. The scene finishes with Jutta asking, "Should I grow old waiting for a man who won't stand by me?" (Papa is obviously not standing by her, since he is sitting on the floor, looking away.) The passivity of both characters and their total lack of passion stand in complete contrast to the youthful vitality of Lola and Manni. Tykwer expends just one minute of the film's eighty-one minute running time on this scene, but the opposing forces are plainly drawn. In a subsequent short scene before Lola arrives, Jutta reveals she is pregnant and Papa agrees to have the child with her. Any credit one might give him for loyalty to his mistress is considerably offset by the lack of commitment to his wife and daughter, standing in sharp contrast to Lola's unwavering love for Manni.

Lola and Manni

The scenes with Manni and Lola emphasize their mutual commitment. Even though they are in separate spaces in the opening phone conversation where Manni pleads for help, the rapid cutting between them, the vivid colors (Lola's red phone and Manni's yellow phone booth), and the intensity of the interaction create an obvious link. So does the graphic match of their faces in close-up. The sense of their connection is particularly strong in the two scenes where they lie in bed together, occurring at the end of the first and second runs. In the first instance, Lola has just been 'killed' by the policeman's bullet and the camera tracks into an extreme close-up of her face as she lies sprawled on the pavement. Her eyes start to go blank as somber death chords play on the sound track. Then a red cast infuses the screen, fading to a scene with Lola lying on Manni's arm in bed. She is smiling slightly, looking relaxed and happy (suggesting postcoital bliss), and she blinks (Figure 8.7). That blink suddenly brings her back to life after the fixity of her gaze in the preceding shot as she lay on the street. Quietly, without turning her

8.7
Lola
returns
to life.

head, she asks, "*Manni. Liebst du mich?*" ("Do you love me?") He turns his head toward her and says, "Of course." ("*Na sicher.*")

Lola has addressed the exact same words to Manni that Jutta did to Papa fourteen minutes earlier. Jutta had to repeat the question three times before Papa, hurrying to meet Mr. Meier, stopped long enough to snap back, "*Ja, verdammt!*" Jutta tells him he has to decide (between her and his wife), he says not now, but she insists, saying she is pregnant. The contrast with Manni and Lola couldn't be stronger. Lola presses Manni in a quiet voice, asking how he can be so sure. He answers: "*Weil du die Beste bist.*" It's as simple as that. He may lack the brains to be a kingpin in the crime world, but his heart tells him she's the best. When she continues to question him, he says, somewhat worried: "Lola, what's wrong? Do you want to leave me?" Her questioning reveals how important his love is to her, and his calm, straightforward answers suggest how honest his feelings are. The scene between Papa and Jutta had been very confrontational at the end, the two of them speaking intensely, and Papa's "Yes" had sounded more like "Leave me alone!" Manni's profession of love, by contrast, seems simple and sincere.

The second scene of Lola and Manni in bed again contrasts clearly with Papa and Jutta. This time it is Manni who has concerns, asking Lola: "What would you do if I died?" (This is an extremely pertinent question since he has just been struck by the ambulance and given a final twitch in the street with Lola hovering over him.) Her answer is just as straightforward as his had been previously: "I wouldn't let you die." The conversation continues, with her smiling slightly at the foolishness of his questions, just as he had smiled at hers, but in both cases the smiles are tender rather than scornful. The question uppermost in each of their minds is "Are you sure you really love me?"—a clear indication of how much the relationship matters to each of them. Again, in a nice parallel, Papa and Jutta had also been questioning one another a few moments earlier in this second run. In the first run, Papa had agreed to have Jutta's baby, but the second time Lola is delayed by a boy tripping her and so arrives later. These additional moments give Jutta time to provide Papa with a further piece of crucial information: the baby isn't his. As a result, Lola arrives to find the two of them in the midst of a furious argument. Papa yells, "Great start for a new love!" and Jutta responds, "If you hadn't neglected me, it wouldn't have happened!" The contrast between their bitter accusations and the quiet togetherness of Lola and Manni could not be greater.

Tykwer says the two bed scenes of Manni and Lola represent "the secret heart of the film,"[25] true for a number of reasons. First, they highlight the contrast between "moribund life" and "vigor" that Frye links with the antagonist and protagonist of the quest adventure. Second, they suggest that, amidst all the external racing about, a small but important internal movement is occurring. Lola and Manni each feel some momentary insecurity about their relationship which is laid

to rest in these two scenes. Resolving those doubts, in part, enables Lola to succeed in her third run. Last, these scenes set Lola back in motion again. At the end
of the first one, she decides she doesn't want to leave Manni and wills herself back
to life. The second time, Manni has asked what she would do if he should die, and
she responds, "But you haven't died yet," and begins her third run in a refusal to
let that happen. The quest hero can only achieve the Grail when pure of heart or,
in this case, when the heart is strengthened by the assurance of love reciprocated.

Lola, Mama, Papa

Lola and Manni's relationship is central in the film, but Lola's relationship
with her parents is also touched on. Her story begins with her at home, living with
her parents, and ends with her out on the street, together with Manni, and holding
a bag with DM 100,000. The film becomes a radically shortened *Bildungsroman*,
with Lola maturing in the space of twenty minutes.[26] This again is an integral part
of the quest journey, since the hero's journey into the underworld to battle with
dark forces represents an interior voyage. A good example is Theseus's defeat of
the Minotaur, by which he proves himself worthy to rule Athens. The monster
resulted from the selfishness of King Minos, who kept for himself the bull sent
by Poseidon for sacrifice. The labyrinth Theseus enters is a figuration of his own
soul; the Minotaur he defeats is his own selfishness, for he risks his life to save
others.[27] Thus the hero's brave actions reflect a corresponding inner growth.

Lola's initial childish state is indicated by her small womb-like room, the
walls bare except for a few taped up photographs and a row of Barbie dolls on
the bureau. Preparing to rush to Manni's aid, Lola quickly sorts through her
mental Rolodex of friends and family and, not surprisingly, ends up narrowing
the choice to just two: Mama and Papa. Mama isn't a viable choice: the one
invariable scene in all three runs is a quick glimpse of her as Lola races past,
lounging in her peignoir, watching TV, drinking, and flirting on the phone with
someone. She is going nowhere and Lola knows she needs to *go* and so heads
to her father's bank. Although turning to family is an obvious move in moments
of crisis, it also signals that Lola is still assuming the child's role, seeking to be
rescued by her parents.

As it turns out, her father is no more help than her mother. In the first run, he
announces that she is not his real daughter ("a cuckoo's egg"), refuses to help her,
and throws her callously out of his bank. In the second run, Lola disowns him just
as decisively, marching him down the corridor with a gun at his neck in a mirror
image of his action the first time (Figure 8.8). Her eyes are somewhat tearful as she
says, "Bye, Dad" and heads off with her loot, but having thoroughly humiliated

8.8 Lola robbing and rejecting Papa.

him and appropriated DM 100,000 from the bank coffers, it seems unlikely she will receive overtures of reconciliation any time soon. Her father, hunched down in the corner of the teller's office, is unable to meet her fierce stare. She has renounced him as cruelly and broken his spirit as thoroughly as he did to her the first time around. In the third run, their relationship remains ambiguous, since before Lola can reach him, Papa drives off with Mr. Meier. They end up in an accident and the final shot shows them slumped unmoving in the car.[28] They could be dead or merely injured, but the film's logic suggests that Papa's and Lola's relationship should be severed.

In these encounters, Papa represents mythologically the "ogre father." More precisely, "the ogre aspect of the father is a reflex of the victim's own ego": the person projects his selfish desires onto the father figure and sees him as an antagonist.[29] Lola's father remains focused solely on his own needs and is unable to show sympathy for her. But in her determination to rescue Manni, Lola risks ignoring the needs of others and becoming, like her father, totally turned inward. Killing the dragon of time and carrying away the treasure he guards is her outward quest, but there must be a corresponding inner triumph. She must break free of her parents and, simultaneously, rein in her ego so as not to emulate their selfishness.

Lola and Schuster

The third run shows Lola coming more and more into alignment with the universe, a change signaled notably by her altered relationship with Schuster. Each of her encounters with him is different and each marks an important milestone in her quest. In some ways, Schuster seems warmly paternal—funny and rotund and welcoming, in contrast to her cold, angular, dismissive father. When she races into the bank the first time, he greets her with an impish smile. "Lolalola," he warbles, "*Die Hausprinzessin!* What a rare pleasure!" His gentle joshing shows a good-natured *bonhomie*. When Lola goes in to plead with her father and in short order is marched back out again, it is Schuster who stands beside Lola as her father coldly informs her she is not his child—the devastation of this announcement emphasized by the sound track's sudden silence. Papa then orders Schuster to throw Lola out, "*Raus mit ihr*," to which the poor man at first cannot respond, standing dumbfounded. At Papa's repeated command, Schuster walks her to the door, holding her arm gingerly, his discomfort made plain by his wide-eyed sideways glances in her direction. Outside, Lola stands silently in tears and Schuster lingers for a moment, obviously seeking some words of consolation. Finally he blurts out, "Well, we all have our bad days," and hurries back into the bank. Clumsy as Schuster's words are, his intentions are for the best and his concern for her is obvious.

When she rushes in the second time, flustered after a more difficult run, the usually genial Schuster is more stern. "Courtesy and composure are the queen's jewels," he counsels her. Lola glares at him and ducks through the security door. She exits some moments later, furious at having found her father arguing with a woman obviously his mistress and having gotten a resounding slap from him when she called Jutta a "stupid cow." (Those were the same words Doris had hurled after Lola a few moments earlier, showing how the contagion of ill humor spreads.) As she rushes out, she collides with Schuster, who calls after her, "Just isn't your day today. Doesn't matter. You can't have everything." In effect, he's calling her a spoiled brat. She halts and looks back at Schuster, who crosses his arms rather defiantly. She strides back, snatches the weapon from his holster in passing, and heads to her father's office. The bank robbery is now on.

Schuster is not nearly as warm and welcoming this second time around, but that is true of almost everybody in this version. It is as if the initial action of the boy who tripped Lola has knocked the entire world out of kilter, including Lola. She bumps into Doris and Norbert with no apology, runs across the hood of Mr. Meier's car without looking back, crashes through the column of nuns, tells the biker he is a thief (she's right, actually), glares at Schuster, and ends up throwing furniture around her father's office. The composure which Schuster urges on Lola might be good advice. Equally important, his comment—"You can't have everything"—is a direct challenge to her selfish worldview in this run and inspires her to take action. Her action will ultimately fail, but if the film is a *Bildungsroman*, her initial failures are a necessary part of her education and will eventually allow her to achieve her goal. The other characters Lola encounters cannot deflect her course of action, but Schuster shunts her in a new direction. His words in each case spring not from any consistent character psychology, but from his role as guiding spirit. In this second encounter, he challenges her not to succumb passively to her father's rejection and also brings out her negative side (which will be self-defeating). The scene ends with Lola rejecting Schuster also, pointing his own pistol at him when he tries to intervene, emphasizing her total focus on herself.

In the third run, Lola arrives at the bank just in time to see her father drive off with Mr. Meier. She stands swearing hysterically in front of the bank, at which point Schuster strolls out the door, lighting up his cigarette. Moving alongside Lola, he says, "You've come at last, Dear." ("*Da bist du ja endlich, Schatz.*") At these strange words, Lola turns her head and stares at him. The camera does the same, tracking in to his blank face, as, with eyes unfocused, he struggles to understand the meaning of the words that have just tumbled from his lips (Figure 8.9). After one last glance at him, Lola is off again, leaving Schuster, still standing in bewilderment. He, Lola, and the viewer have every right to be puzzled, since besides uttering a complete *non sequitur*, he has used the familiar form of address for the daughter of his employer. What do these various encounters, particularly the final one, betoken?

8.9
Schuster
struck
dumb by
his strange
words
to Lola.

Mythologically, Schuster's function is clear: He stands outside the door of the bank vault and Lola must ask his permission to enter. This makes him the "threshold guardian" who stands at the border, representing "the limits of the hero's present sphere, or life horizon."[30] He marks the point at which the hero, at his peril, will cross into the unknown world and face its dangers. Sometimes the guardian will challenge the hero, blocking the path. Other times he may assist the transition. Thus, Schuster joshes Lola both times when she arrives and does not open the door instantly. His joshing is a gentle warning that she is about to enter a whole new territory and gain terrible knowledge. In the first version, she learns that her father has no love for her, is not in fact her biological father, and will leave her to fend for herself. In the second run, after bursting in on his fight with Jutta and getting her face slapped, Lola takes her revenge by robbing the bank. Here, too, she has entered a new and darker world, learning not only of her father's infidelity but of the latent violence within her own heart. After all, in this second run her father does not inform her she is illegitimate, so she points a pistol at a man she believes to be her biological father and at the kindly Schuster also.

In the third run something totally different is happening. Schuster's strange greeting to her (which he himself does not understand) announces that she has finally gotten it right. After two failed attempts to rescue Manni, she is now in the right place at the right time: too late to reach her father and hence forced to find a new, more fortunate path. He is greeting her with words that would more appropriately be spoken by a princess locked in a tower, welcoming the prince come to rescue her. Of course, this is exactly what is happening only, as befits a modern fairy tale, the roles are reversed and the princess is rescuing the prince.[31] In fact, besides rescuing Manni, her prince, Lola rescues nearly everyone in sight. She resurrects herself after the first run and Manni after the second. In this third run, she will rescue Schuster, and his greeting reflects that fact.

Just as Lola has finally arrived at the right spot and received guidance from Schuster, Manni simultaneously is aided by his guiding spirit. The camera cuts from Schuster's face to the blind woman standing outside Manni's phone booth, who has loaned Manni a phone card to make his calls. This woman, like Schuster, serves as a "protective figure," representing "the benign, protecting power of destiny."[32] Folk tale heroes often have helpful forest creatures to assist them and quest heroes, similarly, are aided both by human and divine helpers (e.g., Theseus guided through the Minotaur's maze by Ariadne's thread). When Manni exits the booth to hand back her card, this blind fairy godmother, a seer like the blind Tiresias, points out Norbert pedaling by on his newly purchased bicycle with Manni's bag of money enthroned in the basket. Besides sending the heroes in the proper direction, the appearance of these two helping agents signals a growing unification with the numinous world.

Karma

The narrative gives repeated hints that, although Lola's determination is crucial in shaping the story's outcome, other forces are also at work. Those forces seem to shape the ending of the first two runs. In the first run, when Lola arrives too late and finds Manni already robbing Bolle, she pleads with him to stop and run away with her, but then must deck the security guard who gets the drop on Manni. Manni kicks the guard's pistol to Lola who picks it up and points it at the guard lying prone on the floor, saying "Don't move." When Lola releases the safety catch as Manni instructs her, the gun discharges and buries a bullet in the floor alongside the man's head. Lola takes a firmer grip on the weapon, says "Don't move" again, and the robbery continues. A few scant moments later, Manni and Lola have fled Bolle only to find themselves ringed in by police cars and officers at the ready, weapons drawn. One young officer, extending his pistol in front of him with both hands, calls out, "Don't move!"—repeating Lola's words exactly. A moment later, glancing up when Manni throws the bag of money into the air in frustration, that officer is startled when his weapon unexpectedly discharges, drilling Lola precisely in the center of her chest and killing her—at least in this version. The look of horror on the officer's face as Lola staggers back makes it clear that his act was no more intentional than hers was earlier (Figure 8.10). Wood calls this a moment of "instant karma,"[33] and indeed the two incidents seem connected in some fashion, an example of Jung's acausal synchronicity. It is as if Lola has unwittingly released some cosmic safety catch, loosing forces beyond her control which then destroy her.

8.10
Negative
karma:
The
stunned
policeman.

The same pattern of karmic linking is found in the second version. Lola runs to meet Manni carrying the loot from her father's bank and tries to flag down the red ambulance that races past her in all three versions. The driver refuses but, distracted by her pleas, he fails to see the workmen crossing the street in front of him carrying a huge pane of glass which his ambulance shatters as he skids to a stop. Lola runs around the shattered glass, arrives at Bolle in the nick of time to prevent the robbery, and then watches in horror as Manni walks blithely toward her, only to be struck down by the onrushing ambulance. As before, the two incidents seem linked in some karmic, acausal fashion. Lola, focused on saving Manni at any cost, impedes the ambulance which is rushing a heart attack victim to the hospital. (The forward-rushing ambulance, bright red, its klaxon wailing, seems a particularly apt symbol of forces not to be trifled with.) The shattering of the glass, like the earlier explosion of Lola's gun, signals the unloosing of karmic forces or their deflection in a new direction. The head-on shot of the ambulance plowing through the waterfall of glass shards is replicated a moment later with the head-on shot of it about to strike Manni (Figure 8.11).

8.11 The karmic force deflected: Driving through glass—and over Manni.

In some strange fashion, shattered glass has led to a shattered Manni. For a second time, Lola's relentless forward drive has put her at cross-purposes to the invisible flow of the universe and she has lost her race.

The Lola who makes the third run is much more "in synch" with the world around her, visible and invisible. That new state of being is signaled not only by her altered behavior but by subtle changes in filming. The first two versions emphasize Lola's energy and determination; the third shows her more controlled. For one thing, the later versions drop out many events and the average shot length in the three runs increases from 3.4 to 3.6 to 4.4, smoothing out the action. In the first two versions, the camera is generally close, amplifying her pumping arms. Her Doc Martens have the same effect as Charlie Chaplin's slap shoes, increasing the effort she must expend in running. Many shots track her from the side with objects constantly intervening—parked cars, pillars—that increase the sense of her motion as do the vertical doorways, windows, and walls in the background. In those two initial runs, the editing likewise emphasizes Lola's energy, with five jump cuts in the first version as she runs from the house and down the street. She seems to leap forward in space. Then in the third run, the editing smooths out notably. She gets to her outside door in the shortest time (38 seconds), and reaches Doris just 6.4 seconds later. The camera is farther back, the background sharply in focus (where it had been blurred in earlier versions), and one slow motion shot helps increase the sense of gracefulness. The contrast is most noticeable when she crosses the Oberbaum Bridge. In the first version, she ran and ran, requiring twenty-one shots to cross it. Many of them were from the side with the bridge pillars racing past and the camera zooming slowly in to accentuate her frantic movement. There were also repeated flash cuts between side tracking and straight on shots. By contrast, in the third version Lola zips across the bridge in a single five-second shot, with the camera in front of her. Her greater control is suggested both by the slight up-angle and because she is beautifully framed by the arches of the bridge. In her final run, while Lola is still dynamic, she is filmed in a way to suggest increased grace and greater control.

Lola Asks for Help

That increased sense of control produces an interesting result as Lola searches for some new direction now that her father has driven away with Mr. Meier.
Realizing she does not know what to do next, she asks the universe for help.
In voiceover, she says: "What can I do? Come on. Help me. Please. Just this
once. I'll just keep on running, okay? I'm waiting. I'm waiting. I'm waiting."
Rather than trying to bludgeon the world into submission, she is now willing to
align herself with its unseen forces. This changed direction and changed tactic
are signaled by the changes in filming, as the camera now tracks with her in a
straight down shot from overhead. Such shots were seen in the prologue as Schuster kicked the ball into the air and in the high angle shot of Berlin that began the
narrative proper. There were also the straight down shots of Lola running across
the Gendarmenmarkt in runs one and two, which emphasized both the formal
beauty of the stone patterning and also how diminutive a figure Lola appeared
to be. Such shots suggest a godlike perspective on the action, a sense that human
activity occurs within a wider framework than most of us perceive. Now as Lola
runs, the camera slowly cranes down until it is at chest level, tracking directly in
front of her. If the high angle shot suggests something of a godly perspective, this
move might suggest bridging the numinous and the human.

Next, the shot dissolves into a tracking side shot of her. This, too, seems significant. Outside of one lap dissolve of Lola running across the Oberbaum Bridge
in the first version, dissolves have generally only been used in two contexts. They
were used after each of the flashforwards (which encapsulated potential futures
for the characters Lola bumped into) to bring the film back to the present. They
were also used before and after the two sequences of Lola and Manni talking in
bed together. In both cases, the dissolves signal a movement between two very
different spaces, two very different realities. This dissolve, likewise, suggests that
Lola is transitioning between two realities, as does her voiceover: "I'm waiting."
Voiceover, too, is linked to the concept of bridging. It was used in both the first and
second runs as Lola, straining to reach Manni, called out to him mentally to wait
for her. In those instances, they were shown in split frames, with her voiceover
trying to reach from her space to his as she raced.

All the elements now combine to suggest that Lola is merging herself with the
cosmos. As she runs, the camera slowly tracks in to a very tight close-up, the background blurs, and the film speed slides into slower and slower motion so that she
seems to float through an undefined space. The sound track, too, shifts Lola out of
the real world. In the immediately preceding scene, a somber chord played over
shots of the unmoving accident victims—Papa and Mr. Meier—and that chord
continues as Lola begins running. Now her rhythm track comes in, but with a

notably slower beat: about 92 in contrast to the 120 which was typical up to this point. This beat softens and then drops out, leaving just the somber held chord from the crash scene. The music waits, just as she does. Then suddenly there is the screech of brakes as she dashes in front of a white semi-trailer. This powerful vehicle is the latest incarnation of motorized karmic agents, preceded by Mr. Meier's car sliding out of the alley and the strident red ambulance. Camera, editing, and sound have all helped Lola migrate from her old reality to a new one. Now that her energy is synchronized with the karmic flow, she can accomplish her task.

The Casino

Frozen in front of the truck, Lola spots a sign across the street: *CASINO*. She has arrived at the dragon's lair, filled with hidden treasure. When she enters the gaming room, she is clearly in a strange world, its sound hushed, with only the discrete murmur of voices and the clink of chips. Lola stands out, an obvious interloper with her red hair, punk clothes, and youthfulness among the elegant people in evening dress. Having trespassed in a dangerous space, she must move quickly. Heading straight for the roulette table, she slaps down her bet on number twenty, heretofore her nemesis as the number of minutes allotted to rescue Manni. Brushing off the efforts of a tuxedoed attendant to eject her, she focuses her powers on the roulette wheel, loosing her famous scream which, besides deafening everyone in the room and shattering all the glassware within range, drops the ball neatly into the required slot. All the energy built up by the film to this point as Lola charged forward through Berlin again and again, the dynamism of the techno music, and the frustrations of her repeated failures climax with the explosion of this scream.

The casino scene serves as the narrative's structural climax, since Lola has now obtained the necessary money on her own, not begging or robbing from her father. Notably, the scene recapitulates many themes from the film's opening, the first being the game motif that began with the allusions to soccer. If one of the film's themes is that life is a game, Lola seems to have come into her own as a player. Herberger would be pleased that, no matter what the outcome of the previous match, Lola plunged into the next one with undiminished élan. The casino sequence also uses a number of straight down high-angle shots, recalling the shot down on the crowd from the opening as Schuster kicked the ball into the air. Several of these are of the roulette table with its neatly marked off areas, making it Lola's playing field. The down-angle shots of the roulette wheel, in particular, link to the letter "O" in Lola's name into which the camera dove initially and to all the other circles and spirals in the film: the spiral tunnel in the titles, the spiral staircase she races down at home, the Spirale logo outside Manni's phone booth, the fountain in the Gendarmenmarkt, and all the clock faces. The return of these various motifs in the casino scene brings a sense of closure: everything is coming together for Lola. As she cashes in her chips, the camera tracks back into the gaming room, where the people stand like statues staring after her. Moving between them, it tilts up to a large bronze clock on the wall, its hands at 11:57 (Figure 8.12).

8.12
Time
frozen:
The casino
clock.

Unlike the clock Manni gazed at repeatedly, there is no gliding second hand; the hour and minute hand do not move. This is truly the point of Lola's triumph: momentarily at least, she has frozen time. She has slain her dragon.

Rescuing Schuster

Knights who slay the dragon can claim the gold it guards as Lola has done, but quests are ultimately not about treasure; they are about rectifying the heart. (The reduced importance of Lola's wealth is evident to the viewer who has seen Manni corner Norbert a few moments earlier and retrieve the bag of money.) What is central is the decision she makes at this point. Exiting the casino, she spots the ambulance again as it slows to avoid sundering the sheet of glass and she ducks in the rear doors. (Instead of blocking the karmic forces, she now hitches a ride with them.) Inside, she finds the attendant doing chest compressions on none other than Schuster. (His cigarette smoking earlier in this version and the clutching at his chest in version two are subtle indicators of his heart problems.) When the startled paramedic demands to know what she is doing there, she simply sits down alongside Schuster and says, "I'll stay with him." The sound track cues the importance of this moment. The music sinks to quiet chords, overridden by the distressed pings of the heart monitor, the panting of the paramedic as he continues his compressions, and the accompanying squeak of the gurney. A close-up shows Lola's hands gently surrounding Schuster's hand, and then, as the heart

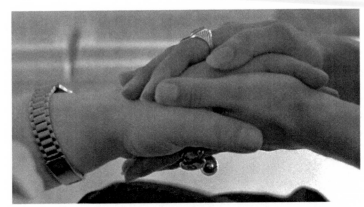

8.13
Lola and
Schuster:
Caring for
her
surrogate
Papa.

monitor suddenly switches to a regular rhythm, there are three more close-ups of their joined hands. They emphasize that Lola's action has somehow, miraculously, brought Schuster back (Figure 8.13). The enclosed space, the tight shots, the slower pace, and the quiet sound track—all contrasting with the preceding scenes—mark this as the emotional climax of the film. It is the third "love scene," capping the two earlier postcoital scenes with Lola and Manni in bed together.

In effect, by remaining with Schuster in the ambulance, Lola is choosing him as a surrogate father and modeling her actions on his. It was he who consistently showed concern for her, for her father, and for the other bank employees. She has an urgent task at hand, getting the money to Manni, but lays it aside to help another human being. This is exactly what her father was unable to do. It is the mark of Lola's transition from child to adult that, after first running to her father for help, she now stops running to help her surrogate father. To some extent, the willful child has taken on the role of protective parent. Her determination and single-mindedness are admirable traits, but to them she adds compassion. Ultimately this is what the quest myth is about: the hero shows the courage to face down the dark forces in the exterior world but achieves greater control over his dark interior forces as well.

Conclusion

Not every hero who ventures into the nether world returns safely, as we are reminded by the film's final scene. Suddenly the camera cuts to an up-angle shot of the building clock which Manni had gazed at repeatedly as he waited anxiously for Lola to arrive. Its hands glide together: it is high noon. Now the ambulance rolls into the intersection, Lola climbs out from its rear doors, and the vehicle speeds off. She is left standing in the middle of the intersection, which is strangely deserted. The camera glides down from its high angle and comes into a medium shot of Lola who looks around, puzzled, calling, "Manni?" The strangeness of the scene is accentuated by the Indian-sounding chant which continues over quiet chords. This is the final stage in the hero's journey, "The Crossing of the Return Threshold."[34] After venturing into nether regions to confront hags or dragons or Minotaurs, some heroes cannot find their way back to the everyday world. Lola ventured into the fearful lair of Mammon, populated by tuxedo-clad deities, and successfully wrested away some of its treasure. She snuck into the red karmic chariot, which earlier had dispatched Manni, and was able to tap into its healing powers to resuscitate Schuster.

Now the hero whose consciousness has merged for a timeless moment with the numinous world must shrink back down and reestablish her ego-centeredness in the quotidian world. (Of course, "the two kingdoms are actually one. The realm of the gods is a forgotten dimension of the world we know."[35]) The camera's craning down suggests this return to normality just as the moving hands on the building clock, in contrast to the frozen ones in the casino, suggest a return into time. Lola struggles to reorient herself, slowly turning to face all the directions of the compass. As she turns 360 degrees, the camera counter-turns 180 degrees behind her, to end up on her opposite shoulder. This shot is very disorienting for the viewer, reflecting Lola's sense of dislocation as she reenters normality. Now, as she looks over her shoulder, Manni appears, climbing out of Ronnie's limo, getting a quick approving pinch on the cheek from him, and then sauntering toward Lola. The contrast in the two vehicles could not be more dramatic: the red chariot of the sun and the black Mercedes of the hoodlum. Manni is pleased with himself at being back in the good graces of one of the minor gods of the underworld. Lola has, for a few moments, aligned herself with the forces of the cosmos. Manni strolls back jauntily, gives Lola a quick peck, and assures her everything is okay. As they stroll off, he glances down and asks, "What's in the bag?" and the film ends on the freeze frame of Lola's sphinxlike smile (Figure 8.14).

8.14
Lola's
final smile:
Full of
secrets.

One notices that Lola does not speak a word in these final moments of the film. How can she possibly communicate what she has experienced?

While Manni orbited his tiny phone booth, she raced from one corner of Berlin to the other. While he lived one life, she lived three. As he was chasing down the shambling old bum, she was invading the domain of the gods. While he brought back the bag of money, she brought back her life, his life, and Schuster's life—and her own bag of money to boot. As Campbell emphasizes, trying to express the wisdom gained from the netherworld experiences is never easy. "That is the hero's ultimate difficult task. How render back into light-world language the speech-defying pronouncements of the dark?"[36] Tykwer breaks off Lola's story at this point, leaving the ultimate outcome uncertain. Bridging the gap between them would seem impossible, given their vastly different experiences, but the strength of Lola's love has already allowed her to accomplish incredible things. Tykwer says, "This woman's passion brings down the rigid rules of the world surrounding her. Love can and does move mountains."[37] This is always the mark of the true hero, to be faced by "miraculous tests and ordeals," and to triumph.[38]

Afterword on Narrative Structure

Tykwer's kinetic cartoon shows what creativity can be unleashed by the new narrative experiments, allowing a punk redhead who resolutely resurrects herself like some character in a computer game to morph into an archetypal hero. Like other forking paths narratives, *Lola* accentuates its major themes by contrasts between the various story versions. Lola's first run sets a baseline of behavior: she simply charges straight ahead. The second version is characterized by general negativity, with Lola crashing into everyone and finally marching her father through his own bank with a gun at his neck. In the final version, everyone is kinder. Lola avoids bumping into Doris and, to avoid charging through the gaggle of nuns, she runs into the street. When this forces the bike rider to swerve, she calls out "*Entschuldigung*" ("Sorry"). Manni, likewise, says "I'm sorry" ("*Tut mir leid*") when he takes back his money from Norbert, recognizing that he is shattering the bum's dreams of an easy life. His giving Norbert his gun in exchange, while admittedly far-fetched, shows his sympathy for someone down on his luck who needs a break. Crucially, it also avoids the violence associated with weapons that popped up in both the first and second versions and inevitably led to disaster. Neither Lola nor Manni waver in their central impulse—Manni to find some money and Lola to rescue Manni—and so when the casino cashier tells Lola, "You can't go in there [dressed] like that," Lola replies, "I have to." But she also says "Please," when asking for a DM 100 chip (since she only has DM 99.20). Hence the film suggests finding a balance between commitment to personal goals and sensitivity to others. This is seen especially in the penultimate sequence as Lola helps resuscitate Schuster, pausing in her personal quest to reach out to another human being. The monitor that signals that Schuster's heart is beating regularly also announces that Lola's heart is in the right place. Unable to speak, Schuster can only reach out his hand to her. But he has already greeted her: *"Da bist du ja endlich, Schatz."* Indeed, she is finally there.

Notes

1   Michael Wedel, "Tom Tykwer," in *The BFI Companion to German Cinema*, Thomas Elsaesser and Michael Wedel, eds. (London: BFI, 1999), 238.

2   Peter Stack, "See 'Lola' Run: German Film Fascinating but Doesn't Go Far Enough," *San Francisco Chronicle* (25 June 1999): C3.

3   David Clarke, "In Search of Home: Filming Post-Unification Berlin," 151-80 in *German Cinema since Unification*, David Clarke, ed. (London: Continuum, 2006); Christine Haase, *When 'Heimat' Meets Hollywood: German Filmmakers and America, 1985-2005* (Rochester, N.Y.: Camden House, 2007); Mettaluk, "Beyond the Butterfly Effect," 29 March 2004, www.epinions.com (24 February 2008); Margit Sinka, "Tom Tykwer's *Lola rennt*: A Blueprint of Millennial Berlin," www.dickenson.edu/glossen/heft 11/lola/html (3 May 2008); Catherine Wood, "Sometimes You Need the Help of the Universe: *Run Lola Run*," *Screen Education* 42 (2006): 107-10.

4   Anthony Kaufman, "Interview: Art Cinema or Piece of Cheesecake? Tom Tykwer Races with 'Run Lola Run,'" 17 June 1999 www.indiewire.com/article/interview_art_cinema_or_piece_of_cheesecake_tom_tykwer_races_with_run_lola_/ (24 February 2008).

5   Michael Töteberg, ed., *Tom Tykwer: Lola rennt* (Reinbek: Rowohlt, 1998), 137.

6   Northrop Frye, *Anatomy of Criticism* (New York: Atheneum, 1969), 187-89.

7   Frye, *Anatomy of Criticism*, 191.

8   Frye, *Anatomy of Criticism*, 187.

9   Frye, *Anatomy of Criticism*, 192.

10 Ray Pride, "Speed of Life," *Filmmaker: The Magazine of Independent Film* 7, no. 3 (Spring 1999) www.filmmakermagazine.com/spring1999/speed_of_life.php (14 May 2008).

11 Frye, *Anatomy of Criticism*, 190.

12 Frye, *Anatomy of Criticism*, 190.

13 Frye, *Anatomy of Criticism*, 187.

14 Joseph Campbell, *The Hero with a Thousand Faces* (Cleveland: Meridian, 1956), 51.

15 Campbell, *The Hero with a Thousand Faces*, 52.

16 Campbell, *The Hero with a Thousand Faces*, 51.

17 Pride, "Speed of Life."

18 Campbell, *The Hero with a Thousand Faces*, 97.

19 Frye, *Anatomy of Criticism*, 187.

20 Stuart Klawans, "Born Cool," *The Nation* 269, no. 2 (12 July 1999), 34.

21 Tom Mes and Joep Vermaat, "Tykwer's Run," www.projecta.net/tykwer3.htm (3 May, 2008).

22 Töteberg, *Tom Tykwer: Lola rennt*, 134.

23 Eric Rudolph, "A Runaway Hit," *American Cinematographer* 80, no. 6 (June 1999): 20.

24 Frye, *Anatomy of Criticism*, 187-88.

25 Clarke, "In Search of Home," 158.
26 Charles Ramirez Berg, "A Taxonomy of Alternative Plots in Recent Films: Classifying the 'Tarantino Effect,'" *Film Criticism* 31, nos. 1/2 (Fall/Winter 2006): 30-31.
27 Campbell, *The Hero with a Thousand Faces*, 13-15.
28 Mr. Meier, in particular, seems totally at odds with the karmic forces. He has to stop sharply in the first two runs when Lola rushes past right in front of his car. Distracted, he rolls forward straight into a car containing Ronnie and two of his thugs. In the third run, Lola spread-eagles herself on his hood (allowing Ronnie's car to pass safely), which also ensures that Mr. Meier will get to the bank before Lola does and drive off with her father. Not two minutes later, Mr. Meier must swerve to avoid Manni chasing Norbert and immediately collides violently with another car. It is Ronnie's.
29 Campbell, *The Hero with a Thousand Faces*, 129.
30 Campbell, *The Hero with a Thousand Faces*, 77.
31 Tom Whalen, "Run Lola Run," *Film Quarterly* 53, no. 3 (2000): 39.
32 Campbell, *The Hero with a Thousand Faces*, 69, 71.
33 Wood, "Sometimes You Need the Help of the Universe," 109-10.
34 Campbell, *The Hero with a Thousand Faces*, 217.
35 Campbell, *The Hero with a Thousand Faces*, 217.
36 Campbell, *The Hero with a Thousand Faces*, 218.
37 Rudolph, "A Runaway Hit," 26.
38 Campbell, *The Hero with a Thousand Faces*, 97.

9

The Double Life of Véronique

A Haunting Sense of Connection

Krzysztof Kieślowski's timing was fortuitous. A graduate of the famous film school at Lodz, he produced many shorts, documentaries, and features beginning in 1966. He was less overtly political than many of his fellow filmmakers, whose central aim was to slip subtle critiques of the Communist regime past the censors, but still became frustrated when his attempts to portray life honestly were blocked. Then, as that regime began to collapse, his ten short films based loosely on the Ten Commandments, the *Decalogue* (1988), brought him international attention, enabling him to obtain outside financing at a time when state funding was drying up. His final four features, completed before his tragically early death at fifty-four, show him at the height of his powers. They include the *Three Colors* trilogy—*Blue* (1993), *White* (1993), and *Red* (1994)—and his intriguing story of two intertwined lives, *The Double Life of Véronique* (1991).

Kieślowski had already experimented with complex narrative form in *Blind Chance* (1981), which traced three separate futures for a young medical student, diverging at the point where he runs along a station platform trying to board a train. In one version, he becomes a devoted Party member; in the second an unpleasant encounter with authority leads him to join the underground; in the third he leads an ordinary life as a doctor. This is a fairly typical *forking paths* narrative, emphasizing how decision and chance operate in a person's life. *The Double Life of Véronique* is something else entirely, telling the story of two young women who seem to be the same person although living in different countries. Weronika, a young woman who loves singing, lives in a small town in Poland, but soon heads restlessly off to Krakow, leaving behind her loving father and gentle boyfriend, Antek. In Krakow, she wins the audition for the solo in a grand concert, but falls dead from a heart attack in the middle of the performance. At that exact instant, the story jumps to the second woman, Véronique. She lives in a small French town, teaches music at a local school, and one of her favorite pieces is the song Weronika was performing when she died. Véronique finds herself courted by a mysterious puppeteer, Alexandre Fabbri (Phillipe Volter), who saw her while presenting his show at her school, and the remainder of her story deals with their developing relationship. The two women are played by the same actress, Irène Jacob, and besides their physical similarity one finds events where their lives seem to overlap: each is a musician, each loves the color red, and each travels from her small town to the big city. Most important, each seems to be seeking some sort of fulfillment in life although they follow different paths in doing so.

Weronika apparently "fails" in her chosen path, for she dies at a young age, her song broken off in mid-phrase. Véronique gives up singing (it's not certain if she had plans for a concert career) and seeks fulfillment in romance. But if this choice avoids heart attacks, it still risks a broken heart. In the end, neither choice provides the happy ending the audience might hope for. In telling these two stories, Kieślowski uses the ***database narrative*** in a manner that is simultaneously very simple and very profound. Like *Virgin Stripped Bare by Her Bachelors* and *Run Lola Run,* his film seems to tell the same story in different versions. But the repeated story is not as clearly a single story, since the two young women follow life paths that, while similar in some regards, are also very different. Further, Kieślowski is looking less at human connections and more at pathways between the everyday and the noumenal. In this investigation, he pushes the art of cinema to new limits, relying on color, image, music, and motif to suggest the hidden connections between human souls and higher mysteries.

Opening

Abstract elements appear immediately in the film's opening in which the two Veronicas are introduced as infants. The images associated with each child, contained in just three densely structured shots, suggest they are connected and yet embarked on different journeys. In the first, the camera pans slowly across a beautiful but mysterious space. The top two-thirds of the frame is black, filled with winking lights. Below the black is a slash of red color and below that a band of intense blue. A woman says in Polish: "That's the star we're waiting for to start Christmas Eve." The second shot reveals a small girl, held upside down, who points her finger at the star as her mother says, "Show me" (Figure 9.1). With the information provided by the second shot, the beautiful but puzzling images

9.1
Suspended
among
the stars:
Young
Weronika.

of the first one become clear. Representing the child's perspective, they show an upside-down night sky: the black expanse with its dots of light is a slumbering town; the blue/red slash a glowing sky with a haze of stars. Rather than putting the second shot first to establish the inverted point of view, Kieślowski presents an abstract image we must first apprehend as a beautiful visual form to which meanings then accrue.[1] Even the "explanatory" shot of the little girl upside down is mysterious, for the screen is dotted with myriad reflected lights in which the child floats as in a second night sky. Kieślowski insists that we stop and look at the world as closely as his camera does, because ineffable sights await our gaze and deeper meanings cry for discovery. This will not be simply a story; it will be a metaphysical journey.

The journey continues in the third shot as an enormous distorted eye stares out at us. Then the magnifying glass is withdrawn, revealing another small girl being instructed by another female voice—in French this time: "Here is the first leaf" (Figure 9.2). It describes the leaf in detail and commands, "Look."

9.2
Focused
on the
real world:
Young
Véronique.

These three shots, occupying just one minute of screen time, create a visually vertiginous world, the shot scale changing dramatically from moment to moment. This foreshadows a film in which scenes will play against one another and meaning will often be generated as much by image contrast as plot progression. The maternal imperative directed at both little girls—to look—is directed at the viewer also, who must be alert to decipher the complex images presented. "We are made aware of how important it is to look with eyes wide open, to understand with lucidity and with compassion."[2]

The three opening shots establish a series of contrasts between the two young Veronicas. Little Weronika is shown upside down whereas Véronique is right side up, making them mirror images of one another. Weronika looks up at the heavens and will frequently thereafter be characterized by skyward glances, suggesting a spiritual quest, especially since the first two shots announce the Christmas season and she is instructed to look for the star that guided the wise men. "The Magi story initiates the film in a mythic mode and serves as a metaphor that generates the theme for the rest of the film: spiritual search."[3] Véronique, by contrast, is being told about the botanical features of a leaf. She wears an ordinary dress; Weronika had on a black velvet holiday frock. It is daylight rather than night and the mysterious solo flute music has dropped out, replaced by quiet outdoor sounds. Instead of the wintry Christmas season it is now spring, for Véronique is being shown the first leaf and birds are heard chirping. Thus the film has jumped in an instant from a nighttime world of mystery to daylight and everyday reality, reinforced by a color palette that shifts from intense blacks and iridescent skies to earthy tones. If Véronique undertakes a quest, her eyes will likely be directed forward, focusing on things of the earth rather than the sky. At the same time, Véronique's season also has spiritual overtones, with spring the period of rebirth. Thus the two girls are linked by being introduced simultaneously, each held by an unseen mother, and each enjoined to look closely at the world. However, the different seasons and colors, with one child looking at a star and the other at a leaf, suggest divergent life journeys.

One Sings, the Other Doesn't

These similarities and contrasts continue although they are not apparent at first because the film's opening portion deals exclusively with the tragically short life of Weronika, presented in just thirty minutes of screen time. Then the remainder of the story focuses on Véronique, during which the linkages slowly emerge. Weronika's passion for life and especially for music is apparent immediately as she first appears as an adult singing ecstatically in front of a chorus. She does not waver as raindrops begin to fall on her face and the other singers hurry away.

9.3
Weronika's
great
passion:
Singing.

She holds the final note for an extraordinarily long time, finishing with an expression of obvious joy (Figure 9.3). The tight camera position, her eyes raised to the skies, and her passionate singing emphasize the intensity of her feeling and the centrality of music to her identity. The same sense of vitality is felt as she meets her boyfriend after the concert and surges forward into his arms, wrapping her leg around him seductively. The subsequent scene of them together in his room is filled with languorous warmth; camera filters heighten the golden skin tones as they lie entwined, half-clothed. The coziness of the scene is emphasized by the rain that continues outside, reflected in the shimmering light on the walls. Weronika lies back contentedly as Antek nuzzles her thighs and her own photograph smiles back at her from the wall, a testament to how she is enshrined in Antek's heart.

The opening portrait of Weronika shows her vitality, her love of music, and her tender regard for Antek, impressions presented primarily through color, image, and sound. There are only ten lines of dialogue, mostly Antek teasing Weronika about her scarred finger, injured when a car door was accidentally slammed on it. (Besides suggesting the role of fate in people's lives, a tight shot of Weronika's finger entwined in the fringe of the bed robe begins a visual motif of fingers and strings.) However, despite her apparent happiness, she decides to leave Antek and travel to Krakow, for reasons that are not clear, even to her. Sleeping at home later, she gasps and sits up suddenly, awaking from some troubled dream at which she whimpers momentarily. Recovering, she goes to the next room where her father is working on a drawing of a village church. She says, "I woke from a dream," but then breaks off, not describing it, although it may have played a part in her decision. She asks her father to give the news to Antek, apparently not wanting to tell him herself. Her excuse for going to Krakow is to see her sick aunt, but her father intuits that Weronika mostly wants to visit the big city. The sense of their close relationship is enhanced by the dusky lighting and the quiet mandolin music he listens to as he works. Weronika confides to him, "I feel like I'm not alone, . . . not alone in the world." (On the sound track, the mandolin chords move in parallel thirds, subtly echoing the theme of the double.) Her father says of course she's not alone and she responds, "I don't know." That same phrase comes up repeatedly in the film, emphasizing that the characters do not understand the reasons for their actions, but are groping forward, following their instincts as best they can. A moment later, as Weronika's father touches her face tenderly, she smiles at him and asks, "What do I really want, Papa?" Here, then, is an additional key trait. Besides Weronika's vitality, her passion for music and regard for Antek, she is marked by some inward force that propels her. As her question suggests, however, she herself has no clear sense of what she is seeking.

Véronique

A comparison of this opening presentation of Weronika with the first appearance of Véronique reveals both parallels and contrasts. The intervening scenes have filled in the brief remaining details of Weronika's life. She arrives in Krakow, wins an audition for a concert solo, but dies of a heart attack in the midst of the performance. The first appearance of Véronique comes as a distinct shock, because the preceding shot was from inside Weronika's coffin, looking up through a glass lid, as dirt came thundering down to blacken the screen. Suddenly a woman's naked torso appears, writhing in arousal, and the din of falling earth is replaced by passionate breathing. When the camera pans up to the woman's face, the viewer sees the visage of the singer who has just died in Poland (Figure 9.4). However, this is Véronique, living in France and currently engaged in casual lovemaking with a former classmate. Besides the obvious visual resemblance, this scene replicates key elements of Weronika's introduction. Both openings forgo any establishing shot and begin with a close-up, held for nearly a minute.

9.4
Veronique's
great
passion.

Both rely heavily on image and sound: as in the lovemaking scene with Antek, there are scarcely a dozen lines of dialogue, which serve to establish this as a casual liaison. Véronique and the boy have not seen one another since graduation. Most important, each woman is first seen at the apex of passion—Weronika singing, Véronique making love—which in turn suggests they will follow diverging paths in their search for happiness.

Similarities and differences continue. The two women are linked through music, since Weronika is a singer and Véronique is a music teacher. Further, Véronique begins her story with an inexplicable decision, much like Weronika deciding to go to Krakow. She appears at the door of her music teacher to announce she is stopping her lessons. When he demands to know why she would betray her God-given talent, she cannot explain. "I don't know," she says. "But I know I have to quit now." Like Weronika, she cannot explain her sudden decision or foresee where she is headed: she simply knows she is being impelled in a new direction. At the same time, there is a striking contrast: Weronika was so strongly drawn *toward* music that she was willing to leave her loyal boyfriend to follow it. Véronique, by contrast, turns *away* from music and will seek fulfillment in romance—a difference signaled by the opening shot of each woman: Weronika singing and Véronique wrapped in a man's arms. Slavoj Žižek suggests that Kieślowski's frequent use of multiple path stories, including *Blind Chance* and *Red* as well as *Véronique*, shows his fascination with "the role of chance in determining the multiple possible outcomes of a dramatic situation."[4]

The Mystic Link

Weronika's decision to go to Krakow is never really explained. Her bad dream may have been a premonition of the brevity of her life, but she does not explain it to her father. The one thing she seems sure of is that she is not alone in the world, suggesting some awareness of her *doppelgänger*. Hence Weronika's decision seems based on instinct. Instinct also seems to operate in Véronique's case, for as she decides to abandon music the scene's imagery suggests her decision may have been caused—entirely without her awareness—by Weronika's fate. For one thing, there is the abrupt cut from the "coffin shot" of Weronika to Véronique making love. This strongly indicates that the moment of burial and of lovemaking are the same, an idea supported by other details. At the height of her passion, Véronique's hand swings down and falls on a table lamp which she spasmodically turns on. Joseph Kickasola suggests this strange action may be "in reaction to the great darkness that has just consumed Weronika."[5] And just as the couple is relaxing into postcoital bliss, the oboe solo that began Weronika's concert piece comes faintly onto the sound track. As it does so, Véronique turns her face and looks off as if hearing the music, although it is obviously nondiegetic. She begins blinking back tears. When the boy asks what's wrong—is she grieving for someone?—she says she doesn't know and quietly asks him to leave. After he is gone, the camera holds on Véronique's tearful face and the music comes back in: the orchestra, the chorus, and then Weronika singing her opening phrase. On this pensive shot the scene cuts suddenly to black.

Véronique cannot explain the sudden change in her mood, but the viewer is cued by the overlapping scenes and the sound track to think that, on some level, she intuits that Weronika has died. That sense is reinforced in the immediately following shot where Véronique in her car emerges from a black tunnel on her way to bid her voice teacher good-bye. This striking image, combined with Weronika's theme continuing on the sound track, suggests that Véronique's decision to give up singing is to avoid Weronika's fate, to escape from the darkness of the grave.[6] However, Kieślowski only alludes to these possibilities; there is none of the careful causation found in a Hollywood film. After all, the basic premise being advanced—that two people living in different countries can somehow be psychically connected—is inherently nonrational. It seems entirely appropriate that the film's characters cannot explain their choices, being moved by unseen forces they do not entirely understand and to which humans generally remain oblivious.

Divergent Paths

The two young women, besides being physically identical, are linked by a host of actions, objects, and motifs, most notably the frequent reprise of Weronika's musical theme in Véronique's story. At the same time, the opening image of the two little girls as mirror opposites of one another reminds us that they differ in important ways and choose dissimilar paths. Weronika's life, while far shorter, seems notably vital; she sets her own fate in motion by her determination to go to Krakow. The scene of her departure is emblematic: a young woman leaves behind all that is familiar and the people who love her, heading off in search of what her heart desires but her lips cannot articulate. The first shot looks out the train window as quaint houses and a brick church roll slowly past. The glass is imperfect, causing the scene to ripple slightly and bringing to mind the famous verse from 1 Corinthians 13 about humans seeing only as through a glass darkly. The quiet mandolin music from the previous scene continues under the clack of the train wheels, giving the sense of Weronika gliding through a tranquil dream. There are just two more shots in this sequence. In the first, the camera looks down from high angle at Weronika, sitting by the train window and, in a stunning action, she looks up and returns the camera's gaze (Figure 9.5). The importance of this moment is underlined by a final mandolin chord, after which the music drops out. With the camera tracking in, Weronika takes a small clear plastic ball and peers through it at the passing landscape. An extreme close-up through the ball shows the buildings gliding by upside down.

9.5
The "iconic" look: Weronika returns the camera's gaze.

In classic filming, characters never acknowledge the presence of the camera in this fashion. Joseph Kickasola terms these camera looks "iconic," suggesting they mimic saints portrayed in the Orthodox tradition who gaze straight at the viewer, bridging the gap between heavenly and earthly realities. Kieślowski uses these looks sparingly to call attention to key scenes, giving them a "metaphysical weight."[7] The mystery of the scene is increased because we do not know what Weronika's gaze implies. She may be looking at us, at some Divine presence, at the double whose existence she intuits, or into her future.[8] The ball, likewise, is "a key visual motif," stretching the scene "beyond normal size" and "hinting at eternal time and space."[9] One has the sense of some reality hovering just outside the frame which we struggle to catch sight of. Weronika's train journey seems to be taking her into a future that is significant but whose outlines, as suggested by the wavy lines of the window, remain tenebrous. Nonetheless, although Weronika cannot be sure where she is headed, she is moving forward determinedly, as her knowing look into the camera lens suggests.

Véronique also takes a train trip, but it occurs near the end of her story, not the beginning. At her school one day, Véronique is captivated by the performance of a visiting puppeteer, Alexandre Fabbri, who is also a writer of children's books. He, in turn, takes note of the pretty music teacher and begins courting her in his shy way. He begins sending mysterious gifts, each of them a clue to be deciphered, usually through reading his stories. The final one is an audio tape filled with mysterious noises: a creaking sound, more rustling and creaking, strange hollow thumps, footsteps, an automobile starting up, a brief excerpt of Weronika's theme, feet climbing stairs, a murmur of voices, and then the tones that precede a loudspeaker announcement at a depot followed by the announcement of a train departure. At the end there is a terrible explosion, with glass falling, the roar of flames, and the klaxons of emergency vehicles. Véronique listens intently and is frightened by the explosion, but takes the cassette out of the player and studies it carefully. Retrieving the envelope the cassette arrived in, she examines the postmark under a magnifying glass to reveal "Gare St. Lazare." Knowing where the letter was mailed, Véronique travels to Paris, follows the tape's audio clues, and eventually arrives at the table in the station restaurant where Alexandre has been sitting for two days, hoping she cared enough to track him down.

The two journeys convey different impressions. Weronika's town passing outside the train window emphasizes her willingness to break with her familiar past. She is leaving her beloved father: the red brick church is reminiscent of the sketch he was working on, their connection also signaled by his mandolin music continuing in soundover as the train begins to roll. Weronika, then, is leaving safety behind, pulled by some mystery that lies ahead. Véronique's train journey is not shown, only her arrival at the Gare St. Lazare. The scientific manner in which she has followed the clues makes the quest somewhat more mundane, and she and the viewer both know that Alexandre has been sending these messages and undoubtedly lies at the end of the journey. However, she is still traveling toward an enigma, having no real insight into Alexandre, given how fleeting their contacts have been. Both women cast themselves into an unknown future, Weronika toward an unknown destiny in Krakow, Véronique toward an unknown suitor in Paris.

Light and Dark

Weronika's life perhaps shows greater intensity than Véronique's, as reflected in the fast pace of events. One moment Weronika is riding on a train and in the next a pair of hands is dealing colorful Tarot cards onto a golden coverlet while an off-screen voice asks, "A blond boy?" The voice then inquires, "You slept with him?" to which Weronika, laughing, replies, "Yes." The inquisitor is Weronika's cheerful aunt in Krakow. This disorienting transition from train window to Tarot cards is typical of the rapid rush of Weronika's life. In almost no time, she auditions for a solo role, wins the audition and then appears on stage in the final act of her life. Besides the fast pace, the very filming suggests the intensity surrounding her. In the scene with Weronika's aunt, the two women are shown in contradictory shots as if Weronika lives in a separate reality. Weronika, in her night slip, sits against an intense red backdrop—a wall or headboard. Her space is indeterminate, intense, and confined (Figure 9.6). The reverse shot of her aunt shows a very ordinary woman in a very ordinary room, with lace curtains and a scattering of

9.6
Weronika's
world:
Intense but
confined.

nondescript furniture. The colors have an earthy tone and the room, while sunny and cheerful, seems typical of Polish everyday life (Figure 9.7). The sense could not be clearer that Weronika exists outside everyday reality.

9.7
Quotidian
reality:
Weronika's
aunt.

The intensity of Weronika's life is increased by constant premonitions of a dark fate awaiting her. For example, as Weronika starts to tell about her tryst with Antek she is cut off by the arrival of her aunt's lawyer, a portent of how her life story will be cut off in a few short months. The aunt explains she is preparing her will: members of their family are short-lived, as was true of Weronika's own mother. (Weronika's excuse to visit Krakow, we remember, was that the aunt was sick.) Giving a final macabre twist to these portents, the lawyer turns out to be a dwarf. The hints become even more ominous as Weronika appears to suffer a mild heart attack after her audition. As she hurries along an empty street, the sky is suffused with dusky light, there are autumnal leaves on a nearby wall, and behind her lies a cemetery. Suddenly, she clutches her chest and stumbles to a nearby bench.

The dry screech of leaves on the wall as she drags her arm across them and the heavy clunk of her shoes emphasize the weight of her body. As she sits recovering, a man approaches, opens his raincoat to expose himself to her, and walks off, this strange incident further marked by the camera canting for an instant. The flasher seems ominous—"a dark figure of death"[10]—but Weronika smiles slightly at him for all that he may be a fatal harbinger. This suggests a determination to follow her fate wherever it leads. As a final dark hint, the *hejnal* is heard in the background, the tune traditionally sounded at dusk in Krakow to memorialize the trumpeter whose warning of an impending attack was truncated by a Tatar arrow.[11] In the preceding audition scene, Weronika's finger had snapped the string on her music folder sharply as she hit her high note, emphasized by the camera tilting down and tracking in. That action, showing the physical strain of singing, juxtaposed with this heart attack scene leaves little doubt of the price to be paid for continuing to perform.

The scene preceding the concert is equally ominous. Trying to calm her nerves as she dresses, Weronika wanders to the window and presses her face and hand against the glass. This image, viewed from outside, is riveting. She is pinned by the window frame on either side. Her fingertips and cheek whiten slightly from the pressure of the glass (Figure 9.8). Eyes closed, lips parted, pushing against

9.8
Weronika
before the
concert:
Yearning
to be free.

the glass, she is the figuration of a soul longing to be free of earthly constraints, seeking some glorification just beyond her reach. Standing there, she spies an old woman outside, slowly trudging with her heavy grocery bags. Weronika quickly opens the window and offers to help, but the woman only glances at her and moves on. After this traditional symbol of death, the crone, Weronika's fate is foreshadowed again a moment later as she puts on makeup and her breath on the mirror blots out her own image. And when she stops and looks to the side, the camera cuts to black, suggesting that she is gazing into a darkness that lies just off camera. Although there seems little doubt as to her impending fate, she stands confidently on stage and launches passionately into her solo. Her collapse as she strains for the top note perfectly encapsulates her essence throughout the film: throwing herself into her art with every ounce of her being, undaunted by the dark shadows that crowd in on her. Her truncated solo embodies her life, cut short too soon. Still, one senses that her life has ended as she would have wished; she leaves the scene singing, just as she first entered it.

While not without intensity, Véronique's life takes place in a more mundane world. She teaches her students, visits friends, and goes to see her father as Weronika did. She too has heart problems, but they are treated much more routinely. One afternoon she stands at the end of the school yard, leaning against a large tree and breathing heavily. She does not clutch her chest, but her isolation, her look of trepidation, the autumnal colors, and the fallen leaves evoke the earlier scene of Weronika having her heart episode. This is confirmed when Véronique subsequently emerges from a hospital cardiology department and is later seen examining her electrocardiogram. Consistent with the first view of her looking through a magnifying glass, Véronique is taking a more rational approach to the problem. This is not to say that Véronique is not an equally vital character, but the events of her life unfold at a slower pace, she seems somewhat more tentative in her choices, and there is less sense of dark forces hovering on the verges of her existence.

The Puppeteer

Véronique's attraction to Alexandre Fabbri is understandable, given his mesmerizing performance at her school, its sensitivity enhanced by subtle shifts in camerawork and musical score. On a darkened stage, the puppeteer's delicate hands slowly rotate a red velvet box, open it, and extract a ballerina puppet. The ballerina floats out and glides across the stage *en pointe* to soft piano music. The schoolchildren watch entranced, as does Véronique, her growing fascination indicated by successively closer camera positions. The ballerina's dance is abruptly cut short when she stumbles and falls to the stage, her leg injured, and then slumps backward, dying (apparently) because she can no longer dance. The music breaks off, emphasizing the pain of the moment, and the puppeteer's hands bring forward a grandmother puppet that has been rocking quietly in the background. In silence, she bends down and spreads a shroud over the crumpled ballerina. At this moment, as Véronique glimpses Fabbri's face reflected in a mirror, a new musical theme comes in softly: it is Weronika, singing her solo. This theme, which links the two women, suggests a potential link between Véronique and the puppeteer she has just seen. Then, to the intensifying music—Weronika, orchestra, and chorus—the puppeteer's hands gently pull off the shroud to reveal the ballerina transformed into a lovely angel with butterfly wings who soars off the stage. This magical fable creates a first bond between the puppeteer and the enraptured music teacher.

The puppeteer continues to be associated with romance and dream, for he next wakens Véronique, telephoning her at 4 a.m. Too shy to speak, he can only play a tape of Weronika singing. Subsequently he sends Véronique a shoelace, which she first discards, but then realizes it is linked to his stories and retrieves it. She begins reading Alexandre's books and her growing fascination is captured in a marvelous image, a tea bag slowly revolving in a glass, with steam rising from it, and a portentous hum on the sound track. The dreamlike force of this image is difficult to explain. It captures the sense of Véronique's spirit—floating—hypnotized by this person she finds herself growing closer to. Quiet chords come onto the sound track and she slowly winds the shoelace around her finger as she reads one of Alexandre's books, blowing softly on the pages to turn them. A following shot has her perusing another book, caressing her lower lip sensuously. In a third shot, she is lying barefoot on her bed, laughing quietly to herself as she reads (Figure 9.9). These wordless scenes testify to Kieślowski's power to tell a story

9.9
Véronique
captivated.

through images alone. Véronique's gentle turning of the pages, her rapt attention and soft smile show her becoming immersed in Alexandre's world. The shoelace she unconsciously winds around and around her fingers as she reads suggests how his words are ensnaring her.

The Meeting

Véronique and Alexandre finally meet face to face when she tracks down the cassette's audio clues and locates him at the St. Lazare station.[12] The camera cuts to shot/reverse shot in medium close-ups to register carefully the expressions of the two characters as Véronique coaxes Alexandre to explain himself. She is obviously touched as she learns he has been there two days already and would have waited two or three more in hopes she would appear. However, he then says this was all a psychological experiment. He plans to write a novel and wanted to see if a woman would answer "the call of a complete stranger." By the end of his story her face is devastated. "Why me?" she demands, pain in her voice. His eyes fall, and he can only reply, "I don't know." She gulps and then flees from the table. Having immersed herself in the fairy-tale world of his children's stories, she undoubtedly felt she was the princess in a tower, awaiting the prince on his steed who would woo her. Now she discovers she is a psychological subject, apparently chosen at random.

The thoughtful viewer is disinclined to take Alexandre's explanation at face value. His brilliance in expressing himself through silent puppet shows and his refusal to speak on the early morning phone call suggest he is less comfortable using words, especially trying to rationalize behavior he may not himself understand. His words—"I don't know"—are the exact ones Véronique used when asked by her one-night lover why she was suddenly depressed and by her music teacher why she was quitting her lessons. In both cases, she had no rational explanation for her feelings or behavior, since a deeper, instinctive sense lay behind them. Alexandre, likewise, seems impelled by forces stronger than a supposed writing project, for he chases after her frantically. He obviously is not the cold-hearted monster she first imagined, but an awkward, smitten swain. When she later checks into a Paris hotel, he has managed to follow her and she finds him waiting by the elevators, distraught. He stares at her, his face haggard from his two-day wait, and murmurs, "I'm sorry. Please forgive me." When she asks, "For what?" he can only shake his head in bewilderment. Although he cannot explain himself, his dogged pursuit of her speaks volumes. Then they are in the hotel room together, and when she steps into the bedroom, she finds the exhausted Alexandre collapsed on top of the bed and already asleep, fully clothed. She tenderly pries loose the glasses clutched in his hand and crawls under the covers, clothed except for her shoes. It seems possible she has found her Prince Charming: awkward but artistic, silent but steadfast.

Weronika Hovers Nearby

The conjunction of Véronique and Alexandre is marked by propitious signs, for many details in the hotel room suggest Weronika is there also. As Véronique lies back to sleep, she rubs her eye and strokes the underside of her eyelid with her ring, the same gesture performed by Weronika before her concert. Apparently they share the folk belief that a gold ring can prevent a sty from forming. At that moment, a shadow falls across her face, there is the gentle sound of wings flapping, and Weronika's theme comes in very softly, with recorder and harp. These ghostly signs suggest Weronika's hovering presence. At many earlier points, Véronique had seemed to be aware of her double, beginning with her breaking off of love-making. Later, she had visited her father and said, "Not long ago, I had a strange sensation. I felt that I was alone. All of a sudden." She cannot know of Weronika's death, but she has sensed some loss. (The scene obviously recalls Weronika's telling her father she felt she was not alone.) And now in the hotel room the connection between the two women seems stronger than ever as that theme is heard again, Véronique's head sinks onto her pillow, and her dream appears. A clear plastic ball fills the screen, in which the inverted image of a red brick church is suspended (Figure 9.10). Slavomir Idziak, the cinematographer, cites this as an example of

9.10
Weronika
hovers
nearby:
The dream
ball.

Kieślowski's "emotional establishing." This "completely illogical" shot—Véronique has not viewed this scene—"helps us understand what's going on in her head." This is the church Weronika saw out the train window on the way to Krakow, as the presence of her music suggests. Hence this is intended as a further link between the worlds of the two Veronicas.[13]

Alexandre later wakens Véronique and they make love,[14] but the most powerful moment in the scene occurs when Véronique finally learns of her double's existence, thanks to Alexandre. He is eager to know everything about her and she playfully dumps the contents of her purse on the coverlet for him to examine. Item after item link the two women. There is a tube of lip salve: Weronika applied some while sitting on the bench following her first heart incident. There is a clear plastic ball, the exact duplicate of the one through which Weronika viewed the buildings on her train and of which Véronique dreamed a few hours earlier. Filled with colored stars and turning the world upside down, it hearkens back to the very first shot in the film, showing Weronika's view of the Christmas sky and hence the key symbol of spiritual quest. Véronique's increased spiritual sensitivity is shown when Alexandre admits he now realizes it wasn't the book he was supposedly writing that made him choose her for his "experiment." Smiling at him tenderly, she says, "I knew that." Her instincts told her that his determined efforts sprang from a deeper impulse. She continues: "All my life I've felt like I was here and somewhere else at the same time. . . . I always sense what I should do." These remarks signal her feeling of connection to her double and a growing confidence in her instinctual sense of where her life should go.

Her connection to her double becomes complete when Alexandre unwittingly reveals her spiritual sister. He picks up another object from the purse—a proof sheet of photos taken when Véronique was on a group tour of Czechoslovakia, Hungary, and Poland—and remarks on a photo of Véronique in a big coat (Figure 9.11). She

9.11
The photo
of
Weronika,
Véronique's
double.

says it can't be her. When he passes her the sheet she stares at the photo, crumples it spasmodically and sags onto the coverlet, sobbing. The woman in the photo is not her, she realizes: it is her other self. She took the picture hastily out the window of a bus in Market Square in Krakow and never noticed that her camera was pointed at her exact double. This woman, she also realizes, is now gone: she had told her father of suddenly feeling alone and this photo shows her who has disappeared.

The Parallel Worlds

With the evidence of the photograph in her hand, Véronique easily accepts her double's reality, something her intuition has long suggested. Having seen both women and the accumulated parallels in their lives, the viewer, too, is persuaded of this mysterious possibility. Such simple acts as Weronika looking directly into the camera, as if looking out of her world into the world of the viewer, have already suggested this. Weronika's music, heard at many points in Véronique's story, also liked the two. For example, as Véronique was listening to Alexandre's cassette she suddenly sat up in bed and looked around and crying out, "Who's there!"

A reverse shot showed the room to be empty but then, as she sat trembling on the bed, a recorder and harpsichord entered on the soundtrack playing Weronika's theme softly. This moment seems to suggest that the spirit of Weronika hovers in some nearby space that can be heard—like the aural space captured on the tape—but not seen.

One scene in particular suggests other dimensions to the world which cannot be explained rationally. One day Véronique finds a strange item in her mailbox: an envelope containing nothing except a piece of dark string. (It is actually a shoelace.) She pitches the envelope and its contents in the trash and heads upstairs for a nap. She is awakened by a spot of light dancing across her eyes and around the room, like Tinkerbell. Going to the window, she discovers the strange apparition emanates from a nearby apartment window where a boy is leaning out and playing with a mirror. He goes in and shuts the window, but when Véronique turns away, the light continues to dance on the far wall, hovering around her music folder. Up to this point, normal diegetic sounds have filled the sound track—her footsteps, the click of the window as the boy closes it, and vehicles passing on the street—but now soft music comes in. Véronique glances back out the window: the boy is no longer in sight, so this light has no logical source. The mystery continues as Véronique kneels alongside the folder and touches the string that dangles from it. She hesitates and suddenly looks up straight at the camera, which slowly rotates counterclockwise, then clockwise, as if acknowledging her gaze (Figure 9.12).

9.12
Véronique's camera look.

Annette Insdorf calls this "one of the film's most haunting scenes,"[15] and, indeed, it is haunted with images from Weronika's life. Véronique's upward look into the camera repeats Weronika doing so on the train, and the mandolin music playing at this moment was heard in the background of that scene. The camera's rotation mimics its sudden cant when Weronika had her heart attack. Finally, the string on the music folder reminds viewers of the string on Weronika's folder which she wrapped around her finger as she auditioned and of the other strings prominent in her story, including the rope used to lower her coffin. All the recurring objects, from balls to lip salve, serve to link the two women, but the strings in particular suggest how they are webbed together. In this case, the mysteries work to enlighten Véronique, who recalls the shoelace she discarded and runs to retrieve it. These elements reinforce the sense that lives may be connected in mysterious ways, that our commonplace view of reality may ignore a vibrant liminal dimension.

Alexandre's New Puppets

At this point, Véronique's life seems to have achieved satisfactory closure. She lies in the hotel room with Alexandre, having found the love she seeks and conjoined with Weronika, whose photograph watches over them as they make love (just as Weronika's photo on Antek's wall had watched over their lovemaking in Poland). If Kieślowski had wanted to create a neatly happy ending, he could have finished here, leaving the hope that Alexandre's love will shelter Véronique as Weronika's spirit had. Instead, Weronika's music enters dramatically and the scene cuts to Alexandre's home where Véronique wakes from her slumbers on some later day and walks through the house. A point-of-view shot has her moving through several doors, past a flickering TV set in an empty living room, and finally to the door of Alexandre's workroom. The music has gradually crescendoed, building toward the climactic moment at which Weronika collapsed onstage, and just as Véronique comes to the workroom door the music crashes to a stop. This musical reprise clearly signals another moment of death. Véronique steps in, surveys Alexandre's work in progress, and breaks out in a laugh: "Is that me?" It is, Alexandre assures her, and she steps forward somewhat tremulously to meet her new double as Alexandre holds up the puppet he has been fabricating. Suddenly she spies a second puppet, the exact duplicate of the first, lying on the table. "Why two?" she asks, her face showing increased concern. Alexandre explains, "They get damaged easily," an answer which has terrible implications. It might explain why God made two Veronicas: the first one got damaged, but fortunately there was a backup. If so, God becomes a detached puppeteer who manipulates His players carelessly but can easily create replacements.

One watches in pain as Alexandre casually and unconsciously destroys the bond between the two of them, so newly formed. Véronique's face is seen almost entirely in close-up, so the play of her emotions registers clearly. She touches her face uncertainly, showing her vulnerability as she hears Alexandre's explanation. He urges her to try the puppet and helps her manipulate its hands, but as he does so the camera tilts down to focus on the second puppet, sprawled on the table. This tilt down from Véronique's sorrowful face to the "dead" puppet on the work table shows just how thoroughly he has killed her love. Véronique's face is shadowed as Alexandre reads the beginning of a fable he is concocting about the two puppets. They were born at the exact same hour but "in different cities, on different continents." As he reads on, detailing their parallel lives, Véronique turns her face, averting her eyes from him. Her eyes tear up, she swallows, and her face gradually sags in sorrow (Figure 9.13). She lifts her hand to wipe the tears that are

9.13
Véroniqe
shattered
by
Alexandre's
betrayal.

forming. When Alexandre asks if she likes it, she half turns her head and doesn't reply. He adds, "I think I'll call it *The Double Life of...*" but hasn't decided what to name them. She stands for a long moment, still not looking at him, then slowly turns and walks out the door in the rear, her shoes clopping on the wooden floor. The final shot lasts 1:12 and registers her slide into utter desolation.

The scene powerfully suggests the end of Véronique's nascent romance with Alexandre, cut off as starkly as the concert truncated Weronika's budding career. Although the scene leaves their future unclear, Kieślowski doubted they would stay together. "I imagine Véronique doesn't spend her life with Alexandre."[16] It is true Alexandre was the person who made Véronique aware of the existence of her double, showing his own sensitivity, but then he used this intimate knowledge for his own purposes. "And the moment he used it," Kieślowski argues, "she understood that he probably wasn't the man for whom she was waiting so desperately" because he had brought out into the open "something which was so terribly intimate."[17] In effect, he is stealing some of her soul and using it for his selfish artistic ends. One could argue that this is what artists always do and critics have noted that this is exactly what Kieślowski does with his actress, Irène Jacob.[18] The key difference is that Kieślowski seems highly conscious of the moral dilemma because he makes the motif of the puppeteer so evident. Notably, he selected Bruce Schwartz to do the puppet work, emphasizing how important it was to have the hands of the puppeteer visible, "the hands of someone who's manipulating something."[19]

Kieślowski emphasizes the pain Véronique feels at this personal violation, whereas Alexandre seems oblivious to it, totally immersed in his artistic project. The viewer may well feel cheated at this point, first seeing Weronika's hoped-for musical triumph snatched from her and now Véronique's dreams of romance dashed.

Conclusion

After Véronique leaves Alexandre's studio, the film comes quickly to a close, with just five shots that show her driving up to her father's home as he works in his wood shop, rolling down the car window, and reaching out to touch a giant tree. One clear effect of this ending is to bring everything full circle. That is, the story essentially begins with Weronika leaving her cozy home and loving father to follow her dreams to Krakow. It ends with Véronique coming home to a father who has always welcomed her warmly. It also brings her back to the tree, which serves as her totem since she was first seen examining a leaf as a child. Kieślowski said of the tree: "This is something that existed when she was small, when her mother was small, and something that will exist when her daughter is small. This tree is; it exists. Something permanent, certain." It contrasts with Véronique's life and with works of art, both of which are uncertain.[20]

This brief, uncertain ending complicates the larger issue of judging the two different paths which Weronika and Véronique take in life. Kieślowski said the story boils down to a matter of choice. "Véronique's constantly faced with the choice of whether or not to take the same road as the Polish Weronika, whether to give in to the artistic instinct and the tension intrinsic in art or to give in to love and all that it involves."[21] Following this suggestion, critics have noted that Kieślowski's own example—literally working himself to death at the end of his life—indicates the proper choice is to give everything for one's art. Paul Coates thinks both choices carry risks, arguing the film shows, on the one hand, that "Polish adventurousness is self-destructiveness." He adds, "Indeed, during shooting he [Kieślowski] even described the Polish girl as one who had abused her talent; Véronique, however, buries hers. She is Weronika reproduced as a doll; she survives, yet not fully alive."[22] R. J. A. Kilbourn concurs: "Véronique merely chooses one type of death over another, the death of a dancer who stops dancing, of a singer who stops singing: stasis, silence, death."[23] Žižek sees Véronique's return, "back to the safe haven under the wings of her father," as an "escape from freedom."[24] By revealing the existence of Weronika, Alexandre has shown Véronique how one's choices can lead in different directions. Rather than following instinctual promptings from Weronika, Véronique needs to decide how her life will proceed. Instead, avoiding that choice, she retreats to her father.[25]

However, Kieślowski termed this return home "a logical conclusion to the film,"[26] saying that in European culture in particular "going back to the family home" is a strong value.[27] Supporting this view, the farm house has been portrayed throughout as solid and comforting and in the final shot it is bathed in a warm, reddish glow. Kickasola says her return home represents "a need to find a solid place from which to renew the eternal search once more."[28] He argues that the two Veronicas are engaged in a spiritual quest. "Both women try to fill the nagging spiritual void with romance, . . . [and] both find romance wanting in this regard."[29] Other visual and aural cues support a positive reading of this ending. Although the sound of his wood-working equipment would have made it impossible to hear her drive up, apparently her father is so attuned to her that he senses her return and shuts off his router. He has always been supportive of Véronique, and so her movement toward him and away from Alexandre, who callously appropriated parts of her life, seems positive. Further, there is Véronique's gesture of reaching out to touch the tree. This links to other shots of hands—Weronika reaching out to touch the cool window glass, Weronika's father reaching down to stroke her face—that signify the human need to be "in touch" with one another, with our own spiritual nature, and with the wider world. As an expansive rather than a contractive gesture, it seems positive. Finally, as Véronique reaches out to the tree, Weronika's solo comes in. While a reminder of her tragic death, it is also expressive of her passion. Its steadily rising scale shows the human determination to rise and achieve. In Alexandre's puppet show, it was linked to the emergence of the angelic butterfly and one reading of this final moment would be that Véronique, after a period of spiritual pupation, is now ready to emerge, spread her wings, and soar.

Afterword on Narrative Structure

With this apparently simple story of two lives, Kieślowski has created one of the most complex uses of the database or multiple-draft narrative. In the end, we seem not to be watching two different lives but two worlds that somehow overlap. The sense of coexistent realities is conveyed most strongly in the scene where the two Veronicas encounter one another near the end of Weronika's story. On her way to her audition, she crosses Market Square in Krakow, ignoring the political demonstration going on in the background and the wail of klaxons as the riot police move into position. Walking forward, she slows and stops at the amazing sight she beholds. A group of tourists is being hustled onto a bus to get away from the potential clash of police and demonstrators, and among them is her double, Véronique, dressed in red scarf and red gloves, the exact apparel Weronika is wearing (Figure 9.14). This unknown young woman hurries through the bus,

9.14
Véroniqe
seen by
Weronika
in Krakow
Square.

snapping photos through the windows, but never catching sight of Weronika, who steps forward to keep this apparition in view and stands transfixed as the bus rolls away.

In folklore, catching sight of one's double is a harbinger of death,[30] but Weronika half smiles and steps forward curiously, appearing not to fear this encounter despite the scene's dark overtones. The demonstrators are from Poland's period of turmoil following the collapse of the Soviet Union, but they are more significant on the metaphysical than the social level. They function like the disturbances in *Macbeth*, where the storms and strange occurrences in the natural world—Duncan's horses breaking out of their pens and eating one another (IV.4)—are a figuration of the breakdown in the moral order. That is, in the medieval view, God's place at the summit of creation is mirrored in the monarch's place at the head of his kingdom. By usurping the throne, Macbeth upsets the divine order, producing equivalent abominations in the natural world. Similarly, at this moment in Weronika's story a monumental disturbance is occurring in the universe. As Žižek brilliantly proposes, the film may not be showing the encounter of two different Veronicas, but of "*one and the same* Véronique who travels back and forth in time."[31] The film's title, after all, is *The Double Life of Véronique*, not *The Two Veronicas*, suggesting that there is a single Véronique who leads two lives. In the Market Square at Krakow those two realities collide and the magnitude of this disturbance is reflected in the surrounding turmoil, with fleeing demonstrators, screaming klaxons, a police vehicle that blocks the view, and the tourists hurriedly clambering on their bus.

The disturbance is also conveyed through the "vertiginous" camerawork.[32] As Weronika walks forward, the camera first leads her and then, when she catches sight of the tour bus, swings around 180 degrees to view the bus from behind her shoulder. After a close-up of Weronika, a closer shot of the bus reveals Véronique boarding it and taking her random photos through the window.

In a return shot, Weronika walks left while the camera simultaneously tracks right and pans left, increasing the sense of vertigo. A telephoto close-up shows the bus turning clockwise away from the camera and then, in a following shot, continuing to rotate completely around before moving away. The combination of tracking and panning camera, moving characters, and pivoting bus create a dizzying swirl of movement. Žižek likens this to the "time tunnels" which link alternate realities in science fiction movies, invariably portrayed as "a terrifying primordial vortex threatening to swallow all consistent reality." If the two Veronicas were actually to meet and recognize one another, he argues, "Reality would disintegrate" because the overlapping existence of two separate space-time continuums "is precluded by the very fundamental structure of the universe."[33] Following this view, the riot police lined up behind Weronika might be taken as a feeble attempt to ward off ontological chaos. In this pivotal scene, Kieślowski foregrounds the thrust of the entire film, seeking to explore dimensions of reality which escape our everyday notice.

The cumulative effect of these narrative and visual patterns is a haunting sense of order, as if we are watching the pieces of a puzzle that fit together in some mysterious way. Kickasola says Kieślowski is revealing that "there is a unity in the world—a beautiful structure that is noticed when the camera distills it to a celluloid image."[34] In his book, *The Liminal Image*, Kickasola argues that these abstract images—such as the very first shot of the night sky—communicate with viewers at a prerational level. They are liminal, bridging the divide between the normal rational world and realities which lie beyond it, creating a moment when eternal order is felt behind the flux of events.[35] This is the hierophanic world as described by Eliade, a world which moves in circles rather than forward, where time is unchanging.[36] By presenting the viewer with images that cannot easily be deciphered, Kieślowski reminds us of the mystery that lies outside our quotidian world. Kickasola argues that all these elements—the formal patterns, the abstraction, the intertwining of plots, the timelessness, and the mystery—show Kieślowski struggling toward a transcendent core at the center of reality. "There is no evidence that Kieślowski ever felt that he concretely found that Transcendent hope," Kickasola, concludes, "but his films stand as testament to the integrity of his search and his longing."[37] The heroine in particular exudes a luminescence, as if we are watching not so much a person in pursuit of a goal but a soul in search of its essence (Figure 9.15). Music and mortal love, we are shown, fall short of the perfection the soul seeks, but that is not disheartening. Rather, the film celebrates the fact that the search continues.

9.15 The puppeteer's angel: Kieślowski's abiding hope.

Notes

1 Joseph G. Kickasola, *The Films of Krzysztof Kieślowski: The Liminal Image* (New York: Continuum, 2004), 66-69.

2 Annette Insdorf, "Audio Commentary," *La Double Vie de Véronique,* Criterion DVD (2006).

3 Kickasola, *The Films of Krzysztof Kieślowski,* 246.

4 Slavoj Žižek, *The Fright of Real Tears: Krzysztof Kieślowski between Theory and Post-Theory* (London: BFI, 2001), 78.

5 Kickasola, *The Films of Krzysztof Kieślowski,* 251.

6 Kickasola, *The Films of Krzysztof Kieślowski,* 251.

7 Kickasola, *The Films of Krzysztof Kieślowski,* 77, 38.

8 Kickasola, *The Films of Krzysztof Kieślowski,* 248.

9 Kickasola, *The Films of Krzysztof Kieślowski,* 75.

10 Kickasola, *The Films of Krzysztof Kieślowski,* 249.

11 Paul Coates, "Metaphysical Love in Two Films by Krzysztof Kieślowski," *The Polish Review* 37, no. 3 (1992): 341.

12 The scene has an immediate dark undertone because of repeated shots out the window of a burned out car and a blackened building (captured in the explosion on the audio tape), apparently resulting from some terrorist attack. Like Weronika's flasher, these intercut shots hint at a world where violence and uncertainty always lurk in the background.

13 Slawomir Idziak, "Interview," *La Double Vie de Véronique,* Criterion DVD (2006).

14 Kieślowski's decision not to depict the sexual liaison of Véronique and Alexandre contrasts with the typical Hollywood romance. Weronika's lovemaking with Antek was shown, emphasizing the depth of her affection for him, and yet she left him to seek artistic fulfillment. Concluding the film with a passionate encounter between Alexandre and Véronique would put the director's imprimatur on their relationship

and endorse romance as the guarantor of human happiness. For all the tenderness to be seen in Véronique's face as Alexandre begins making love to her, such pat resolutions are not generally found Kieślowski's films.

15   Annette Insdorf, *Double Lives, Second Chances: The Cinema of Krzysztof Kieślowski* (New York: Hyperion, 1999), 136.

16   Danusia Stok, ed, *Kieślowski on Kieślowski* (London: Faber and Faber, 1993), 182.

17   Stok, *Kieślowski on Kieślowski*, 182.

18   Emma Wilson, *Memory and Survival: The French Cinema of Krzysztof Kieślowski* (European Humanities Research Centre-University of Oxford: Legenda, 2000), 20.

19   Stok, *Kieślowski on Kieślowski*, 180-81.

20   Marek Haltof, *The Cinema of Krzysztof Kieślowski* (London: Wallflower, 2004), 162-63n.

21   Stok, *Kieślowski on Kieślowski*, 185.

22   Coates, "Metaphysical Love in Two Films by Krzysztof Kieślowski," 343.

23   R. J. A. Kilbourn, "Toward a Non-Euclidean Cinema: Kieślowski and Literature," *Canadian Journal of Film Studies* 6, no. 2 (1997): 46.

24   Slavoj Žižek, "The Forced Choice of Freedom," DVD Booklet, *La Double Vie de Véronique*, Criterion DVD (2006).

25   Žižek, "The Forced Choice of Freedom."

26   Haltof, *The Cinema of Krzysztof Kieślowski*, 117.

27   Stok, *Kieślowski on Kieślowski*, 7.

28   Kickasola, *The Cinema of Krzysztof Kieślowski*, 262-63.

29   Kickasola, *The Cinema of Krzysztof Kieślowski*, 253.

30   Haltof, *The Cinema of Krzysztof Kieślowski*, 118.

31   Žižek, *The Fright of Real Tears*, 84.

32   Žižek, *The Fright of Real Tears*, 84.

33   Žižek, *The Fright of Real Tears*, 84.

34   Kickasola, *The Cinema of Krzysztof Kieślowski*, 84.

35   Kickasola, *The Cinema of Krzysztof Kieślowski*, 62-63.

36   Mircea Eliade, *The Sacred and the Profane: The Nature of Religion*, Willard R. Trask, trans. (San Diego: Harcourt, 1957), 11-12.

37   Kickasola, *The Cinema of Krzysztof Kieślowski*, 89.

10

Conclusion

Tying Up the Threads

When Ilsa Lund walks into Rick's Café Américain twenty-five minutes into *Casablanca*, the audience sits back with a contented sigh because she is so beautiful and because the romance—that standard feature of classical Hollywood films—will now begin. (In the one hundred films sampled for their monumental analysis in *The Classical Hollywood Cinema*, the authors found eighty-five had a romance as the central plot action and ninety-five included it as one of the two central plot lines.[1]) It is interesting, then, that of the eight films with complex plots examined here, only the three *database* (or *multiple-draft*) *narratives*—*Virgin Stripped Bare by Her Bachelors*, *Run Lola Run*, and *The Double Life of Véronique*—have a romance at the center. Although romance plays a reduced role in the various *network narratives* studied here, that is not necessarily true for network narratives generally, a number of which deal centrally with love relations. Nevertheless, the point remains that the viewer of complex narrative films cannot expect romance to appear routinely, nor for other standard generic patterns to appear. In fact, some of the films delight in inverting generic conventions. *Nashville* inverts the musical (since the bickering musicians do not come together in the final grand show but disappear from the stage) just as *Pulp Fiction* inverts a host of earlier clichés—Vincent does not run off with the boss's wife/girlfriend as happened in *Out of the Past* (Tourneur, 1947). Hence the pleasure for the viewer of these films comes not in enjoying familiar tropes but in the interweaving of narratives and the emergence of thematic patterns.

Although the eight films studied here demonstrate the potential benefits of complex narration, complexity alone is no guarantor of artistic success. As noted in the introduction, these forms carry attendant risks, one being attenuated character depth. Sketchy characterization, acceptable in a comedy like *Love Actually,* is problematic in more serious stories. Thus in *Things You Can Tell Just by Looking at Her* (Rodrigo Garcia, 1999), the film's premise—announced in the title—is that the essence of a woman's life is immediately evident in a passing glance. (Conveniently, the central essence of all five women glanced at turns out to be the same: loneliness.) In turn, this allows the film to use mind-reading to portray its characters rather than actual story events. This strategy is announced in the first story where Christine arrives at Dr. Keener's house to do a Tarot reading, and is immediately able to lay out the entire truth of her new client's life. "You're not happy. . . .You don't know yourself well. . . .You've been married but you're presently divorced or separated. . . .You don't have any lifelong friends." And so on. No actual story events confirm any of this and Dr. Keener is generally silent throughout the reading, but from the pained look on her face we infer that Christine has gotten everything spot on. Similarly, in the second story a bag lady shows up, cadges a cigarette from the protagonist, Rebecca, and, again, instantly knows the truth of her life. "You're disgusting. One look at you was enough for me. A sad bitch. You're as lonely as a dog." In the final story, the only clue detective Kathy can find to explain a woman's suicide is that her baby died at birth some time back. Fortunately, Kathy's blind sister, Carol, spins out a very plausible story about the child's death breaking up a relationship, which viewers apparently must accept as gospel since everyone knows blind people are amazingly empathetic. These repeated instances of magical mind reading are made somewhat more acceptable by having a woman rather than a man reveal the "truth" of a woman's life, but to suggest that a person's character can be obvious to a complete stranger glancing at her—as the film's title implies—is trite.

In addition to the risk of shallow characters, a director trying to juggle too many stories may fall back on narrative cliché. Paul Haggis's *Crash* (2004) follows no less than eight story lines over the course of two days in L.A., all centering on the problem of racism, but treats its characters and issues superficially. Thus a racist cop pulls over a well-to-do black couple, sexually fondles the wife in a supposed "pat down," and then forces the husband to apologize to avoid arrest. Later, that cop is shown caring tenderly for his father who has prostate problems, and blocked from receiving proper treatment by a rule-bound health coordinator who happens to be black. Not twenty-four hours later, that same cop risks his life to rescue the affluent black woman, trapped in her car after an accident and about to be incinerated. Furious when he first arrives, she turns to smile and mouth "thank you" to him as she is helped to the ambulance. The scene is powerful in its tension and hopeful in its promise of racial reconciliation. However, the superficial reasons given for the officer's racism, the incredible coincidence that brings him together with his victim again, his radical turnaround, and her instantaneous forgiveness—a pattern found in three more of the stories—belong more to Hollywood's version of race relations than to the real world. David Bordwell notes that successful forking paths narratives generally follow only two or three possible tracks,[2] and this may be a principle which complex narratives in general are wise to follow. Films that move beyond three or four stories often get themselves into trouble.

Besides shallow characters and clichéd stories, a third potential problem is that individual stories may spin away from one another and lose their thematic connection. This is seen in Iñárritu's third feature, *Babel* (2006), where two young boys in Morocco, given a rifle by their father to protect the goat herds, start shooting at random targets and accidentally wound an American tourist, Susan Jones. The United States brands this a terrorist act and Moroccan police subsequently track down the family and kill one of the boys in a shoot-out. Meanwhile, Susan and her husband, Richard, are given refuge in a small village whose residents care for her as best they can until she can be airlifted to a hospital. In a third story, the Jones's two young children back in San Diego end up lost in a desert when their devoted nanny takes them along to Mexico for her son's wedding. A fourth story deals with Chieko, teenage daughter of a Japanese businessman who originally owned the rifle that wounded Susan. A deaf-mute, Chieko is tormented by her outsider status, not to mention the recent suicide of her mother. The film's title, *Babel*, announces its theme as the failure of human communication, which is certainly found in the story of Richard and Susan, their marriage in turmoil after the death of a third child. It is also seen when Richard yells at everyone in his frantic attempts to get help for his wife and when diplomatic bickering worsens the situation. But generally the stories are not linked well, either causally or thematically. The two Moroccan boys get into trouble for a foolish accident, Amelia is caught between being a good nanny and a good mother, and Chieko is suffering primarily from personal angst. The individual stories are driven by accident, linked primarily through coincidence, and fail to connect in any meaningful thematic way, weakening the film considerably.

These potential problems with complex narration make the success of the eight examples studied here all the more impressive. In the case of *Nashville*, for example, the ***mosaic*** construction, with its slowed narrative and fractured characterization, may frustrate many viewers but will reward someone attentive to the film's accretion of details. Consider one minor character, L. A. Joan. She is met at the Nashville airport by her uncle, Mr. Green, who plans to drive her immediately to the hospital to see his seriously ill wife. After announcing her changed name (she was formerly Martha), Joan quickly ducks off to get an autograph from Tom, the lothario folk singer. In the days that follow, she is glimpsed briefly, emerging from various washrooms in some new outfit and wig and walking off on the arm of some new man. She never visits her aunt in the hospital, never utters a single word of sympathy to her sorrowing uncle, and, when her aunt dies, skips the funeral in favor of attending the big concert at the Walker rally. How appropriate, then, that Joan's first moment on screen should be in the same shot where Triplette likewise first appears, stepping forward to greet Del at the Nashville airport (Figure 10.1). Thus Joan, the embodiment of narcissism, shifting identity,

10.1
Persons
of easy
virtue:
L. A. Joan
and
Triplette.

and self-prostitution, is placed visually apposite to Triplette, spokesman for Hal Phillip Walker, the self-proclaimed voice of reform in American politics. This minor character with fewer lines of dialogue than wigs in her wardrobe becomes one more piece, fitting neatly into Altman's overall picture. The longer one studies this narrative—so random-seeming at first viewing—the more finely nuanced its mosaic structure appears.

Likewise, the four examples of network narrative discussed here show how themes emerge as stories are compared and contrasted. *Pulp Fiction* is notable for the range of themes that can be found among its stories, thanks to its mishmash of elements, allusions to previous films, and constantly shifting tonalities. The particular interpretation put forward here, that the altered time order of the stories emphasizes the idea of redemption, touches on only one important aspect. Other critics have discussed how the film's stories represent a struggle to reaffirm masculinity,[3] as the individual's battle against time,[4] or as "sheer cinematic spectacle."[5] Besides demonstrating how complex narratives naturally lend themselves to thematic development, Tarantino—for all his other shortcomings—must be credited with bringing a freshness, a sense of energy, and a playfulness to these new forms. Thus when Butch rides away with his girlfriend at the end of his story, a close-up shot shows that the motorcycle he has appropriated (from the soon-to-be-deceased Zed) is named "Grace." Of course, Butch has redeemed himself for the two accidental murders he committed—that of his boxing opponent and of Vincent—but in this passing detail Tarantino is simultaneously throwing in another reference to spirituality and joking with the audience, which is why *Pulp Fiction* continues to be such an exhilarating example of the multi-plot form.

Amores Perros is also notable for its energy, evident immediately in the gut-wrenching car chase that opens the film. More obviously than *Pulp Fiction*, it plays its stories against one another, letting the viciousness of the dogfights and the bestiality of El Chivo hint at the violence underlying the lives of all the characters. Just as the dogs in each story reflect on their masters, so do the various dwellings. The crowded kitchen in the Concha home, with the characters practically on top of one another (emphasized by the wide-angle lens) suggests the economic pressures weighing on the family. The upscale but ultimately barren apartment of Daniel and Valeria mirrors the lack of any real emotional center to their relationship. El Chivo's squalid dwelling, with his mangy dogs included in every shot, is the objective correlative of his sordid soul; fittingly, he leaves Luis and Gustavo in the domain of the assassin to fight things out. El Chivo vacates that subhuman abode, wanting to return to a space where human beings are connected, to the world his daughter inhabits, to his family. What is most fascinating about the lives Iñárritu compares is how people so widely separated on the social scale can tear their lives apart in such similar fashion.

Code Unknown stands at the opposite pole from *Pulp Fiction*. Tarantino's desperate desire to entertain his audience results in a frenetic pace that leaves no real time to appreciate the interplay of his themes. Haneke's coldly calculated storytelling risks leaving the viewer so uninvolved that she has no interest in unraveling the various connections. Nonetheless, the film is filled with quietly powerful scenes that link to the central theme of isolation. For example, there is Aminate's visit to the marabout (religious teacher) where she relates the dream that led to her ongoing migraine headaches. In it she felt "shapes coming toward the house. . . . They want to get in. They bang and scrape on the walls and door. Then the door bursts open." She wakes up at this point, but cannot move or speak and when she prays to Allah for help, "I hear loud laughter behind me." This nightmare dramatically embodies Aminate's sense of alien forces tearing into the fabric of her life. Besides explaining her husband's decision to abandon his family in France and return to Mali, the violence portrayed here pops up repeatedly in the film, from the maniacal collector who gasses innocent women to Anne's harassment by the angry young Arab on the subway. These are the forces, Haneke suggests, that threaten to tear not just Amidou's family but all of Europe apart. The fragmented lives lived out in very disparate cultural spaces are being pulled apart, not so much by individual decisions as by powerful social tides.

Although *The Edge of Heaven* has more than its share of death and non-communication, it somehow manages to sustain the hope that human beings can come together despite their differences. This is emphasized by the many scenes of communal dining—Ali and Nejat drinking raki together, Yeter preparing börek for Nejat's trip home, Lotte buying Ayten a meal at the student cafeteria, and the bookstore owner in Istanbul offering Nejat chai. This motif has its capstone when Nejat and Susanne dine together in Istanbul and he introduces her to the delights of Turkish cuisine. As they enjoy a glass of raki together, he asks what they will toast to and she says, "To death," a grim recognition of how tragedy has touched their lives. But the beautiful straight down shot of the table displays their colorful meal served in crisp white bowls, suggesting that people of differing backgrounds can somehow find moments of communion (Figure 10.2). Haneke shows lives

10.2
A beautiful communal meal.

unraveling, emphasized by his distanced camerawork, disjunctive editing, and fractured narrative structure. By contrast, Akin's visual rhymes, thematic motifs, and artfully interwoven stories mirror his underlying assertion that broken family connections can be reestablished just as human commonalities unite us.

The three **database** or **multi-draft narratives** each have a romance at the center, but only in *Run Lola Run* does it turn out successfully. *Virgin Stripped Bare by Her Bachelors* might better be described as an anti-romance since, despite the talk of marriage at the end, there is no sense of emotional connection. Not only is the loss of Soojung's virginity made devastating to watch—the scene lasts for two awful minutes with Soojung crying out continually in pain—but afterward she has to wash the blood out of the sheets since Jaehoon cannot manage it. (There is plenty of ineffectuality to go around, since she confesses she doesn't know how to cook, but he gains the clear edge in boorishness by proposing to take the bloody sheets home as a trophy.) Solicitously, he asks if she would like something to eat, but then it turns out he's feeling a little hungry, so it's clear whose needs will always take precedence. The closing moments where they discuss their future life together are not "celebratory," but set forth the "grim prospect of facing another obsessive cycle of the game to which they are now eternally bound."[6] The story throughout has presented two incongruent versions of the courtship and this ending, rather than the blending of two lives into a blissful union, suggests one reality bludgeoning another into submission. This is narrative closure of the grimmest kind.

It is hard to imagine a worldview more different from Hong's than Tom Tyk-wer's. Hong's characters stand or sit in a dreary black-and-white world, talking to no real purpose, their ineffectuality emphasized by many instances where the camera fails to follow them or adopt their point of view. By contrast, Tykwer's camera can barely keep up with Lola as she charges across Berlin, leaping over obstacles, her red hair flying. Although the city she runs through often appears bleak and empty of life, it is a place where human action can effect miraculous change. In terms of narrative, Tykwer also constructs his repeated story very differently. Hong presents contradictory stories which cancel one another out to a degree, creating a narrative paralysis to match the inaction of the characters. By contrast, Lola remains firmly in charge in all three versions of her tale. Even though the first two runs end in failure, she immediately resurrects herself and then Manni and gives it another try. Particularly because Lola learns from each run and plays the game better, the stories build on one another rather than canceling one another out. Critical, too, are the differences in the two endings. Hong emphasizes human impotence by showing that, despite the differing versions of the courtship, the ending—the loss of Soojung's virginity—is inescapable. By contrast, Lola finds a way to make things come out as she wishes. Her motto in life, according to Tykwer, is "I create the world as I wish it to be," and he says the film is about "the possibilities to be found in life."[7] The dramatic differences in just these two films illustrate the creative range offered by the database narrative.

As a final example of that range, we have Kieślowski's *The Double Life of Véronique*. Its time structure is far simpler than that of *Virgin*, which has five jumps in time, and *Lola,* which returns to the beginning twice and throws in seven flash forwards that forecast the future lives of people Lola bumps into on her run. *Véronique* tells one story and, when it ends, shifts to telling the second story in straightforward chronological fashion. However, the steady accumulation of over-laps in the stories, and especially Kieślowski's use of image and sound, evokes the ineffable sense of two coexistent worlds. In one brilliant example, sound is used to suggest parallel realities as Véronique puts the cassette Alexandre has sent her into a player and listens through earphones as she moves through her apartment. She takes off her shoes, gets herself a drink, shucks her coat and sweater, brushes her teeth and flops on the bed, but none of the diegetic sound accompanying these actions is heard. Rather there is the mysterious mélange of the tape's sound track: creaking doors, voices, train announcements, and finally an explosion. The scene "serves as an amplification of the central duality theme that has run throughout the film: the idea that two worlds could coexist (in this case, through nonsynchro-nous aural and visual elements)."[8] The viewer participates in this experience of bicameral realities, simultaneously seeing one reality and hearing another. What begins as the simple telling of two stories ends as a complex portrait of reality in which the lives of two young women following different paths in separate spaces are mysteriously concatenated so that the two women become one.

These eight films, taken as a group, represent a tiny fraction of the hundreds in recent decades that play with narrative structure. They are a representative sample only insofar as their diversity illustrates the many directions in which this experimentation has led. (The appendix lists further interesting examples of films that use complex narrative.) These eight are united principally in their reliance on thematic patterns and on the renewed creative energy they bring to the cinematic enterprise. Film, like other art forms, oscillates continually between the experimental and the familiar. Because movies are a complex commercial enterprise, the safety of the formulaic is attractive; a director who makes interesting but unprofitable films is unlikely to continue directing. Given the considerable financial risks involved, it is remarkable that the sort of innovation found here has continued, at least to some degree. Innovative films must somehow manage to appeal to mass audiences who enjoy a degree of novelty but are most comfortable with established patterns that orient the viewer clearly. Stories that jump backward and forward in time or require staying attentive to several story lines or present contradictory views of events make higher demands than many viewers may wish to pay, wanting only a momentary escape and a visceral rush. But for viewers willing to pay that price, there are commensurate rewards. David Bordwell speculates that a major appeal in these films comes from "the aesthetic pleasure of seeing unconnected events fall into a pattern."[9] That pleasure arises from the satisfaction we find in experiencing artistic order and the corresponding hope that our lives, filled with random events, may yet cohere into something worthwhile. These filmmakers obviously share that delight in artistic order and in that search for meaningful existence.

Notes

1   David Bordwell, Janet Staiger, and Kristin Thompson, *The Classical Hollywood Cinema: Film Style & Mode of Production to 1960* (New York: Columbia University Press, 1985), 16.

2   David Bordwell, "Film Futures," *SubStance* #97, 31, no 1 (2002): 89.

3   Jesse Zigelstein, "Staying Alive in the 90s: Travolta as Star and the Performance of Masculinity," *CineAction* 44 (1997): 2-11.

4   Peter N. Chumo, II, "'The Next Best Thing to a Time Machine': Quentin Tarantino's *Pulp Fiction*," *Post Script* 15, no. 3 (Summer 1996): 16-28.

5   Dana Polan, *Pulp Fiction* (London: BFI, 2000), 7.

6   Kyung Hyun Kim, *The Remasculinization of Korean Cinema* (Durham, N.C.: Duke University Press, 2004), 217.

7   Michael Töteberg, ed., *Tom Tykwer: Lola rennt* (Reinbek: Rowohlt, 1998), 118, 131.

8   Joseph G. Kickasola, *The Films of Krzysztof Kieślowski: The Liminal Image* (New York: Continuum, 2004), 86.

9   David Bordwell, *Poetics of Cinema* (London: Routledge, 2008), 214.

Appendix

Further Complex Narratives of Interest

Described in this appendix are some further films readers might find of interest. They represent only a small sample of those employing complex narrative forms. David Bordwell lists two hundred films with network narratives in his study *Poetics of Cinema*, and mosaic narratives, network narratives, and database narratives, in turn, are only a few forms among the many kinds of complex storytelling that have appeared. Besides Bordwell's chapters in *The Way Hollywood Tells It* and *Poetics of Cinema*, further useful overviews can be found in Charles Ramirez Berg's taxonomy of narrative experiments, Bordwell's analysis of forking path narratives in "Film Futures," Alan Cameron's book on modular narratives and puzzle films, and Jonathan Eig's discussions of films that deliberately mislead viewers, all listed in the Bibliography.

Mosaic Narrative

Amarcord (1974)
Director: Federico Fellini
Screenplay: Federico Fellini, Tonino Guerra

Beginning with the town bonfire to celebrate the arrival of spring, the film traces a year in the life of a small town in Italy in the 1930s. Many scenes deal with a single family, but the real focus is on the entire populace: pranks played in school, the nightly parade of townsfolk in the square, the boys making their confessions to

Don Balosa, a celebration for the visit of a Fascist official, various town legends, everyone sailing out in small craft to witness the passing of the grand new Italian liner *The Rex*, and the wedding of Gradisca, the town beauty, in the following spring. The seemingly random events and quaint characters coalesce to reveal the society's authoritarian nature, fertile soil for the rise of Fascism, but portrayed with Fellini's typical phantasmagoric imagination.

Network Narratives

13 Conversations about One Thing (2001)
Director: Jill Sprecher
Screenplay: Karen Sprecher, Jill Sprecher

Gene, cynical head of an insurance claims department, fires Wade, ostensibly as a cost-cutting move but mostly because Wade's consistent cheerfulness annoys him. Out of work for months, Wade remains continually upbeat, to Gene's amazement. Troy, the up-and-coming prosecutor, glories in making the world better by taking criminals off the street, but when he accidentally hits a pedestrian at night, he doesn't stop to help the victim. Wanting something more out of life, Walker, a university professor, separates from his wife but then is shaken when a student he has been hard on commits suicide. Bea, a perennially optimistic young house-cleaner, winds up in the hospital after being struck by a hit-and-run driver. Moving from story to story and back and forth in time, the film concatenates these lives in fascinating ways as events force the characters to reexamine their worldviews.

Babel (2006)
Director: Alejandro González Iñárritu
Screenplay: Guillermo Arriaga, Alejandro González Iñárritu

Two young boys in Morocco accidentally wound an American tourist, Susan, when shooting randomly with a rifle purchased to kill jackals. Susan and her husband are taken to a nearby village whose locals try to help while awaiting a rescue helicopter. Unbeknownst to them, their two children back in San Diego have been taken into Mexico for a wedding by their loving nanny, but then get into difficulty. In Tokyo, Chieko—whose businessman father was the rifle's original owner—suffers significant psychological problems as a deaf-mute teenager unable to fit in, compounded by the recent suicide of her mother. The various stories do not cohere as strongly as they might, but are compellingly told and brilliantly photographed, with dazzling scenes such as the wedding in Mexico and the rave club in Tokyo.

Beautiful People (1999)
Director: Jasmin Dizdar
Screenplay: Jasmin Dizdar

The war in Bosnia impacts a diverse group of people in England. Jerry, a BBC reporter is wounded while covering the war but even more devastated psychologically by the horrors he witnesses. Griffin, a skinhead, is likewise changed when accidentally dumped into the middle of the carnage. Back in a hospital in England, Portia, a doctor in training, falls in love with a Bosnian refugee; her colleague, Dr. Mouldy, is trying to counsel a Serbian woman whose pregnancy is the result of rape; and a Serb and a Croat who attacked one another on a London bus are treated in the same ward. Our human connectedness, emphasized by the tight interweaving of the stories, makes the ethnic hatreds portrayed all the more lamentable.

Chungking Express [*Chung Hing sam lan*] (1994)
Director: Wong Kar-wai
Screenplay: Wong Kar-wai

In Hong Kong, young cop 223 won't believe that his girlfriend has broken up with him and gives her until April 1 to come back. He marks each day by buying a can of pineapple with a sell-by date of April 1. A mysterious woman has been given a can stamped with that same date from her boss as a message: she has only a few days to recover the drugs and money her "mules" ran off with. On April 30 these two meet. In a second story, cop 633 stops coming to the Chungking Express, a fast food stand, to avoid taking back the keys his ex-girlfriend left there for him. He never seems to notice the changes that begin to occur in his apartment now being used as a refuge by Faye, a worker at the Express, who has secretly appropriated the keys. One day, 633 finds her there. A quirky, funny, melancholy film with two stories that barely overlap but are filled with similar themes.

Crash (2004)
Director: Paul Haggis
Screenplay: Paul Haggis, Robert Moresco

An L.A. cop pulls over an affluent black couple for no reason and "pats down" the wife in a sexual, deliberately humiliating way. The cop, it turns out, is struggling to care for his seriously ill father and he later risks his life to rescue that same woman, trapped in her car after an accident. Getting carjacked by two young blacks allows the wife of the D.A. to give full vent to her vituperative racism. She thinks differently when she has an accident at home, her society friends are all too busy to help, and her Spanish maid gets her to the hospital. A young cop who has been horrified at the racist behavior around him ends up committing an awful racist crime. Several more stories show this same pattern of abrupt character reversals, incredible coincidence, and superficial explanations of racist behavior, weakening a film which audiences loved because of its strong acting performances and emotionally moving scenes.

Exotica (1994)
Director: Atom Egoyan
Screenplay: Atom Egoyan

Francis, an auditor, goes weekly to Club Exotica and has Christina, who dresses as a schoolgirl, do a table dance for him. They seem to have a special relationship, which makes Eric, announcer at the Exotica and Christina's former lover, jealous. He tricks Francis into touching Christina, getting him banned from the club. To get revenge, Francis blackmails Thomas to help him kill Eric and Thomas has little choice since Francis's audit has confirmed that Thomas should go to jail for smuggling birds. An especially somber set of networked stories, with psychologically damaged characters constantly revealing new and darker connections to one another.

Go (1999)
Director: Doug Liman
Screenplay: John August

Facing eviction from her apartment, Ronna agrees to work Simon's shift at the supermarket to get some extra cash. She soon sees an opportunity for more income when two strangers, Adam and Zack, ask her to get them some drugs, since Simon, their usual supplier, is now gone. Short of cash, Ronna has to leave her girlfriend as collateral with the dealer while she sells the drugs. Adam and Zack had been told the drug charges against them would be dropped in return for taking part in the sting operation, but it turns out their handler has further plans in mind. Off to Las Vegas with three friends, Simon finds more adventures than he had counted on, including a hotel room fire, a stolen car, and a bouncer at Crazy Horse who takes exception to patrons fondling the lap dancers. These three fast-paced adventures, taking place in just twenty-four hours, bounce off one another in wacky ways.

Hannah and Her Sisters (1985)
Director: Woody Allen
Screenplay: Woody Allen

Hannah, a successful actress, is happily married to Elliot, a stock analyst. Unbeknownst to her, Elliot begins an affair with Lee, Hannah's younger sister, who is torn between her feelings for Hannah and for Elliot. Hannah's other sister, Holly, a recovering drug addict and failed actress, constantly borrows money from Hannah to finance some new enterprise. Hannah's ex-husband, Mickey, falls into an existential crisis, quits his job as a comedy show producer and begins a desperate search for the meaning of life. A wonderful blend of comedy and drama, with outstanding acting performances, as all the characters struggle to figure out who they are and where they are headed.

Happenstance [*Le battement d'ailes du papillon*] (1997)
Director: Laurent Firode
Screenplay: Laurent Firode

More than a dozen characters constantly cross paths during a single day in Paris, their lives nudged in new directions by apparently insignificant actions and objects. In one story, a café waiter convinces a patron that good actions create good luck and gives him an appliance store discount coupon. At the store, the man steals a coffee maker to replace the defective one the store refuses to fix for an elderly customer, which gets the salesgirl fired. Hours later, that salesgirl sits in a park with a bandage on her face after a minor traffic accident. Sitting behind her is a boy who happened to be riding with her on the subway that morning and who now sports an exactly similar facial bandage. Still trying to do good deeds, the same man had handed the boy a rain jacket (discarded by a pickpocket), which got the boy tackled by the pickpocket's victim (the salesgirl's roommate). With matching visages, under a full moon, they gaze at one another on the day their horoscopes had predicted they would meet their true love. Whimsical.

Happy Endings (2005)
Director: Don Roos
Screenplay: Don Roos

As a teenager, Mamie seduced her stepbrother, Charlie, became pregnant, gave up her baby, and now works as an abortion counselor. The inept Nicky, having information about Mamie's adopted son, blackmails her into helping him make a documentary he hopes will get him into film school. Charlie, now in a relationship with Gil, concocts a plot to ascertain if their friends, Pam and Diane, actually did use Gil's sperm donation. Jude, a footloose young band singer, tricks Otis into sex one time, then blackmails him into letting her pretend to be his girlfriend and live comfortably at his home in return for not revealing he's gay. Then she starts genuinely to like his tender-hearted dad. Then she discovers she's pregnant. Funny, sentimental stories that connect in fascinating ways, with most having happy endings, but not all.

Jellyfish [*Meduzot*] (2007)
Directors: Shira Geffen, Etgar Keret
Screenplay: Shira Geffen

On a Tel Aviv beach, a silent sea child emerges from the water and walks straight to Batya, who takes her home when no parents can be found. Ignored by her own divorced parents, Batya gets fired from her waitress job when the sea child causes mischief at a wedding reception. The reception is for Michael and Keren, who must spend their honeymoon in a third-rate hotel when Keren accidentally breaks her leg at the party and cannot travel. They begin to quarrel and Keren becomes jealous when a mysterious woman writer insists the couple take her suite. Joy (seen at the reception) takes loving care of elderly Israelis and desperately misses her little son back in the Philippines. A poetic meditation on people being carried in new directions by the tides of life, with mysterious psychic overlaps and constant imagery of the sea.

Love Actually (2003)
Director: Richard Curtis
Screenplay: Richard Curtis

In a concoction of multiple romances, the British Prime Minister falls in love with his tea girl, his sister worries about her husband's fidelity (with good reason, because a coworker has set her cap for him), a widower helps his young son court a classmate, an office girl has her romantic hopes repeatedly dashed by needing to care for her mentally ill brother, two porn film stand-ins start to find one another attractive, a man falls in love with his Portuguese housekeeper despite not speaking her language, a man has a crush on his best friend's wife, a young Brit goes looking for richer sexual pastures in America, and a brokendown rock 'n' roll singer discovers that love has been nearby all the time. No great profundity, but a strong cast, witty script, and endless amusement.

Magnolia (1999)
Director: Paul Thomas Anderson
Screenplay: Paul Thomas Anderson

A quirky prologue offers examples of strange synchronicity, followed by interlinked stories all connected to dying TV producer, Earl Partridge. While Earl's wife arouses the suspicion of pharmacists in her frantic search for drugs to ease his pain, Earl begs his caregiver to locate his estranged son, Frank. The bitter Frank has become a sex guru, teaching men how to "Seduce and Destroy." Jimmy Gator, long-time announcer on Earl's quiz show that pits kids against adults, is dying from cancer and wants to reconcile with Claudia, his drug-addicted daughter. Other stories involve the current child star contestant dominated by his father, a former quiz kid on the show struggling to make a new life for himself, and a gentle cop who begins courting Claudia. An amazing mélange of wacky story lines, awful parent-child relationships, and a deluge of frogs that helps sort all the stories out.

Monsoon Wedding (2001)
Director: Mira Nair
Screenplay: Sabrina Dhawan

Daughter of a successful businessman in New Delhi, Aditi Verma has agreed to an arranged marriage with a young Indian man studying engineering in Houston. She's worried because she's still having an affair with a married man. Because of past history, Aditi's cousin, Pia, is worried about Uncle Tej coming from America. Pretty Ayesha wishes her handsome cousin, Rahul, come to the wedding from Australia, would be her partner in the dance she'll perform at the engagement party. In the midst of all the cousins and the chaos, the comical P. K. Dubey, setting up the wedding tents, becomes interested in Alice, the Verma's shy young maid. This transposed version of *Father of the Bride* is filled with ceremony, music, and dance in a charming portrait of contemporary life in India.

Mystery Train (1989)
Director: Jim Jarmusch
Screenplay: Jim Jarmusch

Three very different groups of people occupy rooms on the same night in a seedy hotel in Memphis. Jun and Mitsuko are Japanese teenagers who have come to visit the shrines of rock 'n' roll: Graceland and Sun Studios. Having broken up with her boyfriend, Johnny, Dee Dee plans to leave Memphis and, since she is broke, is fortunate that an Italian woman stranded overnight, agrees to share a room with her. Having lost his job on the same day Dee Dee broke up with him, Johnny has drunk too much, gotten into trouble, and is now hiding out in a third room with his two erstwhile friends. Without directly becoming involved in one another's stories, these groups keep overlapping—saying the same phrases, walking past the same places, hearing the same radio programs, etc. Separate journeys through life mysteriously become a journey together.

The Safety of Objects (2001)
Director: Rose Troche
Screenplay: Rose Troche, A. M. Homes

Four families in a suburban neighborhood struggle through changes in their lives. Esther cares for her son, comatose after an accident, and neglects his younger sister and her husband. Annette struggles to raise her two children on her own, the youngest one autistic. Helen fills her days with exercise and healthy diets, but still finds her life unsatisfying. Jim is devastated when passed over for a promotion he worked so hard for. Meanwhile, the children in these families face their own issues of maturation. Although the problems have been seen before, the extraordinary editing creates constant visual rhymes as the stories race along together.

Short Cuts (1993)
Director: Robert Altman
Screenplay: Robert Altman, Frank Barhydt, Raymond Chandler

Based on Raymond Chandler's dark short stories, the film manages to interweave nine stories portraying people from varied strata in L.A. Couples are unfaithful, parents fail to meet their children's needs, and people hurt strangers by accident and those closest to them intentionally. Sex, in particular, proves continually disruptive and normal misfortunes add to the pain in the world. The complexity of the storytelling is matched by that of the character portraits—good is mixed with bad, indifference with kindness, anger with humor—created by a first-rate cast. Along with Tarantino's *Pulp Fiction*, this is probably the film that most influenced other filmmakers interested in narrative experimentation.

Things You Can Tell Just by Looking at Her (2000)
Director: Rodrigo Garcia
Screenplay: Rodrigo Garcia

Five separate stories each center on a woman trying to find (or hold on to) romance. A lonely doctor, Elaine, gets her fortune told by Christine. A bank manager, Rebecca, discovers she is pregnant, but her boyfriend is married so she has an abortion, performed by Elaine. A writer, Rose, is intrigued by the dwarf, Albert, who moves in next door. Christine cares for her lover, Lilly, dying of cancer. Kathy, a detective, talks to Albert while investigating a woman's suicide while her blind sister, Carol, dates Walter, Rebecca's coworker. The stories are united less by the occasionally overlapping characters than by the consistent theme of the loneliness of women's lives and strengthened by excellent performances.

Traffic (2000)
Director: Steven Soderbergh
Screenplay: Simon Moore, Stephen Gaghan

An ordinary Tijuana cop, Javier, tries to combat the drug trade but faces powerful opposition from the drug cartels and the corrupt general serving as Mexico's drug czar. Two DEA agents, Montel and Ray, pressure a lower echelon drug dealer to testify against his boss but then must keep him alive. Meanwhile, with her husband in jail, the boss's socialite wife is forced to start learning the business. The newly appointed US drug czar, Judge Wakefield, becomes increasingly disillusioned with the government's efforts to stem the drug trade. The issue comes cruelly home to him when he finds his own daughter is an addict. Despite this final all-too-predictable irony, the stories are compelling, with the episodes in Mexico particularly powerful.

Yuva (2004)
Director: Mani Ratman
Screenplay: Anurag Kashrap, Mani Ratnam

Fighting Indian political corruption, Michael organizes his fellow students to persuade local villagers to stand for election. He also tries to persuade his girlfriend Radhika to move in with him, although he won't promise to marry her. Arjun is applying for a visa to study in America, but then he meets Mira. Unfortunately, she is about to be engaged. Lallan loves his wife, Sashi, but refuses to listen to her pleas to give up his life of crime. Then Lallan is sent to eliminate Michael and the shooting is witnessed by Arjun, changing all six lives. This hub and spoke story is a crazy mixture of romance, activist political tract, and music video, with a little kung-fu action thrown in for good measure.

Database Narratives

Blind Chance (*Przypadek* 1981)
Director: Krzysztof Kieślowski
Screenplay: Krzysztof Kieślowski

In Communist Poland, Witek halts his medical studies after four years and impulsively runs to catch a train to see his dying father. In the first version of his story he barely catches the train, meets an idealistic old Party leader, and does his best to change society as a Party member. In the second telling, he misses the train, tangles with a station guard, and ends up in the underground resistance. In the third, he misses the train, goes back to his medical studies, marries and has a family. This film, that virtually invents the forking paths narrative, is one of the most profound investigations of the role of chance, destiny, and individual volition in shaping a person's life.

The Butterfly Effect (2004)
Director: Eric Bress, J. Mackeye Gruber
Screenplay: J. Mackeye Gruber, Eric Bress

Evan endured a series of traumatic events in his early years, but blacked out each time and is unable to remember exactly what happened. They all involved him; his childhood sweetheart, Kayleigh; her brother, Tommy; and Evan's buddy, Lenny. As a young man, Evan discovers that if he fixes his mind on one of the events, recorded in the journal a psychologist encouraged him to keep, he can return to the moment and change its outcome. Each time he does so, trying to eliminate the damage to his friends or himself, a new chain of events is set in motion that produces an even more awful result. Since Evan's father was insane, these alternate futures may possibly result from Evan's unbalanced mind.

Elephant (2003)
Director: Gus Van Sant
Screenplay: Gus Van Sant

It's an ordinary day at a high school. One boy has to take over the driving when his dad is too drunk to get him safely to school. Another walks around taking photos of classmates to complete his art portfolio. A trio of girls in the cafeteria discusses the fat content of salad dressing and whether they will go shopping together. And two boys march into a side door dressed in camo and carrying ominously heavy duffel bags. The camera tracks one person and then another as they cross paths and head toward disaster. A thought-provoking examination of an event which evades any satisfactory explanation.

Groundhog Day (1993)
Director: Harold Ramis
Screenplay: Danny Rubin, Harold Ramis

Obnoxious TV weatherman Phil Connors is sent to the small town of Punxsutawney (which he despises) to film the annual ceremony (which he detests) of the emergence of the renowned rodent, Punxsutawney Phil (whom he loathes). Stranded in the town overnight by a blizzard, Phil awakes the next morning to find that Groundhog Day is starting all over, and then again the next day. Each day he tries something new, from seduction to stealing to suicide, only to awake the next morning still trapped in his small-town purgatory. Delightful.

Lawless Heart (2001)
Director: Neil Hunter, Neil Hunter
Screenplay: Neil Hunter, Tom Hunsinger

The same story is told three times, seen through the eyes of three men at the funeral of Stuart, a gay restaurateur in a small English town. Dan, Stuart's brother-in-law, encounters temptation in the form of the local florist, a free-thinking French woman, who wants to help him break out of his routine life. Nick, mourning the loss of Stuart, his lover and partner, finds his life thrown into turmoil when he offers a room to Tim, Stuart's old friend, and then finds Charlie, a promiscuous young woman, also invading his space. Tim has been away for eight years, not feeling at home there, but now encounters a charming young lady. As scenes repeat and additional ones are thrown in, new dimensions to each character are revealed.

Sliding Doors (1998)
Director: Peter Howitt
Screenplay: Peter Howitt

Unexpectedly fired from her job, Helen heads home to tell her live-in boyfriend, Gerry, but misses the subway the first time because her way is blocked by a child. At this point the film "rewinds," and in Helen's second run the child is yanked out of the way by her mother so that Helen makes it on board. This allows her to encounter James, a funny Scotsman who bucks up her damaged ego somewhat, and also means she arrives home in time to find Gerry in bed with his former girlfriend. Neither of those events happens in the first version, and the rest of the film alternates constantly between the two different paths that Helen's life follows after this forking moment, with many scenes that cleverly echo one another.

Bibliography

Akin, Fatih. "The Making of *The Edge of Heaven*." DVD featurette. *The Edge of Heaven*. Corazón International, 2007.

Alleva, Richard. "Beaten to a Pulp." *Commonweal* 121, no. 20 (18 November 1994): 30-31.

Altman, Rick. *The American Film Musical*. Bloomington: Indiana University Press, 1989.

Arroyo, José. "*Amores Perros* ('Love's a Bitch')." *Sight and Sound* 11, no. 5 (May 2001): 39-40.

Azcona, Maria del Mar. *The Multi-Protagonist Film*. New York: Wiley-Blackwell, 2010.

Barnes, Alan, and Marcus Hearne. *Tarantino A to Zed: The Films of Quentin Tarantino*. London: B. T. Batsford, 1996.

Berg, Charles Ramirez. "A Taxonomy of Alternative Plots in Recent Films: Classifying the 'Tarantino Effect.'" *Film Criticism* 31, nos. 1/2 (Fall/Winter 2006): 5-61.

Berghahn, Daniela. "No Place Like Home? Or Impossible Homecomings in the Films of Fatih Akin." *New Cinemas: Journal of Contemporary Film* 4, no. 3 (2006): 141-57.

Bernardoni, James. *The New Hollywood*. Jefferson, N.C.: McFarland, 1991.

Bordwell, David. "Beyond Asian Minimalism: Hong Sang-soo's Geometry Lesson," in *Hong Sangsoo*, Moonyung Huh, editor, 19-29. Seoul: Korean Film Council, 2007.

———. "Film Futures." *SubStance* #97, 31, no. 1 (2002): 88-104.

———. *Poetics of Cinema*. London: Routledge, 2008.

———. *The Way Hollywood Tells It: Story and Style in Modern Movies*. Berkeley: University of California Press, 2006.

Bordwell, David, Janet Staiger, and Kristin Thompson. *The Classical Hollywood Cinema: Film Style & Mode of Production to 1960*. New York: Columbia University Press, 1985.

Bowles, Stephen E. "*Cabaret* and *Nashville*: The Musical as Social Comment." *Journal of Popular Culture* 12, no. 3 (1978/1979): 550-56.

Branigan, Edward. "Nearly True: Forking Plots, Forking Interpretations. A Response to David Bordwell's 'Film Futures.'" *SubStance* #97, 31, no.1 (2002): 105-14.

Brooker, Peter, and Will Brooker. "Pulpmodernism: Tarantino's Affirmative Action," in *Pulping Fictions: Consuming Culture across the Literature/Media Divide*, Deborah Cartmell, et al, editors, 135-51. Chicago: Pluo, 1996.

Cameron, Allan. *Modular Narratives in Contemporary Cinema.* New York: Palgrave Macmillan, 2008.

Campbell, Joseph. *The Hero with a Thousand Faces.* Cleveland: Meridian, 1956.

Chang, Chris. "Amores Perros." *Film Comment* 37 (March/April 2001): 72.

Chumo, Peter N., II. "'The Next Best Thing to a Time Machine': Quentin Tarantino's *Pulp Fiction.*" *Post Script* 15, no. 3 (Summer 1996): 16-28.

———. "Script Review: *Amores Perros.*" *Creative Screenwriting* 8, no. 2 (2001): 10-12.

Chung, Hye Seung, and David Scott Diffrient. "Forgetting to Remember, Remembering to Forget," in *Seoul Searching: Culture and Identity in Contemporary Korean Cinema,* Frances Gateward, editor, 115-39. Albany: State University of New York Press, 2007.

Clarke, David. "In Search of Home: Filming Post-Unification Berlin," in *German Cinema since Unification,* David Clarke, editor, 151-80. London: Continuum, 2006.

Coates, Paul. "Metaphysical Love in Two Films by Krzysztof Kieślowski." *The Polish Review* 37, no. 3 (1992): 335-43.

D'Lugo, Marvin. "Amores Perros," in *The Cinema of Latin America,* Alberto Elena and Marina Díaz López, editors, 221-29. New York: Wallflower, 2003.

Dassanowsky, Robert van. *Austrian Cinema: A History.* Jefferson, N.C.: McFarland, 2005.

Davis, Todd F., and Kenneth Womack. "Shepherding the Weak: The Ethics of Redemption in Quentin Tarantino's *Pulp Fiction.*" *Literature/Film Quarterly* 26, no. 1 (1998): 60-66.

Deutelbaum, Marshall. "The Deceptive Design of Hong Sangsoo's *Virgin Stripped Bare by Her Bachelors.*" *New Review of Film and Television Studies* 3, no. 2 (November 2005): 187-99.

Dowell, Pat. "Pulp Friction." *Cinéaste* 21, no. 3 (1995): 4-7.

"Eid al-Adha." islam.about.com/of/hajj/a/adha.htm (23 July 2009).

Eig, Jonathan. "A Beautiful Mind(fuck): Hollywood's Structures of Identity." *Jump Cut* 46 (Summer 2003). http://www.ejumpcut.org/archive/jc46.2003/eig.mindfilms/text.html (28 July 2010).

Eliade, Mircea. *The Sacred and the Profane: The Nature of Religion.* Willard R. Trask, translator. San Diego: Harcourt, 1957.

Farber, Stephen. "A Half-Dozen Ways to Watch the Same Movie." *New York Times* (13 November 2005): A18, A26.

Feuer, Jane. "*Nashville*: Altman's Open Surface." *Jump Cut* 10/11 (June 1976): 31-32.

Frye, Northrop. *Anatomy of Criticism.* New York: Atheneum, 1969.

Gray, David. "*Virgin Stripped Bare by Her Bachelors.*" (21 March 2007) www.hellonfriscobay.blogspot.com/2007/03/david-gray-on-virgin-stripped-bare-by.html (24 February 2008).

Haase, Christine. *When Heimat Meets Hollywood: German Filmmakers and America, 1985-2005.* Rochester, N.Y.: Camden House, 2007.

Halle, Randall. *German Film after Germany: Toward a Transnational Aesthetic.* Urbana: University of Illinois Press, 2008.

Haltof, Marek. *The Cinema of Krzysztof Kieślowski.* London: Wallflower, 2004.

Hart, Stephen M. *A Companion to Latin American Film.* New York: Boydell and Brewer, 2004.

Hartzel, Adam. "*Soojung!* Attends the *Monster's Ball.*" (27 July 2003). www.koreanfilm.org (23 February 2008).

Hoberman, J. "*Nashville* Contra *Jaws*, or 'The Imagination of Disaster Revisited,'" in *The Last Great American Picture Show: New Hollywood Cinema in the 1970s,* Thomas Elsaesser, Alexander Horwath, and Noel King, editors, 195-222. Amsterdam: Amsterdam University Press, 2004.

Hoeij, Boyd van. "Auf der anderen Seite." 25 May 2007. www.european-films.net/content/view/740/118/ (3 February 2009).

hooks, bell. *Reel to Real: Race, Sex and Class at the Movies.* London: Routledge, 1996.

Hornaday, Ann. "'Edge of Heaven' Comes Close to Perfection." *The Washington Post* (20 June 2008): C01.

Huh, Moonyung. "Interview," in *Hong Sangsoo*, Moonyung Huh, editor, 39-91. Seoul: Korean Film Council, 2007.

———. "On the Director," in *Hong Sangsoo*, Moonyung Huh, editor, 1-15. Seoul: Korean Film Council, 2007.

Idziak, Slawomir. "Interview." *The Double Life of Véronique.* New York: Criterion, 2006.

Insdorf, Annette. "Audio Commentary." *The Double Life of Véronique.* New York: Criterion, 2006.

———. *Double Lives, Second Chances: The Cinema of Krzysztof Kieślowski.* New York: Hyperion, 1999.

James, Nick. "Code Uncracked." *Sight and Sound* 11, no. 6 (2001): 8.

Kagan, Norman. *American Skeptic: Robert Altman's Genre-Commentary Films.* Ann Arbor: Pierian, 1982.

Karp, Alan. *The Films of Robert Altman.* Metuchen, N.J.: Scarecrow, 1981.

Kaufman, Anthony. "Interview: Art Cinema or Piece of Cheesecake? Tom Tykwer Races with 'Run Lola Run.'" (17 June 1999) www.indiewire.com/article/ interview_art_cinema_or_piece_of_cheesecake_tom_tykwer_races_with_run_lola_/ (24 February 2008).

Keyssar, Helene. *Robert Altman's America.* New York: Oxford University Press, 1991.

Kickasola, Joseph G. *The Films of Krzysztof Kieślowski: The Liminal Image.* New York: Continuum, 2004.

Kilbourn, R. J. A. "Toward a Non-Euclidean Cinema: Kieślowski and Literature." *Canadian Journal of Film Studies* 6, no. 2 (1997): 34-50.

Kim, Kyung Hyun. *The Remasculinization of Korean Cinema.* Durham, N.C.: Duke University Press, 2004.

Kinder, Marsha. "Hot Spots, Avatars, and Narrative Fields Forever—Buñuel's Legacy for New Digital Media and Interactive Database Narratives." *Film Quarterly* 55, no. 4 (2002): 2-15.

Klawans, Stuart. "Born Cool." *The Nation* 269, no. 2 (12 July 1999): 34-36.

Klein, Michael. "*Nashville* and the American Dream." *Jump Cut* 9 (October/December 1975): 6-7.

Kulaoglu, Tuncay. "Der neue 'deutsche' Film ist 'türkisch'? Eine neue Generation bringt Leben in die Filmlandschaft." *Filmforum* 16 (February/March 1999): 8-11.

Lawrenson, Edward, and Bernardo Perez Soler. "Pup fiction." *Sight and Sound* 11, no. 5 (May 2001): 28-30.

Leitch, Thomas M. "Know-Nothing Entertainment: What to Say to Your Friends on the Right, and Why It Won't Do Any Good." *Literature/Film Quarterly* 25, no. 1 (1997): 7-17.

Lippit, Akira Mizuta. "Hong Sangoo's Lines of Inquiry, Communication, Defense, and Escape." *Film Quarterly* 57, no. 4 (2004): 22-30.

Lyons, Tom. "Amores Perros." *Eye Weekly* (26 April 2001), www.eyeweekly.com/archived/article/51755 (15 September 2006).

Mes, Tom, and Joep Vermaat. "Tykwer's Run." www.projecta.net/tykwer3.htm (3 May 2008).

Metalluk. "Beyond the Butterfly Effect." (29 March 2004) www.epinions.com (24 February 2008).

Michel, Andreas. "The Two-Fold Outsider as Insider: German Turks in the Movies of Fatih Akin," in *Selected Papers: 2008 Conference. Society for the Interdisciplinary Study of Social Imagery*, Will Wright and Steven Kaplan, editors, 377-80. Pueblo: University of Southern Colorado Press, 2008.

Michener, Charles, with Martin Kasindorf. "Altman's Opryland Epic." *Newsweek* (30 June 1975): 46-50.

Mott, George. "Quentin Tarantino and the Pulp of Enjoyment." *The Psychoanalytic Review* 82, no. 3 (1995): 466-69.

Naqvi, Fatima. "The Politics of Contempt and the Ecology of Images: Michael Haneke's *Code inconnu*,"in *The Cosmopolitan Screen: German Cinema and the Global Imaginary, 1945 to the Present*, Stephan K. Schindler and Lutz Koepnick, editors, 234-52. Ann Arbor: University of Michigan Press, 2007.

Newman, Michael. "Character and Complexity in American Independent Cinema: *21 Grams* and *Passion Fish.*" *Film Criticism* 31, nos. 1/2 (Fall/Winter 2006): 89-106.

Niogret, Hubert. "Entretien avec Alejandro González Iñárritu: Aller au fonds des choses." *Positif* no. 477 (November 2000): 24-28.

Oppenheimer, Jean. "A Dog's Life [Interview with Rodrigo Prieto]." *American Cinematographer* 82 (April 2001): 20, 22, 24, 26, 27.

Petek, Polona. "Enabling Collisions: Re-thinking Multiculturalism through Fatih Akin's *Gegen die Wand/Head On.*" *Studies in European Cinema* 4, no. 3 (November 2007): 177-86.

Podalsky, Laura. "Affecting Legacies: Historical Memory and Contemporary Structures of Feeling in *Madagascar* and *Amores Perros.*" *Screen* 44, no. 3 (Autumn 2003): 277-94.

Polan, Dana. *Pulp Fiction*. London: BFI, 2000.

Pride, Ray. "Speed of Life." *Filmmaker: The Magazine of Independent Film* 7, no. 3 (Spring 1999): 56-58+. www.filmmakermagazine.com/spring1999/speed_of_life.php (14 May 2008).

Ray, Robert B. *A Certain Tendency of the Hollywood Cinema, 1930-1980*. Princeton, N.J.: Princeton University Press, 1985.

Rudolph, Eric. "A Runaway Hit." *American Cinematographer* 80, no. 6 (June 1999): 20, 22, 23, 24.

Quart, Leonard. "Code Unknown." *Cinéaste* 27, no. 2 (Spring 2002): 35-36.

Quart, Leonard, and Albert Auster. *American Film and Society since 1945*. 2nd ed. Westport, Conn.: Praeger, 1991.

Sansal, Burak. "Turkish Jareed (Javelin)." All About Turkey. www.allaboutturkey.com/javelin.htm (15 September 2009).

Shaw, Deborah. *Contemporary Cinema of Latin America: Ten Key Films*. New York: Continuum, 2003.

Sinka, Margit. "Tom Tykwer's *Lola rennt*: A Blueprint of Millennial Berlin." www.dickinson.edu/glossen/heft11/lola.html (3 May 2008).

Smith, Evan. "Thread Structure: Rewriting the Hollywood Formula." *Journal of Film and Video* 51, nos. 3/4 (Fall/Winter 1999-2000): 88-96.

Smith, Gavin. "'When You Know You're in Good Hands': Quentin Tarantino Interviewed by Gavin Smith." *Film Comment* 30, no. 4 (July/August 1994): 32-43.

Smith, Murray. "Parallel Lines," in *American Independent Cinema*, Jim Hillier, editor, 155-61. London: BFI, 2001.

Smith, Paul Julian. *Amores Perros*. London: BFI, 2002.

St. Jean, Shawn. "Cases of Myth-Taken Identity in *Pulp Fiction*." *Studies in the Humanities* 24, nos. 1/2 (1997): 75-84.

Stack, Peter. "See 'Lola' Run: German Film Fascinating but Doesn't Go Far Enough." *San Francisco Chronicle* (25 June 1999): C3.

Staiger, Janet. "Complex Narratives: An Introduction." *Film Criticism* [Special Double Issue on Complex Narratives] 31, nos. 1/2 (Fall/Winter, 2006): 2-4.

Stok, Danusia, editor. *Kieślowski on Kieślowski*. London: Faber and Faber, 1993.

Stuart, Jan. *The Nashville Chronicles*. New York: Limelight, 2003.

Tarantino, Quentin. "Quentin Tarantino on *Pulp Fiction*." *Sight and Sound* 4, no. 5 (May 1994): 10.

Thompson, Kristin. Personal correspondence. 3 August 2011.

Töteberg, Michael, editor. *Tom Tykwer: Lola rennt*. Reinbek: Rowohlt, 1998.

Tröhler, Margrit. "Les films à protagonists multiples et la logique des possibles." *Iris* 29 (Spring 2000): 85-102.

Vogel, Amos. "Of Nonexisting Continents: The Cinema of Michael Haneke." *Film Comment* 32, no. 4 (July/Aug. 1996): 73-75.

Wedel, Michael. "Tom Tykwer," in *The BFI Companion to German Cinema*, Thomas Elsaesser and Michael Wedel, editors, 238. London: BFI, 1999.

Wexman, Virginia Wright. "The Rhetoric of Cinematic Improvisation." *Cinema Journal* 20, no. 1 (1980): 29-41.

Whalen, Tom. "Run Lola Run." *Film Quarterly* 53, no. 3 (2000): 33-40.

Willis, Sharon. *High Contrast: Race and Gender in Contemporary Hollywood Film*. Durham, N.C.: Duke University Press, 1997.

Wilson, Emma. *Memory and Survival: The French Cinema of Krzysztof Kieślowski* European Humanities Research Centre-University of Oxford: Legenda, 2000.

Wood, Catherine. "Sometimes You Need the Help of the Universe." *Screen Education* 42 (2006): 107-10.

Wood, Robin. "Pulp the Hype on the Q. T.: Slick Shtick." *Artforum* (March 1995): 62-69, 104, 108, 110.

Zigelstein, Jesse. "Staying Alive in the 90s: Travolta as Star and the Performance of Masculinity." *CineAction* 44 (1997): 2-11.

Žižek, Slavoj. "The Forced Choice of Freedom." DVD booklet. *La Double Vie de Véronique*. N. Y.: Criterion, 2006.

———. *The Fright of Real Tears: Krzysztof Kieślowski between Theory and Post-Theory*. London: BFI, 2001.

Index

About the Author

Peter F. Parshall is professor emeritus of film and literature at Rose-Hulman Institute of Technology, where he taught for thirty-four years, thirteen of them as head of the Department of Humanities and Social Sciences. He has published in *The Journal of Film and Video*, *The Journal of Popular Film and Television*, *Literature/Film Quarterly*, and *Film Criticism*, among others. He received a Lilly Endowment Open Faculty Fellowship for post-doctoral study of film at the University of Wisconsin, Madison, and was Fulbright Lecturer in American film at the Technische Universität Dresden in 1999-2000. In retirement, he teaches film courses independently and for the College of Continuing Education at the University of Minnesota.

CPSIA information can be obtained at www.ICGtesting.com
Printed in the USA
BVOW021649170612

292851BV00003B/2/P